THE
CREATIVE
PRESENT

THE
CREATIVE
PRESENT

Notes on Contemporary
American Fiction

EDITED BY

Nona Balakian
and
Charles Simmons

Second Edition

GORDIAN PRESS
NEW YORK
1973

CONTENTS

vi   *Contents*

INTRODUCTION

Part I

The American writers whose work is discussed in the ensuing ten essays written for this volume do not represent a distinct school or movement. Nor are they the only writers of importance who have placed their stamp on American fiction during the past two decades. But they are among those who, we believe, should by now have been more widely recognized for what they have contributed to the development of the American novel and short story.

When this volume was first conceived, the two major American novelists of our day were still alive. Hemingway and Faulkner towered over the literary horizon, their rich reputations and undiminished personal vitality dwarfing the achievements of their gifted younger contemporaries, making it difficult for readers to regard the newer writers with the seriousness they deserved. It was the rare writer whose "discovery" did not hinge on his potential capacity to emerge in the artistic image of these indisputable giants. Unreasonable as this was, and frustrating to the young writer—who was often as sensitive to the particular tone and texture of his time as his two elders were once to theirs—it was equally inhibiting to readers, who were deterred, if not blocked, from seeking new literary experiences. In large measure, it contributed to the vapid impression which our current literature has left on the public at large since the end of World War II.

Though a whole new generation of writers—prolific in the novel and the short story—had come of age, many of them with a wider readership than the early Hemingway and Faulkner, the identity of the individual writer remained for a long time strangely blurred. To all except the discriminating reader, who explored for himself, and a few bold critics, who had the courage of their enthusiasms, the younger group of writers presented a near-anonymous facade—an amorphous tangle of intentions and viewpoints from which nothing tangible or cohesive could emerge. And while individual works were hailed, the writers themselves appeared generally interchangeable. As recently as the summer of 1962, when the unexpected death of Faulkner prompted a literary parlor game to name his and Hemingway's successors, it proved easier for critics to cite possible candidates than to say *why* one writer was a better choice than another. Past splendor still obscured a clear view of the immediate present.

Yet all the while, in the full wake of the considerable impact of Hemingway, Faulkner, Steinbeck and Dos Passos, our newer literature—with little help from American commentators—had made its way abroad. More than five years ago, in a massive special issue titled "The American Imagination," the *Times Literary Supplement* burst into a paean to American literature that was tantamount to admission into the Commonwealth of Cultured Nations. It announced to its readers —and such Americans as might be caught napping—that we had not only a creative *past* to boast of but a creative *present* of "vigor" and "independence." The pronouncement was not so extravagantly generous as it might seem, for it merely confirmed what had been widely acknowledged in Europe for some time: the unprecedented rise in popularity and prestige of American letters abroad since the end of the war.

"Translated from the American" became a magical catchword in western Europe, where critical attention began to turn from the Nobel Prize-winning Americans to the younger writers—J. D. Salinger, Carson McCullers, Norman Mailer, James Baldwin, Jack Kerouac and others of their vintage. In France, where not long ago Jean-Paul Sartre picked an American, John Dos Passos, as the greatest living writer, book-length studies of the new American literature became readily available. Indeed, if we are to believe what we read in the foreign press, visiting American writers (who long ago lost the starry-eyed look) were treated with a deference formerly accorded only to favorite American generals and movie stars. Considering the eagerness of European writers to extend their literary horizons, one could almost foresee a reversal of the literary situation of the twenties: a transplantation that could prove profitable this time to a generation of writers from the opposite side of the Atlantic.

One would expect such an accolade to have a significant influence on critical attitudes at home. Yet the contrary proved true. Except for the inevitable attention accorded Hemingway and Faulkner, and to a lesser degree Steinbeck and O'Hara, contemporary American fiction has, until quite recently, suffered a lukewarm, indifferent and even hostile reception from the majority of established critics. And this despite the increasing seriousness with which the current novel is regarded by many readers, by college students and even Ph.D. candidates. (In some universities it is now possible to obtain the highest academic degree by writing a novel in lieu of a thesis.) The very qualities which the foreign critic admires in the new American fiction—its boldness, directness, diversity—were often seen by American critics as flaws. What the foreign critic calls "vitality." the critic at home has called "sensationalism" and "lack of discipline"—a general sign, as some still claim, of the moribund state of the novel as a literary form.

True. there were always champions of individual writers —of these none has been more consistently generous than Granville Hicks—but the appreciations were scattered in isolated reviews and more than counterbalanced by niggardly praise and negative responses. It was only in 1961 that a young critic, Ihab Hassan, dared to fill a whole book (*Radical Innocence*) with sympathetic criticism of the writers he called "postmoderns." Unfortunately his study was less widely circulated than an article published at about the same time, in which a well-known critic damned with faint praise the talents of this same group of writers. The fact remains that the generation of the creative present has not yet attracted to itself a critic of Edmund Wilson's diagnostic power, nor even found an ally in a literary historian who could do for them what Malcolm Cowley did for an earlier group of moderns.

In the absence of a single encompassing and wholly authoritative viewpoint, it seemed not only useful but necessary to pool the separate resources and insights of those critics in our midst who had proved most receptive to the new literature and confront them with a selection of our most gifted and striking writers. Each was asked to consider, on the basis of his particular interest and previous study, one or two or three of these authors and write a comprehensive evaluation of their works which would represent at the same time the critic's personal interpretation. The reader would thus not only be helped in defining the essential quality of each writer but, through the collective impact of the essays, would possibly find clues to the new direction, or directions, of American literature. For undoubtedly the course has changed and is still changing, though one is hard put to set it all down in a systematic light.

Scanning the new faces of American fiction, one can discern a certain family likeness. Though they are turned in different directions and range in expression from semi-comic to deadly serious, they do not seem uncomfortable in each other's presence because of certain basic impulses and concerns they share.

Particularly striking among these is the high value they place on technique in its most fundamental sense. Baldly stated, this observation seems ironical, considering how often these writers have been chided for lacking distinction of style. The answer lies in the altered understanding of "style." Though there is little innovation today in the experimental manner of the writers of the twenties, the serious writer, nurtured on James, Joyce, Woolf and Faulkner, is more keenly aware of the uses of his craft. What the authors of such diverse works as *Dangling Man, A Curtain of Green, The Catcher in the Rye, Rabbit, Run* and *Other Voices, Other Rooms* mainly have in common is a concern for style, not in the sense of literary language or personal vision, but as a tool with which to shape an autonomous work of art. More consciously and to a greater degree than ever before, the writer is striving to make the language, the tone, the very cadence of his prose, as well as the story's essential form, contain and control his meaning.

The aesthetic distance thus achieved has both its dangers and its rewards. If it complicates communication by placing a greater load on the reader's power of interpretation, it also makes communication more creatively challenging. Freed from the subjective element, the fictional contours are sharpened, the perception sensitized to a more subtle understanding of reality: the world seen obliquely through a consciousness which the writer scrupulously authenticates and only barely identifies with his own. It is, in a sense, the stream-of-consciousness technique without the artificiality of the stream, the inner-direction without the free-association which sought to capture character in the process of formation.

The emphasis appears to have shifted from the elusive psychological states to the more or less "finished" product: the characters of Bellow, Nabokov, Welty, Malamud do more than ruminate and display the exposed nerves of their sensibilities. In a world whose tangible reality is ever imminent, though unreliable, outward behavior has become meaningful again, and engagement once more an issue—if only in the passive sense of Salinger's recently reconstructed Christians. But with this difference, that the motives and impulses behind a character's actions remain obscure to the character and "unexplained" to the reader.

Nor are the inner and outer man strictly separated as they once were, if by "inner" we mean a conscious subjectivity. (The inner and outer Holden Caulfield or Augie March are, in each case, substantially the same.) To disengage the authentic self from the many illusory selves that cling to the individual a deeper layer of being, containing instinctual man, has had to be tapped: it is all that is left of the unconditioned self, the self that faces up to major crises and sets its own values. Though self-delusion may still persist for the character at that fundamental level, the reader is now at a greater advantage: to verify his impression of what is true, he needs only to be alert to his own deepest responses.

Yet the reader's insight is not made to seem superior to the character's. What matters is not who is right and who is wrong (there is no Jamesian moral imagination at work) nor even whether right and wrong exist (though moral values are often questioned) but rather to show the elusiveness of truth and its irrelevance to the particular reality we experience.

In their preoccupation with the nature and limits of reality, these writers at times suggest the Proustian tension between illusion and essential truth, but a basic disenchantment with absolutes makes them more often congenial to the main impulse of European existentialism. Like the existentialists, they can conceive of an anguish or anxiety that is independent of circumstantial events, whose source is psychic and sometimes even spiritual. But whereas the European writer is inclined to "use" fiction to demonstrate a viable philosophy or ideology, the American writer, far more pragmatic by tradition and bound to the literal fact, is more readily prepared to apply his philosophy to the particular human situation, whether it involves war, racial conflict or simply love in its many guises.

The philosophically inclined writer, however earth-bound, can in effect denature the novel, and there is more than a modicum of truth in Mary McCarthy's complaint that character is disappearing from contemporary fiction, with the concommitant possibility that the novel may disappear as a form. The source of her pessimism is, of course, her refusal to imagine "character" in any sense other than that established by earlier conventions of the novel. An astute critic of fiction, Miss McCarthy is aware that it was the modernists who started the destructive process when they deprived character of its expected consistency and permanence. But she overlooks a more recent and perhaps stronger influence, the disbelief of the existentialists—by now widely publicized—in the very premise of a fixed and given human nature. Because it has had some scientific support, the idea has struck with force.

You are what you want to be or have the courage to be, is the existentialist message—or, as Norman Mailer has put it in his famous essay, "The White Negro": "each man is glimpsed as a collection of possibilities . . . Character being thus seen as perpetually ambivalent and dynamic." To survive in the modern world, man must be prepared to "create a new nervous system."

Traces of this new nervous system or new pattern of human responses are already to be glimpsed not only in the hipster-dominated world of Mailer, Kerouac and Baldwin, but in the surreal-fantasy world of Capote, Flannery O'Connor and James Purdy, in the transcendent-underground world of Ellison, McCullers and Salinger, in the tragicomic world of Bellow, Malamud and Nabokov. But until a new psychology is also invented to cope with this new "ambivalent and dynamic" man, the concern of the writer is less likely to be with character analysis and development than with a direct portrayal of characteristic attitudes and symptomatic behavior.

The protagonists in contemporary American fiction whom we remember—Holden Caulfield, Augie March, the Invisible Man, Lolita, Dean Moriarty, Rabbit Angstrom, Margaret Sargent—are not the kind of human beings whom we must strain to understand on more than one level (as we strain to understand persons close to us in real life) but variously expressive voices that speak for segments of contemporary experience. Because their strong drives and expectations make them blatantly audible most of the time, the merest suggestion of an inner contradiction (the mystery of character) affects us as if we had intruded on something secret and inviolate. In the end, instead of the unraveling of character, we have the revelation of an experience, an "epiphany" in which character and destiny become merged.

"We live in a society in the process of defining itself," Ralph Ellison has said, "and we must affirm that which is stable beyond the process of social change." As a program for today's writer, that statement represents a striking departure from the aims of a previous generation of American writers. What *is* stable "beyond the process of social change"? Man's will? His fate? Certain immutable truths—like love and death —by which he lives? If the scope of fiction has contracted, its base has invariably been broadened.

No wonder "the novel of manners"—and by extension, the novel of social criticism—is dying, as was demonstrated some time ago. And not only because in our fluid, diversified society the writer has no traditional base from which to view the human comedy. It is dying chiefly because the writer has ceased to believe that the social world can reveal the direction of man's soul. "For the advanced writer of our time, the self is his supreme, even sole, referent," as Diana Trilling so well explains in her essay on Mailer. The serious writer whose faith in exterior reality is shaken, if not wholly shattered, who questions even the concept of "inner" man (now no longer immune to social conditioning) is turning increasingly to the inmost self, examining it both in relation to the higher levels of being which it controls and the outside world by which it is set in motion.

This organic concept of life and the determination to remain open to experience, to accept nothing on faith, has brought a new veracity to contemporary American fiction at its best. Undeniably, it has also brought some less attractive things: violence, vulgarity, a morbid fascination with the grosser aspects of man. For modern man's curiosity, once roused, knows no bounds. The miracle is that out of darkness has come light—the truth, mercilessly probed, revealed in its lyric, poetic essence. One ventures to say that never before has the American fiction writer been so sensitive to the pathos of the small inner voice of sensibility, straining even in defeat to affirm a reality outside itself; nor has he ever perhaps so acutely sensed the ironic possibilities of unheroic heroes tilting at windmills they never sought.

One must be willing to relinquish a little of the past to be able to envision and create the future. While Hemingway and Faulkner were alive, they were so vivid that we forgot that the world was moving and that a new generation was steering its course. Their distinguished presence blinded us to those who were close behind. Though it is still too early to pass judgment on the permanence of what these younger contemporaries have achieved, it is hardly too soon to acknowledge the revitalizing influence they have had on modern fiction.

If death has come to the novel, as was long predicted that it would, it has come only to certain kinds that have prevented us from recognizing the novel's newest guise. Whether one accepts it or not, the new American fiction—no longer so new—is a reality. So far, in one basic respect, it has retained its link with the discipline of Hemingway, who taught the art of examining experience at its source, directly and impersonally at the same time. The reputation which he gave to American writing for vigor and immediacy is thus still upheld. Yet a striking change in emphasis has occurred. The writer who takes fiction seriously has developed an insight into the basic human condition that allows him to transcend the evidence of the senses and the more surface ironies of modern life.

Though deep fervor is generally missing from his work, at times his quest for a more profound apprehension of life has drawn him close to the inspiration of the classic American novel. Dealing with the redeeming power of love, with the almost mystical need to connect with others and yet preserve the self's inmost truth, he has bordered on a new spirituality. Beneath the surface negativism of his work is a growing faith in the possibilities of man, which in time may help him reclaim for American fiction some of the dignity and beauty of its earliest flowering.

Nona Balakian

INTRODUCTION

Part II

Gore Vidal once used an apt little phrase to describe the writers who, at a given time, are to be taken seriously. They are "O.K. writers," and together they make up an "O.K. list." Mr. Vidal explained that he had been on the O.K. list, along with such contemporaries as Truman Capote and Calder Willingham, but, of the three, only Capote was left.

There was a defensive but a cutting edge to Mr. Vidal's phrase, because he knew that more than talent goes into making an O.K. list. Or, to put it another way, if talent does define the list, then talent is judged in different ways at different times. The writers discussed in this book may seem to form an O.K. list. Mainly to lessen that effect I would like to say something about how this book was made.

It was begun three years ago; at least the idea for it occurred to Miss Balakian three years ago. The first step necessary to advance from an idea to a working plan was, sure enough, to make an O.K. list. In order to do this, Miss Balakian and I talked with each other at great length. We both had our favorites, so that there were times when we found ourselves almost trading writers as if they were marbles. But, beside the talk, we read books we hadn't read before; we reread others. We asked the advice of friends and colleagues, and listened gratefully to their arguments for and against individual writers. One or two writers, we agreed, had to be included (whatever our feelings about them) because of the broad, intelligent public interest in their books. We ended, however, where we had begun: by consulting our tastes—enlightened perhaps and extended, but our tastes nonetheless. Luckily our tastes (those difficult products of personal history and current needs, so much easier to exemplify than describe) turned out to be, if not congruent, at least compatible.

Well, all O.K. lists, even those as admittedly subjective as this one, are transitory. This list was made, by and large, three years ago. Have our tastes changed since then? To a degree, yes; and it may be of some help in explaining why we chose the writers we did to say how this book would be different if we were beginning it again today.

First of all, John Updike, who gives the illusion at times of being able to do anything he wants to with words, would probably have his own essay instead of being dealt with in the company of two other writers. Philip Roth, whose ambitious novel, *Letting Go,* was published after the essays were in progress, would be O.K. Contrariwise, Jack Kerouac, who has continued to produce but not to grow, might be dropped —even though David L. Stevenson's comments on him are enormously useful in understanding contemporary American fiction.

Three years ago I personally felt that Calder Willingham had been the cleverest new writer of the postwar years. It had been shocking to see how, as his books got better, the reviewers deserted him. *Geraldine Bradshaw,* which at this writing is not even in print, is one of the funniest American novels ever written. If there had been some way to deal with him in light of the fact that he apparently had given up fiction for screen work, I would have argued hard for his inclusion. After this collection of essays had taken form, however, galleys of Mr. Willingham's *Eternal Fire* became available, and his omission did not seem such a loss.

J. P. Donleavy's *The Ginger Man* is a great wild, mocking lyric of a book; but one novel and a handful of stories did not seem enough to set a course by. The same must be said of the work of Anatole Broyard, who owns the distinction of having sat for perhaps more characterizations in other writers' books than he has fashioned characters himself. Nonetheless his few published stories, particularly "What the Cystoscope Said" (available in Herbert Gold's anthology, *Fiction of the Fifties*) have been brilliant. If the number of essays extended beyond ten, the books of James Purdy and Flannery O'Connor would have been discussed. One of the critics who contributed to this volume made an eloquent defense of Wright Morris, and although Miss Balakian and I respect this critic's judgment highly, we had not found Mr. Morris's novels so interesting as the critic had and we decided not to include him.

Telling what we might have done and did not do will give the reader a clearer idea of our criteria for choosing these writers than a definition can. Nevertheless a definition must be attempted. To start negatively, these writers are obviously not young, although an aura of youth hangs about them as a group. They might not all even seem to be American, although they are. (Vladimir Nabokov considers himself an American writer—as if *Lolita* were not evidence enough for naturalization.) They are not all post-World War II writers in the sense of first coming to public attention after the war. What, then, differentiates them from, say, John O'Hara and John Steinbeck, or—they were alive three years ago—Faulkner and Hemingway?

They are distinguished by their potentiality. Although possible, it was doubtful that John O'Hara would write a better book in the future than any of the books he had written in the past. So also with John Dos Passos, Steinbeck and Robert Penn Warren. On the other hand, although Vladimir Nabokov is a near-contemporary of these men, who can say what will come after *Pale Fire?* Who could have foreseen *Pale Fire* when *Lolita* was published? Carson McCullers writes in physical pain and with difficulty, but is anyone willing to declare that she will not write another masterpiece? Mary McCarthy made a place for herself in American letters a quarter of a century ago, but Miss McCarthy's is still one of the liveliest minds in this live land.

All these writers seem to have a future. It has become a commonplace to bury Norman Mailer; Mr. Mailer himself with his strenuous statements of grandiose creative intentions seems at times most of all to doubt his future; but who knows whether that "unpublishable" book he talks about may not turn out to be something large and important?

Thus the criteria for choosing these writers was accomplishment and potentiality. The potentiality must be speculatively judged; the accomplishment is revealed in the subsequent essays.

Finally, speaking for Miss Balakian and myself, I would like to thank publicly the eminent critics who have given their energies and insights to this book. It is their book, so perhaps it is not a breach of modesty to say that we think it is a good one.

Charles Simmons

PREFACE

Since the original publication of this group of essays in 1963, the literary scene in America has changed so drastically that one may wonder why a book about the writers of the 1940's and 1950's should reappear, seeking the readership of an upcoming generation. Hasn't the book dated, and if it is being revived, shouldn't the more recent faces of American fiction be given a place in it? The possibility of revising some of the essays and including new ones was not overlooked. If the decision went against doing so, it was because the writers gathered here seemed in retrospect even more cohesive than at the time they were chosen, while as yet the place of their successors of the '60's and '70's beside them remained indistinct. On one other count, too, the book seemed to stand on its merits: speaking generally, it dealt with these writers' major works, since only in rare instances have their subsequent writings measured up to the work by which they became known. (I might add, parenthetically, that this is not uncharacteristic of American writers who, perhaps more than writers of other countries, are subject to quick reversals of literary climates.) Yet if their fame is receding, their reputations remain secure, with the literary excellence of their best work now even more apparent than when "the creative present" was theirs alone.

In personal terms, too, this postwar generation of writers has proved a hardy lot, with no tragic cop-outs or suicides. Two of the 17 have succumbed to illness and died (Mc-Cullers and Kerouac), one (Salinger) has gone into hiding, hopefully to emerge with a magnum opus, and five (Mc-Carthy, Jones, Baldwin, Styron and Nabokov) have sought exile for non-political reasons. Like the rest in the volume (and we might add such contemporaries as Jean Stafford, Wright Morris, James Purdy and John Cheever) they are holding on fast, if at times only by the skin of their teeth. It has not, apparently, occurred to them — as it has to an equivalent generation in England — to turn from fiction writing to television work or other similarly lucrative fields. Some are publishing simply not to perish, others are walking a tightrope, waiting perhaps for that inevitable change of climate.

In some instances, the writer's native bent has been diverted by the practical demands of publishing. One thinks of Eudora Welty, Bernard Malamud, Herbert Gold and John Updike, all short story writers basically, who have learned to accommodate to the public taste for longer fiction. (In Miss Welty's case, she has happily adapted the story form to the episodic novel.) At times it seemed their talents would barely escape being straightjacketed. For some others, popularity has been bought at the expense of an initial artistic vision. Updike, by writing too often and too profusely, has lost the poetically serene and piquant quality that distinquished his early fiction. His "Rabbit Redux" is rich in topical details but weak in substance and in the power to move when compared with its predecessor, "Rabbit, Run." Though one admires the essayist-philosopher Saul Bellow of "Mr. Sammler's Planet," one misses the exuberant, earthy characters that made his earlier novels overflow with life. Mailer, of course, is our weathervane, turning in all directions, his brilliant mind creating fictions out of the day's events almost at a moment's notice. Unlike G. B. Shaw, he has not yet been able to incorporate his socio-political insights into true fiction (very possibly he does not seek to do that at all). Only Nabokov and Welty, it would seem, have retained the original stamp of their talent, though for some readers Nabokov must appear to grow more and more esoteric. A teasing, erudite parodist, he is less read these days than collected.

The reader may well wonder why an extraordinary group of writers such as this has so soon relinquished its preeminence on the literary scene. One reason, I would suggest, lies in the limitations which the current socio-economic scene is placing on the growth of the imaginative writer. To make a living by writing, the novelist today must seek an increasingly wider audience. The more costly book publishing becomes (manufacturing and production costs have loomed very large in recent years) the less willing publishers are to take on manuscripts of limited or special appeal. In order to survive, the writer must keep up with literary trends and fashions whether or not these are congenial to him or block his own natural process of growth. Under pressure to publish, he often ends up by simply repeating himself, or at best gleaning the surface innovations of the contemporary scene.

Beyond the survival factor, there is a self-inflicted form of restraint: the feeling of futility the writer of fiction experiences in a world where a galloping technology and automation diminish the human capacity for responding to art. To capture the attention of readers for whom time is increasingly fragmented and precisely measured in Eliot's proverbial coffeespoons becomes no small feat. Yet these novelists have not ceased writing — defying the prophets of doom who have ordained silence for the novel — and some are holding their own even as a new crop of energetic talents is surfacing.

As for the newest recruits of contemporary fiction — they are quickly learning to accommodate to present circumstances. Not surprisingly perhaps, a dominant response of the fiction writer since the late 1950's has been that of passive resistance through parody and burlesque. With their feet on neutral ground (where neither great new dreams are dreamed nor old ones mourned), they are the generation of the Cold War in American fiction. Unhappy with the world as they find it, but reluctant (or unable) to engage in a struggle that might destroy the good with the bad, they succeed best when they dilute their outrage with grim laughter. These black humorists, as they have come to be known, have learned to exploit their sense of futility, locking their fears and hallucinations in a fantasy world that mimics the irrelevancies of real life.

Putting aside the metaphysical concerns of Sartre or Camus, post-existentialist novelists like Joseph Heller, Thomas Pynchon, Kurt Vonnegut, Jr., John Barth and William Burroughs want only to *render* the chaotic absurdity of modern life, in terms that can be instantly and directly understood. At the center of the stage is no longer Man or a particular aspect of contemporary experience, but the overpowering, faceless presence of Society within which Man all but disappears. Closely controlled in form if not in other aspects of literary technique, their novels often read like extended metaphors which, by repetition, achieve something of the effects of a ballet, a *dance macabre*.

If at times we detect in their work traces of the expressionism of a Nathanael West or Bertolt Brecht, it is because, like them, these black humorists are negators and distrusters of Utopias. But there is a pithy longing for stability behind the despair of a West or Brecht — an unwillingness to accept the void — that is alien to the more disenchanted writer of our day. Irrational, irresponsible, outrageously irreverant, these latterday satirists mock and desecrate many things, not least of all the common impulse to resist abuses. They are wary of all attempts to circumscribe the truth or lend order to the universe — and frequently the offender for them is as vast and unassailable as Civilization itself. All too rarely, excepting Vonnegut's early work, does the rough laughter in which they wallow bring about the cathartic release of true satire.

Because fiction itself has become an object of parody, many young writers deliberately avoid the accepted qualities of literary art. Two-dimensional characters, a series of disconnected incidents, and a vague or monotonous narrative that repeats its simple statement ad infinitum — these and other characteristics are turning the novel form inside out, without at the same time contributing concretely to its reconstruction. At its most ordinary entertainment level, the models most often followed are the Western, pornography and science fiction. One could not begin to list the undistinguished titles in this category (mostly by one-novel writers) published within the last ten years.

On a higher level of achievement — apart from those already mentioned — is the work of Richard Brautigan ("Trout Fishing in America," "The Abortion," "In Watermelon Sugar") — playful, anarchistic, improvised. There are the inverted narratives of Donald Barthelme ("Come Back, Dr. Caligari," "Snow White," "City Life") — surreal fragments steeped in the fairytale mode. And there are the cryptic novels of Thomas Pynchon ("V." "The Crying of Lot 49") with their futuristic islands and their original concept of "entropic" modern man.

Others — and not necessarily black humorists — who have aroused the expectation of readers are: Robert Coover, Joan Didion, Irvin Faust, John Gardner, William Gass, John Hawkes, James Leo Herlihy, Jerry Kosinski, John Leonard, Alison Luri, Tom McHale, D. Keith Mano, Leonard Michaels, Joyce Carol Oates, Cynthia Ozick, Marge Piercy, Ishmael Reed, Anne Roiphe, Wilfrid Sheed, Charles Simmons, Charles Wright, Sol Yurick and Marguerite Young.

And these are only some of the new names which are in the process of plenishing the immediate Creative Present and forming separate unities. Very possibly, a new form of the novel is in the making, one in which the attention will be riveted not to psychological dimensions (so acutely probed by the writers in this volume) but to the forces which go into the making of these dimensions, shifting and altering their nature so that no fixed portrait becomes possible (as, indeed, has long been the case in modern painting).

But wherever these writers are leading us, one thing, one hopes, will remain unchanged: the novelist's awareness of himself as a thing apart from the circumstantial world. The nihilistic present in which the novel has settled is tending to blur the distinction between man and matter, and by so doing denying the very need to *read* fiction. If we cannot be made to feel concern for ourselves, for others, for the world as it relates to our fate as human beings, we need not expect the literary arts to survive. What we want now, it seems to me, are writers who can see through their dark laughter a purpose (however remote from their grasp) which makes the writing of imaginative fiction a valid occupation.

A POSTSCRIPT:

Two writers who would seem to belong in this volume and whose names have not come up in the foregoing discussion are Anais Nin and Flannery O'Connor — both masters of the art of fiction whose reputations since the late '60's have been on the rise. I can only excuse their exclusion by noting that both writers bring a quality of timelessness to their work. Because they have woven their novels and stories out of an inner landscape they belong in every "creative present."

—Nona Balakian

THE
CREATIVE
PRESENT

JAMES BALDWIN

AND TWO FOOTNOTES

JAMES BALDWIN

"As a writer of polemical essays on the Negro question James Baldwin has no equals. He probably has, in fact, no real competitors," Fred Dupee wrote in a recent review of a Baldwin book. In contemporary American letters there is no case, even a case so special as this, of such obvious precedence. Baldwin, with his dark passion and lighted language, has provided a unique description of the Negro's situation in America, which readers the world over have attended. If Baldwin had written only his three novels and no non-fiction (on which this precedence is based) he might not have been represented in this book; but his novels are statements by an important writer. They help explain him, and to the extent that two of them deal with American Negroes, they too are important. His first novel, *Go Tell It on the Mountain,* stirred up considerable interest and was generally praised. His second, *Giovanni's Room,* in which one theme was homosexuality, was turned down by his original publisher, but found a friend in Dial Press. *Another Country,* his third and most popular novel, received an eloquently mixed press. One critic said that Baldwin's publisher should be horsewhipped for having squeezed a sensational best seller out of him; other critics, overlooking or explaining away the novel's novelistic faults, hailed it as a highly charged and unique accomplishment. Baldwin was born in 1924, raised in Harlem and attended De Witt Clinton High School. He lived in Paris for a number of years, not as an expatriate, because, having experienced the deep sense of alienation that comes to many Negroes in the United States, he reports that he did not think of himself as an American. While in Paris, however, and during his numerous travels since, he discovered his American-ness. One of the jobs he has set himself is explaining it to us.

RALPH ELLISON

Ralph Ellison, who was born in Oklahoma City in 1914, turned to two other art forms before he took up writing. At Tuskegee Institute, which he attended on an Oklahoma State Scholarship, his interest was music—he majored in composition; in 1936 he came to New York to study sculpture. For a while he went back to music, studying under Wallingford Riegger. Finally he turned to writing, participating in the New York City Writers' Project. In 1945, having published many stories, articles and critical pieces, he was awarded the Rosenwald Fellowship to complete work on his novel *Invisible Man*. Critically acclaimed when it was published in 1952 and winner of the National Book Award in the following year, it thrust Mr. Ellison into the limelight not merely as a Negro writer of promise but as a distinguished American talent. On the basis of this, his first and only novel to date he received the Prix de Rome from the Academy of Arts and Letter in 1955. A quiet, modest man, who in conversation reveals an intense devotion to the novel as art, Mr. Ellison does not readily divulge his literary plans, but his publisher reports a novel in progress. He has spent much of his time in recent years teaching Negro culture and folklore, as well as literature and writing at New York University, Columbia, Princeton and other universities.

WILLARD MOTLEY

Willard Motley, who was born in Chicago of middle-class parents in 1912, has said that it was not until he voluntarily moved to the

Chicago slums in his twenties that he discovered himself and his purpose as a writer. Before that, as a sports enthusiast, he made a cross-country trip to New York on a bicycle and shortly afterward traveled to California, working successively as migratory farmer, cook, waiter, football coach, janitor and ranch hand. Back home, while working for the housing division of the Federal Writers' Project as photographer and radio script writer, he discovered Chicago's slums and got his earliest material for stories, and later for his first novel, *Knock on Any Door*. Published in 1947, it was critically acclaimed. Next, in 1951, came another novel of Chicago—this one dealing with labor and politics—*We Fished All Night*. His third novel, *Let No Man Write My Epitaph*, is a sequel to the first one.

JAMES BALDWIN

AND TWO FOOTNOTES

by Harvey Breit

We modern civilizations have learned that we are mortal like the others. Paul Valéry wrote: *"Elam, Ninevah, Babylon* were vague and splendid names; the total ruin of these worlds, for us, meant as little as did their existence. But *France, England, Russia* . . . these names too are splendid. *Lusitania* is a lovely name. And now we see that the abyss of history is deep enough to bury all the world. We feel that a civilization is fragile as a life. The circumstances which will send the works of Keats and Baudelaire to join those of Menander are not at all inconceivable."

Valéry formulated his melancholy thought shortly after the end of World War I. What would he have said now, after Hungary and Tibet, after the Congo and the Bay of Pigs, after Goa and Algeria? What view could he wish for and hold to? Most assuredly, a man of Valéry's stature and sensibility would continue to write. But how? What tone would he take? What detachment would he discard? Surely he would have found existence far more intolerable and the pursuit of pure logic far more difficult.

It does not require nearly so much intelligence as Valéry

possessed to know that at certain historical moments abstract essays, however brilliant, may strike the reader as ineffectual. And that, at a perilous time when the very architecture of the cosmos is threatened, references to Keats and Baudelaire, charming as they are, may seem only charming or, what is worse, naïve and vain. Would the urgency of time have impelled Valéry elsewhere? Or would he, heeding the immediacy of metaphysics, continue to write his pure poetry and his superb, if paradoxical, essays?

With blocs of nations at war against other blocs, with nations at war against themselves (race against race, color against color), what commitment does a writer have, how is he to choose his destiny? How completely can he—and may he—shun the outside? How deeply does he become deflected? When life becomes particularly imperious the writer is often tempted to try to solve real problems, to try to put to rights some agitated facet of existence. Either to do too little or to do too much about the world: if we are not Stendhal or Tolstoy we can hardly help doing one or the other; if we are not Stendhal or Tolstoy we are in varying degrees Commissar or Yogi, man of action or man of thought—that tragic, human, scale-tipping flaw that Goethe knew too well: *action animates but narrows, thought expands but lames.*

Of course, one is discussing writers. It is never a question of giving up writing; rather it is a question of the mode of commitment, the degree, however infinitesimal, of deflection. Conceivably, one could create an aesthetic based on these criteria, the commitment to action and the deflection from literature, visible in a blunting or thickening of sensibility, in a disregard of shape (of vision really), in a naked outburst that is life itself rather than art. Thomas Mann felt himself trapped in art, the great Turner exclaimed, "Damn paint," Lawrence wrote *Lady Chatterley.* Even Dostoyevsky's *The Devils* seems more an action than a work of art. How much reality can a writer take in, how many real problems can he solve, without obstructing the creative process, without confounding the very end of art itself?

It seems to me something of this sort is at the bottom of the problem of James Baldwin, unquestionably one of the most brilliant young writers in America today. A mad reality confronts all our writers today. But it is more mad—and possibly even more maddening—for Baldwin, a Negro, who, because of his brilliance, his eloquence, his honesty, his courage, his superb intelligence, has become a spokesman, in a sense a captive spokesman, for his people and, as well, a kind of minister without portfolio for both black and white on black-and-white relations. Evelyn Waugh once remarked with his marked irony to an English friend who had turned American, "Ah, to have been born in England and yet not to be an Englishman!" Pitiable? Absurd, one may well reply, why in God's name not? But for a Negro writer today not to write as a Negro, particularly if he has manifested critical acumen and a grasp of the problem, is a life-and-death matter, something played out on another stage, truer, grimmer, humorless; the antithesis, really, of Mann's insight that literature could be viewed as serious frivolity or, to employ his exact phrase, seriousness at play. In spite of Shakespeare's wisdom, Brecht's radicalism or Robbe-Grillet's scientism, literature is play, and one can imagine the moment of unending absolute shock Ezra Pound must have experienced when, having cavalierly mixed literature and reality, he discovered he had called down on his head an American division armed with machines of real, unliterary death. It is (sad, true, ironic, bad) James Baldwin's unique problem. He has the talent, the sensibility, the psychology, the humanity to be a writer unqualified by race, color, nationality or class. But he is a Negro leader. It is a new eventuality. The pressure on him is infinitely severer, the necessity infinitely graver. The problem is new, less amenable to solution, more tragic in its impasse.

Inevitably, this "imprisonment" is progressively reflected in Baldwin's work—three collections of essays and three novels, all appearing within the past ten years. Baldwin's first book, *Go Tell It on the Mountain,* published in 1953 when the author was 29 years old, is the most free because the special role both forced on him and created by him did not yet exist. It is fiction but it is also a memoir, a contemporary shape for which there is no clear-cut term and into which one could place Carlo Levi's *Christ Stopped at Eboli* and Malcolm Lowry's *Through the Panama*. The novel is a recollection, not in tranquillity (though it is poetic in the best sense), within a harsh and bitter asphalt landscape of growing up. Here the shadows gather in the halls and the hard boys gather on streets and stoops. What to make of it, over and beyond the perennial fear? One must not only endure when young, one must grow up. It is Jimmy Joyce's Dublin transposed to Jimmy Baldwin's Harlem: "When you wet the bed, first it is warm then it gets cold." But the spindly-legged, four-eyed, banished little black prince will never be able to say, with the young Stephen Dedalus, "Daddykins." There is no daddykins! There is only the grim street and, once, an albino Fifth Avenue with albino women sauntering by the immaculate shops. There is only the permanent hymn in the store-front church—and his own weak voice, but these tell him, go, flee, move, search, know. And in this sense, though free, creative and bold, the book is orderly and normal (what an irony of vocabulary) because it is the sensitive confrontation of one's impossible beginnings out of which one yet manages a possible plateau. It is a book which, in spite of (or because of) its torment and despair and its scarecrow hero, one loves. (Must one always be plunged into the language of chaos?) I would suppose it is the honesty one is drawn to, an unadulterated honesty utterly cut off from malevolence or "side" or even reverberation, so intact and pure that for a moment one is awed by the possibility of the human organism and proud of its skilled, complex and precise techniques.

In 1955, Baldwin published his first collection of essays, *Notes of a Native Son*. Again, his candor was a significant factor in the considerable impact the book made. Candor, a search for the immutable truth, a confrontation of his own and society's evasions, a recognition that he was "a kind of bastard of the west," all constructed his revelation: "I brought to Shakespeare, Bach, Rembrandt, to the stones of Paris, to the cathedral at Chartres, and to the Empire State Building, a special attitude. These were not really my creations, they did not contain my history; I might search in them in vain forever for any reflection of myself. I was an interloper."

Interloper and stranger, but, like Joyce, exile too. In one of the essays, "Stranger in the Village," an account of his stay in a tiny Swiss town, he writes: "Some thought my hair was the color of tar, that it had the texture of wire, or the texture of cotton. It was jocularly suggested that I might let it grow long and make myself a winter coat. If I sat in the sun for more than five minutes some daring creature was certain to come along and gingerly put his fingers on my hair, as though he were afraid of an electric shock, or put his hand on my hand, astonished that the color did not rub off. In all of this, in which it must be conceded . . . there was certainly no element of intentional unkindness, there was yet no suggestion that I was human: I was simply a living wonder." If isolated, how simple the experience would have been for Baldwin. But he is American; he walked, as in a frieze, a small black boy on grand white Fifth Avenue. And so he adds: "Just the same, there are days when I cannot pause and smile, when I have no heart to play with them . . . Joyce is right about history being a nightmare—but it may be the nightmare from which no one *can* awaken."

If *Go Tell It on the Mountain* is his most free, most creative book, *Notes of a Native Son* is his most natural and graceful one. So much of the essays derives from the novel, or the other way round. The pattern has not yet been fixed, the pressures have not yet multiplied. It is a portrait of the author *not* in search of a theme. All thought flows, all is grace, because Baldwin is writing solely from himself, from an inner necessity, which generates a variety of approaches and an affluence of themes and variations. It is a most satisfactory book of essays, new, contemporary, tempered and exhilarating. If there are mysteries in the collection, they are good mysteries, that is, rewarding, and the dominant clarities require them. At the finish of the "Autobiographical Notes," which form the introduction to the collection, Baldwin sounds a momentous thought, which, one feels sure, continues to haunt him: "I consider that I have many responsibilities, but none greater than this: to last, as Hemingway says, and get my work done. I want to be an honest man and a good writer." That he is an honest man and a good writer is, one can only suggest after finishing his first two books, an understatement. That he has many responsibilities is a certainty too; but that his greatest responsibility is to last and get his work done, though literally and verbally true, requires closer scrutiny, perhaps bringing us up before that treacherous frontier of psychology. For it seems that in the light, or dark, of his subsequent work, the pressures on Baldwin begin to take effect, and it is possible (as it is also possible that I am far off the mark) that he has become deflected from what he considers his greatest responsibility, that is to write truthfully and well.

Now, deflection has as many disguises as the devil himself. It does not necessarily dictate a noisy, bad book screaming with class hate and race horror, typical of the kind of thing that went on during the nineteen-thirties. It can be a good book. It can be, even, a *Lady Chatterley's Lover,* something meant, primarily, to put things to rights. And if the medium gets neglected and the ends of art get obscured, well, damn the medium and damn the ends. In *Giovanni's Room* (published in 1956), Baldwin's concern is homosexuality, and deflection takes on its first disguise in Baldwin's work, this one an entirely personal mask. It is some extra-literary need to clear the decks, to get rid of something, to put things in shipshape anterior to getting at the main job. Baldwin, in moving Ingmar Bergman to talk about *The Seventh Seal,* has the film director make a statement that is admirably applicable to *Giovanni's Room:* "You just do it because you must and then, when you have done it, you are relieved, no?" But there exists a decisive difference between a personal necessity and an aesthetic one. Too often the former is a confession, an escape, a relief, and art has a way of punishing the artist who would use it for therapeutic ends.

The second novel is a more exacting work than the first; it is more mature, its intensity is restrained and organized, its drama describes a difficult passion with taste, dignity and —perilous word—bravery. Yet it is, by far, less significant than *Go Tell It on the Mountain*. The three major figures are shadow-players, lacking in the minute particulars, commanding little response. The refreshing qualities of immanence and spontaneity that were at the heart of the first two books are missing in the third volume; it is more conscious and less instinctive; it is mature, but it has sacrificed too much. Has the writer failed because he has ventured from the world he knows so profoundly, that world of black and white people in momentary communion and in everlasting alienation? It can hardly be the reason. For even though he has written a "white" book—that is, a book devoid of all colors—the author knows Giovanni's sort of room profoundly too. And even if Baldwin did not know the homosexual world as deeply and humanly as he knows the black-and-white world, it is still essential for a writer to have his own try-works, to discern his limits, to discover his scope. After all, there are marvelous failures. But in that sense the failure here is small. The novel constricts, never gets close to employing the author's gifts. For all its thought and its images of honor and beauty, it is a partial effort, compartmentalized, conscious, flawed by monomania (which can only become a virtue in an hallucinated work), a have-to-do book and then you are relieved, no? From the psychological point of view, I would think *Giovanni's Room* constitutes an exorcism, a plucking out, a purgation; from the aesthetic view, one might conceive of it as a bridge, as a necessary catwalk at whose end one might be able to strike out into a broader highway.

In 1961, five years after *Giovanni's Room,* James Baldwin brought out his second book of essays, *Nobody Knows My Name.* Those five years had not been silent years; nor were they a period of retreat. On the contrary. The author had during that time traveled considerably, taken on assignments and published the essays (before they were collected) in various journals. Most of the pieces were mainly concerned with the question of color, and though for Baldwin the question of color is the question of humanity, it is in this interval, because of a number of brilliant essays ("The Discovery of What It Means to Be an American," "Princes and Powers," "Faulkner and Desegregation," "Alas, Poor Richard," "The Black Boy Looks at the White Boy") that he becomes The Spokesman. I am tempted to say Captive Spokesman, but the dialectic between "captive" and "voluntary" is subtle and elusive. There is nothing I can think of that James Baldwin is not aware of; of course he is aware of the problems implicit in his statement that his greatest responsibility is to last and get his work done. But between the resolve and the execution lies an abyss. Between the thought and the act falls the shadow. *Nobody Knows My Name* is a rare and great book, yet one senses in it a kind of tragedy—not flaw, but tragedy. Society has somehow got hold of him in the wrong sort of way. Some subtle deflection has set in. The essays correspond to a part of himself only. He is engaged profoundly, yet partially. There are, one feels, enormities in Baldwin that are not engaged—curiosity, mysticism, bawdiness, laughter, poetry (dark and haunted), tenderness. Is he doing, metaphorically, what Lenin did, refusing to listen to Beethoven because it made him gentle? In order to be most effective must one become monolithic, steel, Stalin?

Baldwin has written that the essays in *Nobody Knows My Name* are part of a logbook. But the logbook contains no secrets, no sighs, no unfinished poems, no daydreams. It is a log only in its unwavering and admirable effort to come to record people and ideas. Somewhere in a novel of Céline's, a man, Céline writes, constantly sweats in an effort to be honest. It is the opposite with Baldwin. There is no confusion about his goal of complete candor, there are no subterfuges, no conflict of interests. In these essays it is no longer a question of being honest, but only of conveying honesty. The victory is so much his that it becomes a problem of technique, of craft, of finding and forging the exactitudes for all that is inexact in experience. And he succeeds. His truths are put down, stone on stone. The essays are among the most honest and honorable in our time.

And yet again—and one says this in peril—it is a constricting book. How does one reconcile something that is great and yet constricting? One's own dilemma, I feel, is also Baldwin's. The greatness, I think, is in the plunge that Baldwin has made. To echo Melville, he has dived deep. He is the only writer who has dealt with these painful things of Negro and white love and hate. He is the only writer who sees these questions whole and steadfastly and in all their interlockings and ramifications and dialectics and permutations. On these matters—and they are some of the most harrowing and grave in our time—he is the only writer we *believe* in. It is as simple as that: the Black Prince declaring war on the black-and-white dappled dragon. Through his special gifts, Baldwin has been chosen, a kind of Dalai Lama; and he has accepted the responsibility, possibly with a heavy heart and even with a sense of doom. But those dilemmas, those life-and-death dilemmas of American society, the extraordinary, fundamental paradox of a people working together yet alienated, loving each other yet hating and hostile, so extraordinary that they had been buried away deep within, now, however perplexing, frightening and insoluble, had to be disinterred. And it remained for the Black Prince to pursue them to their ends, to their musty lodgings, to wherever they might lead, and to bring them up into the uncompromising cold light of day. These essays of Baldwin exorcise old ghosts and conjure up new challenges. They marshal us, confront us with their own confrontations, deprive us of neglect and cynicism and indifference and all the other vestigial armor one employs in order to maintain an unreal solipsism.

Yet in spite of these political and moral and human revelations, the pivot is narrow, the medium through which he sees, though immutable and necessary, is obsessive. One longs for relief, for range, for a relaxed stretching. And Baldwin longs for it too, the longing discernible perhaps in the essays on Bergman and Gide, but these are lesser pieces. On the whole, the essays lack texture and resonance, a continuity with history; they lack *literature*. Somehow, by its very oppositeness, T. S. Eliot's *The Sacred Wood* becomes apposite. Obviously, it is not a poetic prose that one is praising. Eliot has managed the strictest sort of prose, cool, denotive, bare to the point of aridity. But the ideas reverberate and lead one to a variety of provocative and fertile facets of a problem—to language, to communication, to distinctions and generalizations, to the root of genius even. And though Eliot is almost exclusively concerned with literature in these essays—with Marlowe and Jonson, Blake and Dante, poetic drama and poetic tradition, Cyrano and rhetoric—they illuminate his creative concerns, they are absorbed into his special creative machinery, into the poems and the dramas. One feels that the creative and critical faculties are working together, discrete yet in harmony, supplying and nourishing each other.

Is it sheer nonsense, or even lunacy, to examine these two books of essays together? The incongruous juxtaposition (perspective by incongruity?) may nevertheless throw light on certain significant differences between the writers—not of talent (both talents are more than sufficient) but of purpose, of direction, of deflection. I would regard both writers as exemplary. Eliot, I have always felt, is the exemplary writer acting as the guardian of literature, a devout and an austere husbandman, the least distracted. He may have made his own sallies across political and social frontiers, but these were brief, local, essentially alien, and consequently, if not helpful, at least economical to his interests and his vitality, and could not but fail to modify his literary purpose or his creative power. In a sense, structurally, he is the writer sticking to the last, a Flaubert for whom the right word was of the highest significance, a Cézanne who continued to paint his landscapes while the Franco-Prussian war raggedly raged near by, an artist closed to the world, influenced, of course, but undeterred by it. Baldwin is the exemplary writer completely open to the world, a high-priority target, bombarded by its whirlwinds, by the imminent collapse of society, by the complication of being an American, of being Negro, of being an intrinsic part of the culture of *apartheid,* of being black yet not being African, of being a stranger, an interloper, an exile, heritageless together with his people, yet not being even a part of them. What has Rostand's rhetoric to do with all this true, living and dying drama? Baldwin's book is in effect an action.

Having experienced the potentially fatal wound in American life and believing that the wound can only be healed by an absolute human equality between black and white, Baldwin cannot ignore his knowledge; nor can he refuse to act. Abdication would mean a betrayal of his American-ness, an abandonment of his Negro-ness: the struggle for America is real, crucial, now—and all the rest is literature! How remote this captive Baldwin is from the Berlioz who wrote: "And why did I dispatch my hero to Hungary? Because I wished to include a piece of music with a Hungarian theme. I would have sent him anywhere in the world if I had found the slightest musical reason for so doing." To the dedicated essayist and moralist, to the man who wrote, "The time is always now," the passage may seem ultimately capricious, a piece of bravura. To the novelist of *Go Tell It on the Mountain,* though, the credo strikes a different gong, and must insinuate itself as a dear and precious freedom, as one of the few manifestations of grace man is permitted to know on earth. To feel free as Berlioz! To shake the world, to shrug off the shackles, to yawn at the pressures and determinisms of society! And if no man is an island, if each is connected to the main, then it is sheer good luck, a hurrah for communications. Because there is the other betrayal, the abdication of one's self, the abandonment of one's gifts, the failure to be one's self at every single instant. Yeats suggests the loss:

> *. . . And there's a politician*
> *That has read and thought,*
> *And maybe what they say is true*
> *Of war and war's alarms,*
> *But O that I were young again*
> *And held her in my arms!*

Baldwin must win a war, and because he must wage an exterior war he may be losing the interior one. That is the danger, the price, the expense. His newest novel, *Another Country,* fails him a little. Through eight people, most of them living either in Harlem or Greenwich Village, Baldwin explores love: Negro man and southern white woman, Negro woman and white man, white man and white woman (married), and a homosexual partnership between an American and a French youth. It is undeniably an advance over *Giovanni's Room,* not only because of greater scope and density; the people in the earlier novel never achieved more than silhouettes of themselves; these new people are truer, more credible, incantatory, life-size, shadowed. And though these are not the only criteria for judging a novel (they are not the values, for example, by which one would measure Kafka, or Faulkner, or Robbe-Grillet or the Argentinian Borges), they are some of the elements the author found desirable and set out to do, and the achievement is noteworthy.

But though the characters are true and moving, the novel itself, its totality, design, shape, vision, its indivisible and unique life, its existence as a physical, or metaphysical, entity, falters and, paradoxically, contradicts the life force of its people by a basic schematization. It is a moving novel that fails to be a great one because it has been inspired by the essays in the wrong way, by *scoring points as it were.* The social and political and moral content of the essays get into the novel but these are not enough; as for the more salient and creative ingredients of the essays, the hard-headedness, the irony, the objectivity, the coldness, the clarity, these the novelist has fled from. It is, it seems to me, an escape from the essays, a rush toward "creation," and a headlong flight from objectivity to subjectivity, from logic to emotion, from classicism to romanticism. Love and hate, gentleness and toughness, tenderness and anguish, aspirations and fears get into the novel, but they get in raw, untempered, unassimilated, melting and naked. For all its radical personae how conservative the novel is! And for all its iconoclastic events how conventional! Must he—the Negro, "the interloper without heritage"—write a white man's traditional novel so that by creating it he will possess, in a kind of magic, the very tradition, the whole magnificent and disreputable tradition? It is a psychological possibility. But the disparities within the novel are more basically determined by the duality in Baldwin, that is, by the double role he is forced to play out. It is the attempt to correct an imbalance.

The Fire Next Time (1963), Baldwin's newest essay, which deals with the Muslim movement, only corroborates and strengthens the point I have been making. It is a more philosophic essay than his earlier pieces, dealing with the author's sense of the American past, and contains considerable wisdom and considerable truth. But it is also too prophetic, a mixture of the gospel preacher and the political activist, and it appears to me that Baldwin has in *The Fire Next Time* taken his deepest plunge. One wants to pull him back a little. And no matter how essential and necessary the essay, no matter how true it is that only Baldwin can force us to see and feel the fierce dilemma (the fiery furnace), one continues to feel anxious about his future as a creative writer.

For all the steadfast admiration I have for him, I continue to think of Baldwin as a trapped artist at a crossroads. But he is only at the beginning, or at the beginning of the middle of his life and work, and this is no epitaph. "Enough," one longs to say, "you have done enough, you have fought one kind of fight too well and too long. Now forget it all as it was. Sit down and write us our contemporary *Brothers Karamazov, War and Peace, Moby Dick, Charterhouse of Parma*, those marvelous novels that are at once both works of art and instruments of power." But longing is a state of mind that foresees the improbability of attaining a goal. Overwhelmingly sensitized to the dark that has gathered, to the outcry of the world, a thousand times reiterating that splendid and useful poem: "But at my back I always hear . . ." Baldwin must heed all the agonies, a roll-call of all the peoples at bay. Even if one had the power to intervene, can one ask him not to be a Negro for the sake of his art, demand that he change his fine, living, thin skin, dissuade him from his confrontations and consequently his deflections, negate his eloquence, his unique eminence? Can one pull him out of the front lines? Offer him a less ravaged space and a more spacious time? There is never time, Baldwin has written, giving to his profound dilemma a definite bias: "The challenge is in the moment, the time is always now."

FOOTNOTE ONE

It was inevitable, no doubt under the stimulus of the works of Evelyn Waugh and Graham Greene, that our fashionable literary symposiums of a few years back discussed the question of whether a Catholic novelist was first a Catholic and second a novelist or the other way around; the question seems so remote now, and so fictive, that one forgets even how to formulate the formula. It is not proposed here to commit a similar folly with respect to the Negro novelist, though presumably a far more relevant case could be made out. Being a black American means being a second-class citizen, deprived of economic opportunity, divorced from a decisive landscape, alienated from its great works, barred even from those places where a free people freely work together and freely consort. Birds inhabit the air, fish the water, four-legged beasts the earth, but man has nowhere to lay his head: not Catholics, but Negroes experience this melancholy truth.

What happens is that a people fight back, existentially as it were, each man and woman and child developing a constellation of strengths through the trial of fire and ice: patience, alertness, endurance, resourcefulness, perceptiveness, shrewdness, wisdom, even quick physical reflexes. (Of course, tragic weaknesses are developed too; a program of discrimination to develop black Spartans would be a monumentally fatal and inhuman mistake.) Thomas Mann's play on the phrase "in spite of" becoming, in certain instances, "because of" is not altogether remote.

Consider only the narrow, only recently desegregated world of sports. The American Negro dominated our Olympic victory. The last great heavyweight pugilist was Joe Louis, a Negro. The most glamorous and gifted fighter in the ring was until recently Archie Moore, a Negro. The premier athlete in professional football today is Jimmy Brown, a Negro. Two of the greatest players in modern basketball are Negroes, Elgin Baylor and Oscar Robertson. And baseball has Willy Mays, the greatest natural ball player in the big time. It would be wrong to regard such prowess as merely a matter of muscular co-ordination of power and control. The mind is constantly at work. Within this admittedly limited field, there must be what William Blake called "copiousness of glance," the ability to take in the entire *gestalt* at once, to make an instantaneous choice and decision and then to make the right moves (the correlations), to gauge the opponent and to know a great deal about him. The difference between a good athlete and a great one is not so much physical skills (most athletes possess these to a sufficient degree) as intellectual agility, a capacity to learn and a generalizing power.

The wound is unrelenting. The white man shares the wound with his black brother, but there is a calculable difference between a concrete wound and a symbolic one, just as there is between a true Christian who never sleeps because of Christ's agony and a comfortable Christian who re-enters the myth only on Sundays. The Negro endures his wound every day and every night, even in deepest sleep. If a candlelit room and a woman's fingers moving over the ivory keys of a piano shape a child's life, as Rilke suggests, how much more savagely, if less hauntingly, does the roll-call of taboos, ostracisms, *verbotens,* inhumanities and dehumanizations shape a life? "What doesn't kill me makes me strong," Nietzsche said, and, flawed as such aphorisms always are, sometimes this is true; sometimes a resiliency is born, an underground life is concocted from necessity, a subterranean vision is evolved that is all the more remarkable for its point of vantage, as if a periscope were held up to an unsuspecting and consequently disarmed society.

The most successful, the most eloquent and brilliant detective of this underground world, since the novels of Dostoyevsky and Kafka, is the hero of Ralph Ellison's novel, *Invisible Man,* published in 1952. He literally lives in an underground, an embezzled basement, and when he finally emerges, with (one imagines) eyes webbed against the sunlight, he has become totally familiar with all the terrible subsurface machinations of an apparently smooth-working order, from politics to love, from relations between black and white to black and black and white and white.

Written in a straightforward, unadorned prose, the novel yet has the quality of a poem; a tough, harsh, uncompromising poem, perhaps because of its sustained curve, the equal pressure on all the parts, on each phase and phrase; perhaps because of the vision, checked against the sightings of the periscope. It is a vision of objective reality. No matter how much one learns of existence from the underground novels of Dostoyevsky and Kafka, one ultimately learns more about the observer than the things observed. In Ellison's novel, psychology plays a lesser role; one is not driven back to the "subjectivity" of the observer, to pathology as a rationale for a view of life, and in that sense *Invisible Man* is less provocative but a truer recording of the machinery of society.

The notion that is being strained for is perhaps best summed up in an essay by James Baldwin: "No one in the world—in the entire world—knows more—knows Americans better or, odd as this may sound, loves them more than the American Negro. This is because he has had to watch you, outwit you, deal with you, and bear you, and sometimes even bleed and die with you, ever since we got here, that is, since both of us, black and white, got here—and this is a wedding." In Ellison's novel it is a violent wedding, but it is presided over by a priest who watches us, outwits us, deals with us, bears with us, loves us, and perhaps even dies for us. Ellison's sensibility is unique and his novel is original—not because he has created a new form (in that sense he has written a traditional novel), but rather because he holds a view we have not known before, or only half knew, and because he has managed to penetrate to a heart of our society which we have hidden, or half hidden, from ourselves. It is a vision of the underground man who is also the invisible Negro, and its possessor has employed this subterranean view and viewer to so extraordinary an advantage that the impression of the novel is that of a pioneer work. This impression was corroborated by James Baldwin, who in *Notes of a Native Son* wrote, "Mr. Ellison, by the way, is the first Negro novelist I have ever read to utilize in language, and brilliantly, some of the ambiguity and irony of Negro life."

No white man, however great his gifts for fiction, could have written *Invisible Man*. Nor could he know this world with Ellison's degree of intensity, exactness, bitterness and truth. It is a work of enormous concentration, purposeful and undistracted. Somehow, luckily for us if not for Ellison, the author managed to slip through the web of our war which began over a hundred years ago and retreated long enough into a strict privacy to work out his contemporary masterpiece.

FOOTNOTE TWO

At the risk of losing the points of this speculation altogether (for they are already half lost), I feel that a brief if muted tribute to Willard Motley is in order. He has written at least one novel that rises far above even the excellent naturalistic fiction of our generation. In his first novel, *Knock on Any*

Door, published in 1947, Motley tried to write a color-blind story and succeeded admirably. His improverished, oppressed, harassed and fleeing people were any people; for the purposes of his fiction they were white. It was, in effect, a distinct coup. Motley, feeling himself a human being whatever his color, wanted to be read as a writer, not a white or black writer, but as a writer of no color or of all color, and not, one must rush to add, because of shame, humiliation or fear. It obviously was Motley's way of striking back at any patronizing attitudes or qualifications; it was his way of striking a blow for a free art, for a fair (even if more destructive) reading, and against segregated criticism.

How magnificently he succeeded is illustrated, I think, by E. M. Forster's asking me with open incredulity if Willard Motley could be a Negro. His response, when I affirmed it, was a mixture of awe and admiration. "Marvelous," he muttered, "marvelous!" There is enormous pleasure in the triumph, as there is in the virtues of the novel. *Knock on Any Door* is naturalistic, in the Dreiserian tradition, and breaks no new ground. What rescues it is the author's compassion, sensitivity, love—the soul laid bare. (Once again I am in the language of chaos.) It would be a mistake, of course, to claim these universal attributes for the Negro alone (though an amalgam of tenderness and toughness, an amalgam that makes for more than mere survival, seems peculiar to the Negro); one can claim them, these seemingly paradoxical combinations of tenderness and virility, gentleness and brutality, for the underground man, the invisible man, the wounded man, who yet refuses to be maimed by hate or mutilated by cynicism. In spite of abrupt shifts of every sort in *Knock on Any Door,* so that pride and shame and love and envy become inseparable, it is Motley's special grasp of life as essentially tragic, and more specifically, poignant, that transfigures his novel into a significant, moving and highly personal art. Against the blank stare of the universe and the hostile stare of society, Motley appears battle-worthy, armed with a kind of intransigent wisdom and compassion, perhaps even—one hesitates to say it—with a touch of saintliness that is completely unpretentious.

Both Baldwin and Ellison are in the vanguard of what Baldwin might call the War of Love, whose end can only be the creation of a society in which no minorities will be permitted to exist. Motley, more withdrawn and hermitlike, is engaged in an older war, which, after the new war is won, will yet have to be fought. Conceivably it is going on now, concurrently with the other, a ground-bass continually repeating itself beneath the strident top sounds. It is, I would suppose, the war against the deadly sins that are in each of us and that too often prevail.

Ah, buddy

J. D. SALINGER

In the twelve years since the publication of his first book and only self-contained novel, *The Catcher in the Rye,* Jerome David Salinger has become something of a legend and lively target of controversy. Unlike Fitzgerald and Hemingway, however, he has achieved notoriety not through a glamorous public image but, *in absentia,* through the projection of a startlingly contemporary vision. In Holden Caulfield and later in the "mad" and "crazy" Glasses, he has suggested a portrait of the sensitive young American, postwar version, which some have swallowed whole and others denounced as phony. Although *Catcher* has sold in the millions and has been widely read abroad, its author lives simply. Since 1953, he has secluded himself in a one-storey house in Cornish, New Hampshire, writing his stories and books in an adjoining skylit concrete cell. Whether out of shyness, an instinct for self-preservation or—as has been hinted—a sly flair for publicity, he has given out no statements to the press and supplied the barest biographical information to his publisher. This includes the following: He was born in New York City forty-four years ago of Jewish and Scotch-Irish extraction. After attending public school there, he entered Valley Forge Military Academy at the age of fifteen, graduating in 1936. Briefly he toyed with the idea of joining his father's Polish ham business and with this in mind he took a trip with him to Vienna in 1937. But returning that same year to New York, he instead registered at Columbia and took a course in short story writing under Whit Burnett. Though drafted in 1942, he continued writing and his stories appeared successively in *Story* magazine, the *Saturday Evening Post* and *The New Yorker*. (It was in the latter that he built his reputation—even before his first book was published—as a writer of polished and subtle short stories.) Mr. Salinger served in the Army from 1942–46, participating in most of the European campaigns, and ended the war as staff sergeant. Before returning to New York, he was briefly married to a European physician. Soon after the war, as an habitué of Greenwich Village, he discovered Zen. Possibly under the influence of this oriental philosophy, and because he was now completely absorbed in his writing, he began a series of withdrawals. He lived for a while in Tarrytown, then in Westport, Connecticut, and finally retired to Cornish, where even his closest neighbors do not know him. In 1955, he married an English-born Radcliffe graduate, Claire Douglas. They have two children, a boy and a girl.

Ah, buddy:

SALINGER

by Donald Barr

"I don't care where an actor acts. It can be in summer stock, it can be over a radio, it can be over *tele*vision, it can be in a goddam Broadway theatre, complete with the most fashionable, most well-fed, most sunburned-looking audience you can imagine. But I'll tell you a terrible secret—Are you listening to me? *There isn't anyone out there who isn't Seymour's Fat Lady.* . . . Don't you know that goddam secret yet? And don't you know—*listen* to me, now—*don't you know who that Fat Lady really is?* . . . Ah, buddy. Ah, buddy. It's Christ Himself. Christ Himself, buddy."

J. D. Salinger

J. D. Salinger's entire reputation rests on four smallish books. He has written a great deal more, but the other work is forgotten as thoroughly as if he had published it under a pen name.

His only novel, *The Catcher in the Rye,* appeared in 1951.

It is apparently a story about a furious, heartsick boy who has flunked out of prep school and who is both going home and *never* going home at the same time. But it is really a story about an apprentice saint and his indignant love for this bad world. It has been in turn a popular success, a casebook for amateur social diagnosticians, a classic for critics, and a collegiate fashion.

In 1953 the collection *Nine Stories* appeared, displaying as its epigraph a koan (one of those remarks of the Zen masters so extraordinarily pointless as to be considered a demonstration of the impotence of reason) and containing

(1) "A Perfect Day for Bananafish" (first published in *The New Yorker,* January 1948). This is apparently an exercise in morose literary precision in which a young man goes to Florida on vacation with his wife with whom he cannot communicate either sexually or verbally, invents some sad whimsies with a child on the beach, and commits suicide. But really, as it has turned out, the story is a sort of eleven-finger exercise, a statement of paradox. The paradox of sickness and wisdom in the same man (or neurosis in the artist, or, looking at it from the other side, the *in*side, the hatefulness of that world which it is incumbent on saints to love) is one which Salinger, like a man trying to make up his mind to eat his first artichoke, has been nervously exfoliating ever since . . .

(2) "Uncle Wiggily in Connecticut" (*The New Yorker,* March 1948). This is apparently the transcript of a boozy afternoon in Fairfield County during which a young matron and her business-girl friend talk over old times; but it is really a random walk through hell . . .

(3) "Just Before the War with the Eskimos" (*The New Yorker,* June 1948) is apparently the matter-of-fact record of an adolescent girl's meeting with a schoolmate's brother and the homosexual who is seducing him; but really it is an *almost* inarticulate cry of dismay at the inarticulateness of any genuine human pity . . .

(4) "The Laughing Man" (*The New Yorker,* March

1949). Here what seem to be some affectionate reminiscences of a boys' recreation group organized by a needy law-school student with a gift for telling horror stories really constitute a work of elaborate artifice in which the internal tragedy of a rather nondescript lovers' quarrel is acted out by a cast of imaginary monsters and a Greek chorus of nine-year-olds . . .

(5) "Down at the Dinghy" (*Harper's,* April 1949) looks like a prose diagram of the stresses caused in a Jewish household by a maid's anti-Semitic remark; but it is not really schematic at all, but a snapshot of terror, taken just as a mother (the sister of the sensitive young man who killed himself in the "Bananafish" story) confronts her doubt that her own abnormally sensitive child is viable in this malicious world . . .

(6) "For Esmé—with Love and Squalor" (*The New Yorker,* April 1950) comprises two fragments of an American sergeant's overseas experience in World War II, one an encounter with a charming little English girl, the other the strong and swift working of her charisma when he is about to break under the moral torture of his assignment. In this story, there is no apparently/really dialectic; the form is gashed open so that the content spills into the reader's awareness . . .

(7) "Pretty Mouth and Green My Eyes" (*The New Yorker,* July 1951) is a brittle, ironic anecdote about an adulterous couple interrupted in bed by a phone call from the betrayed husband; but it becomes really a kind of whimpering homage to love, which can make us nearly as foolish as saints . . .

(8) "De Daumier-Smith's Blue Period" (unpublished previously) is the lightly told but acutely felt recollections of a young man who is afraid to be altogether genuine and who goes to work as a "teacher" in a correspondence school of art, until he has a mystical experience resembling *satori,* the abrupt enlightenment sought by followers of Zen, after which he gives up his postal assault on a nun and goes home to ogle girls . . .

(9) "Teddy" (*The New Yorker,* January 1953) is a literal portrait of a Zen-plus-Saki child prodigy who wanders learnedly around an ocean liner writing in his diary (excerpts given) and correctly prophesying the moment and mode of his own death.

In the ten years since this collection appeared, four more stories by Salinger have been printed in *The New Yorker* and have been paired off in the books, *Franny and Zooey* and *Raise High the Roofbeam, Carpenters,* and *Seymour, an Introduction,* each of which became an immediate popular success.

"Franny" (January 1955) is a meticulous account of a college football date, in which the boy shows himself as something between a prig and a decent young *homme moyen sensuel,* and the girl (another sister of the "Bananafish" suicide) shows herself as something between a practicing mystic and a preachy neurasthenic.

"Raise High the Roofbeam, Carpenters" (November 1955) is apparently a detailed account of a wedding at which the bridegroom (who happens to be the "Bananafish" suicide) fails to appear. But in reality it is very likely the *longest* goddam koan in the world.

"Zooey" (May 1957) is a long, long sequel to "Franny" consisting of a succession of dialogues in which the girl's youngest brother explains the family curse to his mother from the bathtub and psychologically pummels his sister into clarity and healthy sleep.

"Seymour, an Introduction" (June 1959) is a fantastically long and devious prolegomenon to the short life of the "Bananafish" suicide, supposedly written by one of his brothers.

It is not hard to see this development as organic, if perhaps somewhat monstrous. The earlier stories, which are controlled and even conventional, seem to begin in ordinary hurts— hurts caused by social snobbery, anti-Semitism, the bitchiness of girls. The world is cruel; nice people are vulnerable. There is a sort of decently oppressed, underdoggy feeling about the stories. Then the center of anxiety shifts. How to be loved is no longer the problem, but how to love. Lovers are not viable. Then, after *The Catcher,* the center of anxiety shifts again. The diary and the harangue, instrumentalities of what we perhaps must call wisdom-writing, now start to displace the acts of love—the kiss, the lie, and the cry of rage. So Salinger draws in and draws in his awareness, from a general sympathy to a personal worry.

These changes in Salinger's concerns are accompanied by changes in his technique. The prose thickens to a chowder of learning and expostulating; the descriptive phrases *reach* more wildly; Salinger's easy mastery of colloquial rhythms and of the insensate little violences of the metropolitan idiom is now exploited to propel longer and longer flights of abstractions.

And with those changes comes a personal change—a complicated intrusiveness, a substitution of coyness for control, an attempt perhaps to force author, book, and reader into some sort of clammy mystical union. Salinger is a writer, one now sees, for whom publication is an intimacy. Probably no other writer, not even Dickens, has depended so much on his audience. Let us consider Salinger and his audiences.

"All progress in the social Self," wrote William James, "is the substitution of higher tribunals for lower"; which is to say, everyone devises a Self or some Selves by means of which he copes with the world, and from time to time he chooses different bits of the world to deal with in a very particular and anxious way. We may consider an author's works as (though of course not *only* as) purposive utterances of his "social Self"—as bids for the world's pity or its concern or its approval. Hemingway's strong-maimed, laconic-lonely, tender-destructive, enviable-pitiable heroes are artful projections of himself, the more worthy of pity because they do not ask for pity. Mailer, simultaneously acting the naughty boy and the scolding moralist, circulates among his characters demanding that society be shocked and shamed. Sinclair Lewis, helplessly mocking his own persistent dream of the plebeian male in clumsy pursuit of the slim high-bred girl, is always inviting us to smile fondly at himself with him.

Every infant lying helpless, uncertain even of the boundaries of Himself, in the center of a menacing universe, a vast turbulent Outside World, learns three languages: the cry of weakness and pain, the roar of anger and demand, and the gurgle of placatory agreement. (He may in time learn the language of withdrawal or silence too.) All the languages he learns afterwards are combinations and elaborations of these, and whatever else he may express with them, they continue to serve him as these originally did, to control the universe and to reassure the terrified baby still colicking inside him.

But the primal shock—the discovery of the World outside the Self—never wears off for any man. The control and the reassurance are never complete, so that he is always on trial, so to speak, before some department or other of the universe; and always, mingled with his percepts and his concepts and the rest of the less self-conscious business of his mind, there is the image of that audience, that personified bit of the Outside World—what James calls the "tribunal"—from which he seeks clemency or a favorable verdict. As the boy matures (if he does mature), he appeals from tribunal to tribunal; he appeals from his peer-group on the sandpile to his chosen friend; then to his father's mystical body, society; and perhaps ultimately he carries his appeal to the old spiritual fox hidden in his tunic, God.

It is instructive to look at this progression in the audiences for which a writer writes; for the writer's social Self progresses by that progression, and at the same time the social Self is continually growing *in* on him. Like the Happy Hypocrite's mask, or the Jungian *persona,* it ultimately modifies the most private Self. Let us, for example, compare what has happened to Salinger with what happened to Hemingway. Hemingway began by writing poetry for *avant-garde* magazines, found a sophisticated audience for his meticulously worked fiction, achieved broad literary popularity, and "progressed" at last through the book clubs to *Life* magazine.

And as his audience opened out from clique to populace, his work broadened (in the theatrical sense of "broad") out to *The Old Man and the Sea.* In contrast, J. D. Salinger began writing for the mass-innocent audience of *Collier's* and the *Saturday Evening Post* and the mass-sophisticated audience of *Esquire,* then progressed to the Book-of-the-Month Club and the class-sophistication of *The New Yorker,* and now, still publishing in *The New Yorker,* seems to be writing for a more and more special audience, a clique that he treats like a cult. The changes in his work accompany the changes in his audience. (We have to distinguish between the audience a writer writes for and the audience he actually gets to. Salinger does not write best sellers. His books just sell very well.)

Appeals from one tribunal to another are not usually extemporaneous; they are prepared for by dreams, the profoundest kind of study. Jerome David Salinger's career began, like any other, in the infant's fitful awareness that the Outside World—the darkness and the stinging wetness and the warm, quenching nipple—came and went in regular fashion and sometimes could be controlled; Himself cried, and Outside World comforted; Himself roared, and Outside World obeyed; Himself smiled, and Outside World gave; there were *people* in the Outside World; by cleverness the Outside World could be trained, but sometimes it was easier to just *think* of another Outside World, a more docile one; there were people in the Outside World who counted for more than others, and knew how to make the rest of the Outside World take notice, and there were words they said, ways they walked, important things they did with eyes and hands which could be secretly copied; most people in the Outside World were pretty easy to train, but some were awful dumb; "Jerry has a good mind but does not apply himself"; nobody *really* had eyes in the back of their head; it was also possible to just *think* of being another Self in the same old Outside World; I was *stupid* last year, I was a *stupid kid;* if all the people who knew me when I was stupid would only *die;* "Jerry has a good mind but does not apply himself"; if you look people in the eyes, they will believe you even if you're lying, but if you drop your eyes, people will think you're lying even if you're telling the truth; I'd like to see their faces if I *died;* even if I wasn't telling the truth, she had no right to say I was lying, because she had no way of knowing it wasn't the truth, so she could *just as well* have been calling me a liar when I was telling the truth . . . and all the rest of it.

All of that is conjectural, presumable, universal. But who knows why some imaginations become palpable and record themselves, while other imaginations continue to work feebly in the tattered shadows of sleep and grief? It is said that young Salinger had a talent for dramatics, but for disciplined school work he seems to have had more limited talent. He did all right but not *too* well in New York City public schools on the upper West Side; flunked out of the McBurney School (a good Y.M.C.A.-sponsored private school with good students); dreamed by the statue of Kossuth on the Drive and stared across the river at the Linit sign; was sent off to Pennsylvania to Valley Forge Military Academy; wrote stories; dreamed of a writing career in Hollywood; finished school all right; tried N.Y.U.; went off to Europe with his father, a Jewish importer of Polish hams; took a short-story-writing course with Whit Burnett at Columbia; and sold a story to Whit Burnett at *Story*. This (March-April 1940) was a sketch of an unhappy girl at a party, interesting because it shows Salinger's uncanny acoustics, but otherwise a conventional exercise in uncommercial short fiction.

For five years after this, Salinger seems to have taken pride in his ability to lead a literary double life—to bang out stories with "professional" callousness for the *Saturday Evening Post* and *Collier's* and, when he felt like it, to write "artistically" for *Story*. This was his first phase. The serious work is of far less interest now than the commerical writing. Both show the completeness of his response to his audiences: the serious stories presented, in the approved room-temperature manner, life as a cumulation of petty defects and joyless vulgarities;

the commercial stories began with two short-shorts for *Collier's* about army life, written before Salinger went into the Army and indistinguishable from five thousand other patriotic lies of the time except that, with their You-see-I-was-that-soldier and You-see-that-man-was-my-father trick endings, they are so patently dishonest that they have a sort of inverted candor, as if the writer were saying: "I am writing this way on purpose. I *could* write well. As you like it, bub!" When the first of the *Collier's* stories appeared (July 1941), Salinger wrote a gaggy piece for *Esquire* (*Esquire* labelled it *"satire"*) about his professional problems as a *Collier's* writer.

But (and this is significant) it was in the commerical writing that Salinger's true development took place. For all his much-publicized interest in Zen Buddhism, which teaches that enlightenment comes from sudden flashes of perception —perception of anything, frog, flower, or phrase—rather than by pondering, Salinger has preferred to work analytically, worrying his way deeper and deeper into the same material. Like most short-story writers, he has formed a sort of *commedia dell'arte* or troupe, with a limited number of *maschere* or rôles and a limited number of *scenarii* or narrative lines, which he uses over and over. It was not in his would-be-serious stories that this *commedia* developed; it was in the *Saturday Evening Post*. In a sentimental *Post* story about songwriters (July 1943), we first glimpse two of the most permanently obsessive of the Salinger *maschere:* the Dead Brother whose spirit works in the living, and the Artist-Martyr; in this case they are combined in the same character, In a *Post* story about a soft-hearted sergeant (April 1944— Salinger was now in army training), we glimpse the Hurt Saint.

In the spring of 1944, Salinger was shipped overseas, and that July the *Post* published the first of four stories about a pair of sergeants named "Babe" Gladwaller and Vincent Caulfield. A chronicle of Sergeant Gladwaller's last furlough before going overseas introduces us to the *maschera* of the Little Sister with her marvelous infectious sanity, the *maschera* of the Beautiful Wrong Girl whom the otherwise deeply perceptive hero cannot help loving, and the *maschera* of the Boy Errant—the Boy Errant in this case being Caulfield's kid brother, who has run away from school. . . .

The *Post* (March 1945) published "A Boy in France," in which Sergeant Gladwaller, sick with revulsion, breaking, reads a letter from his Little Sister and feels a healing sleep creep over him. Five years later, this was to be the *scenario* of Salinger's finest short story, "For Esmé—with Love and Squalor."

Esquire (October 1945) published "This Sandwich Has No Mayonnaise," in which Caulfield is stationed in Georgia, mourning Holden, the Boy Errant, who now figures as the Dead Brother.

Collier's (December 1945) published "The Stranger," in which Babe Gladwaller returns and, taking his Little Sister along as an amulet against despair, goes to tell Vincent Caulfield's former girl friend, now married to another man, how the once cynical Sergeant died, apparently transformed by the Dead Brother's spirit.

So in place of Harlequin and Columbine, Pantaloon and Captain, the troupe had its melancholy modern clowns—flailing with words instead of swords, railing with thoughts instead of words, with the choice and proportion of the three languages wholly altered, but still, like their comic predecessors, endlessly acting out their allotted fractions of man's fate and protest.

Then, in December 1945, *Collier's* published "I'm Crazy," in which the sixteen-year-old Holden Caulfield tells how he left the prep school where he had flunked, made his way home, and talked with his Little Sister, who was his amulet against despair. One year afterwards, in "Slight Rebellion off Madison," more of Holden's narrative of his Boy Errantry appeared, expressed this time in a blend of the three primal languages (of tears, of wrath, and of laughter) nearly as beguiling as that in which, more than four years later, it was to

appear as Chapter 17 of *The Catcher in the Rye;* and this
story was published in *The New Yorker.* . . .

And from this time forward (although there were still to
be two fairly dismal treatments of the Artist-Martyr in *Cos-
mopolitan* and a sort of leftover artistic-type story in *Mademoiselle*), J. D. Salinger was a *New Yorker* writer. This was
his second phase. His apparent pride in a bifurcated creativity
subsided. Now *The New Yorker,* with its curious position in-
termediate between mass and class, was his one tribunal. He
wrote *New Yorker* stories.

New Yorker people say there is no special kind of story
that one could refer to as a *"New Yorker* story," and doubtless they are right. But it is worth describing anyway, because
if only it existed, it would be one of the excellent things, one
of the seminal forms, in American literature. In fifty or a
hundred years, Salinger will be thought of as more singular
than he is—singular, but peculiarly responsive to his age—
because the ordinary *New Yorker* story, from which he has
learned so much, will have been forgotten.

At its worst, the *New Yorker* story of the nineteen-forties
was (or officially was not) a tight-souled, snobbish story in
which embarrassment replaced all other emotions—embarrassment at a social error or embarrassment at emotion itself
—and its humor was the ironic exposure of ignorance or dull-
ness. But at its best, it was a generous anecdote with great
moral energy. Its pathos arose from the defeat of the gentle
by the crass. Its humor was a sardonic exposure of inadequacy, measured by the world's standards but not accepting
the world's standards. By "sardonic" I mean a slightly bitter
amusement at oneself; many *New Yorker* stories were therefore about children.

It was "realistic"; that is, it found wisps of tragedy and even
a modest heroism under commonplace surfaces, instead of
embodying universal themes in striking or mythical events as
Shakespeare or Homer did. Thus it depended on observation
rather than invention, and it concealed invention where invention became too strong. Many *New Yorker* writers de-

veloped immense virtuosity in using details—using brand names, gestures, turns of phrase, patterns of taste, all pregnant trivialities—to *make* the surfaces commonplace.

The *New Yorker* story tended to imply rather than state, to develop revealing scenes rather than use narrative summary, to perch on a character's shoulder instead of allowing the narrator to flit omnisciently from point of view to point of view. It was written in a clean, effective English; the *New Yorker* editors insisted on style but discouraged Style, which is the product of a writer's leftover intelligence.

The tone of the *New Yorker* story was related to a spiritual attitude, harmlessness. The creators of this ethos, Robert Benchley, Dorothy Parker, James Thurber, E. B. White, and S. J. Perelman, contributed a cluster of humane notions and emotions—unmuscular agnosticism, fullback-hating, laughing in a relieved way at one's own lack of power, pregnant triviality, admiring people who have faith as one would admire gamblers who had won, and measuring oneself ruefully against the literature of competence and strength that flourished in the boyhood of the world before World War I.

The next story Salinger wrote for the magazine was "A Perfect Day for Bananafish." It is well within the established *New Yorker* modalities. Seymour Glass, the husband who shoots himself, is a development of a *maschera* first suggested in "Babe" Gladwaller, the Absolute Lover, the man who loves deeply without regard to the shallowness of the creature he loves. The believer said, *"Credo quia impossibile."* The Lover says, *"Amo quia impossibile."* Later, Salinger melded this *maschera* with those of the Artist-Martyr and the Guru; but here Seymour Glass is not prinked out with aesthetic and religious implications; he is only an unhappy young man. (Some critics have suggested, on the basis of a Freudian analysis of the "symbols" in this story, that Seymour is despondent over his sexual inadequacy; and it is true that, even in the latest and fullest treatment of him as Artist-Martyr-Guru, Salinger seems to refer to him as an "underadjusted bachelor"; but all this is below the level of a plain reader's awareness.)

The little girl with whom Seymour occupies his last hours is a kind of *ad hoc* Little Sister, but her power of healing is insufficient, and the "fun" is a disguise for the whimper of the Absolute Lover's breaking spirit; we hear the crack of pain in Seymour's laughter, as we do in Holden Caulfield's; Salinger has always been a master at this business of combining the language of the cry for pity with the language of the winsome laugh.

Two other of Salinger's classic stories are concerned with Seymour's kinfolk: in "Uncle Wiggily in Connecticut," the boozy young Westport matron is haunted by Seymour's dead brother, Walt; and as we have seen, in "Down at the Dinghy," the young mother trying to squeeze through her son's fantasy to comfort him is Seymour's sister Boo Boo. Thus, characteristically, began the assembling of the Glass Family, with which Salinger's latest work is concerned.

His third phase began in January 1953, when *The New Yorker* published "Teddy," a complicated and unsuccessful attempt to render mysticism, clairvoyance, and religious resignation in the person of a small boy clambering around an Atlantic liner. "Teddy" experiments with one or two elements which have since been added to the history of the Glasses—the paradox of the scholarly child of a theatrical family, for instance, and the fatuity of the psychologists poring over a child's genius. More significantly, it shows an open, almost proselytizing, concern for religion and betrays a real impatience with the *New Yorker* tone. From this point forward, the demands Salinger has made on his readers have grown remorselessly; it is clear that he is beating at the doors of someone's attention—not the *New Yorker* audience at large, nor yet the audience of any of the solemn academic-literary reviews, nor yet the scolders and sneerers of the various Generations that have recently set up shop, but *someone*. He is appealing to a new tribunal, but not one that already exists.

And the progression is not complete. In spite of his recent eremetical thimblerig in New Hampshire, where he hides from all but a few trusted friends, and even in his latest stories, with their appalling lucubrative gravity, Salinger has probably not yet reached the stage of addressing himself privately-in-public to God; but God only knows what some of his current writing means.

He is an instance—to me he sometimes seems an exasperating instance—of James's law of the progress of the social Self. Lately, when I find him describing a young man's conversations by simply stating that they had the same effect as Beethoven's later works ("and maybe I'm thinking especially, though it seems a trifle picky, of the B-flat-major and C-sharp-minor quartets") or when I have to extract implications from his offhand comparison of a ten-year-old boy's technique of marble shooting with Zen archery, or when I have to think over his *obiter dicta* on Kierkegaard, Freud, Issa, Lao Ti-Kai, and Shelley, I for one tend to group myself with the audience Salinger has deliberately left behind and to murmur that there is such a thing, damn it, as the social climbing of the social Self.

The progression is not complete. Nor is it irreversible, for the fact is—and this fact preserves Salinger's freedom to choose between continuing and escaping his present obsessive *longueurs*—that the intended audience is one thing, the actual audience another, as I have suggested. For example, the stories "Franny" and "Zooey" (which first appeared, like nuns in a lingerie shop, in *The New Yorker* in 1955 and 1957 respectively) were not intended for popularity; they are unrelentingly discursive, and they emphasize a certain bowelless mysticism pointedly different from the popular taste in spirituality, which runs to cute priests and ravishing platitudes; surely Salinger *wanted* these stories to be caviar to the general; yet as soon as they were reprinted in book form in 1961, *Franny and Zooey* became a top-ranking best seller.

One reason, doubtless, was publicity. Another reason was the continued popularity of an earlier (and very different) work, *The Catcher in the Rye.*

First, publicity.

Salinger as a publicity-hero is, once again, almost the paradigmatic opposite of Hemingway. The public Hemingway was a hairy-chested and worldly-wise old confection; motile but accessible; given to decerebrate, bloody, splurging amusements—*big*-game hunting, *deep*-sea fishing—but filled with recondite lore about them; a great liver of life; a great poser for photographs; just what (let us say) a filling-station attendant might dream of being. Privately, Hemingway was an intellectual.

The public Salinger is very private; he is camera-shy, and looks out of the two available adult photographs of him with a slight mingling of apprehension and self-satisfaction, his eyes liquid and opaque; he is domestic but aloof; gentle; squeamish; faintly neurasthenic. He obviously has had one experience of being at some time or other more than a little sickish. He is a tall fellow who lives in his head, emerging at long intervals for an ice-cream soda; a mystic unafraid of the universe but uneasy with his neighbors; an autodidact; a wounded man. Privately, Salinger might be much more public.

But what relation the publicity-Salinger bears to the "real" Salinger is not at all clear—could it be significant, I wonder, that it was *Hemingway* who created the impotent Nick Adams, and *Salinger* who created the quixotic Holden Caulfield? In such cases, the relation between public figure and real man is always subtle, because each personage helps to create the other; but in Salinger's case the problem is greatly complicated by the stories themselves, for in these a third personage, who is not exactly the public figure and not exactly the real man but a projection of both, is darkly in evidence.

The author's Greta Garbo bit up in Cornish, New Hampshire, made excellent copy for *Time* and *Life* in 1961 when the book *Franny and Zooey* went on sale; and whether it was done by the publicity Salinger or the "real" Salinger is not important, for it really owed its effect to the curiosity which had been aroused by that third Salinger, whom we might call the "chimera" Salinger and who is a truly unusual and formidable bit of fantasy.

Most authors do a certain amount of pseudo-objectifying: they disguise their emotions as inventions. For instance, Hemingway's Nick Adams is profoundly involved, in some complicated ways, with Hemingway himself, and as we read the Nick Adams stories we become aware of this involvement, and aware that writing about Nick Adams is serving some need of Hemingway's (I have put this in the present tense because it is not a matter of scholarship but the aura of the stories), and aware moreover that our awareness of this serves a need of Hemingway's. But at the same time, Nick Adams is *ostensibly* an independent entity, ostensibly an ordinary fictitious fact, and this pretense of objectivity also serves a need of Hemingway's, as does the celebrated flat-sentence style with its ironically exaggerated matter-of-factness.

Salinger, on the other hand, now engages in the strange practice of pseudo-*sub*jectifying: he takes fictitious facts and pretends that they are glimpses of himself. This is new. Earlier in his career he drew, like any author, on the particulars of his own life—on his difficulties with a succession of schools, on his first trip to Europe, on his army service—and he donated these cherished possessions to various characters; but at the same time, he donated to these characters identities of their own, a kind of limited human existence in their own right. Now, instead, he melds his own life with his inventions in a kind of eerie literary prosthesis, and pretends that the resultant monster or chimera is himself, the old primal Himself and not part of the alien Outside World. He has been relying more and more on narrative techniques that give a strained confessional tone to incidents he has invented—on first-person techniques that slyly hint that the inflections of the author's *ego ipse,* speaking from the concrete study at Cornish, can be heard under the accents of the author's conventional *alter ego* speaking from the page; first-person narration so cunningly inconvenient that we feel it *must* mean something special; first-person narration that sometimes turns abruptly into third-person narration. . . .

The key to the relations between the real Salinger, the chimera Salinger, and the publicity Salinger lies in what he does (or they do) with first-person narration; for it is evident that, to J. D. Salinger, first-person narration is no longer merely a way of solving the technical problems of storytelling. Like Conrad, he relies upon it for more than it can do; he needs it because he is revising Himself.

About the end of 1947, for instance, he began to experiment with the *New Yorker* "casual," a special sort of personal reminiscence (or story plausibly cast as a reminiscence) which one could find towards the back of the magazine almost any week in the late forties, trailing its cozy pathos between the ads for expensive gin, effeminate ties, resorts in the British Commonwealth, and leather goods. Written by dozens of *New Yorker* regulars and occasionally by a *New Yorker* hopeful, the "casual" was nonetheless (and this is the gravamen of Salinger's experiments) a set form, one of the very few set forms we have had in modern prose writing; it had a style and structure which—inasmuch as *The New Yorker,* an essentially conservative magazine, has always been able to make a fashion look like a tradition and vice versa—had become so well established in readers' minds that, glancing at the first sentence, they settled back into amused nostalgia, ready to learn all over again that human nature was uniformly surprising and that the past (even the war, which was somehow made to recede further into the past) was full of characters. The "casual" opened with a quiet exordium, usually including a "peg" or timely excuse for reminiscing, usually involving a movement of the mind from the large stage for events to the small, and always establishing a specific date—something like this: "Reading about Vice-President Dawes' gravestone recently, I could not help thinking about my own brief career in the lapidary trade, or art. Back in 1931, when I was beginning junior high school, my

Uncle Chester was one of the . . ." Throughout the "casual," diction and texture of thought were smooth but plain; all the arts of concealing art were used; as were, demurely, the rhetorical figures appropriate to what the Latin critics called the low-density style (*adtenuatum figurae genus*), such as *diminutio, effictio,* and (in a mild way) *praeteritio.* The "casual" often ended with a falling close: "I saw Harkavy only once after that, in a . . ." Sometimes, however, the "casual" would end in a sort of easy-going caricature of a James Joyce epiphany, with some heavily commonplace phrase or other enriched in some sophisticated way or other by the context: "Harkavy looked at my uncle and said, without a vestige of malice, 'Well, what you don't know won't hurt you.' At the moment, that seemed to sum it all up as well as anything."

Salinger's experiments with this form, then, trace a cardinal change in his attitude towards first-person narration.

Initial stage. The first experiments show Salinger studiously working up the rhetoric of *The New Yorker,* which he had broken into a year before with "Slight Rebellion off Madison"; he was now, as it were, assembling features for a social Self which was to be suited nicely to the new tribunal. A young girl's first experiments with lipstick do not always get her kissed, however; and "A Girl I Knew," his first "casual," appeared in February 1948—but in *Good Housekeeping.* (In those days, *Good Housekeeping* had the reputation of being about the only place one could send a rejected *New Yorker* short story without fundamental rewriting.) The story is a waveringly luminous reminiscence of a year in Vienna, drawn presumably from a business trip on which the eighteen-year-old Jerry Salinger accompanied his father to Europe after dropping out of N.Y.U. in 1937; perhaps it was tinted by the twenty-six-year-old Salinger's marriage after the war to a European lady physician. For all its fidelity to the rules and tricks, "A Girl I Knew" fails as a "casual" by finally allowing a streak of unmitigated pain—the murder of a Jewish girl—to pierce its safe anecdotal world. Whether this was because of Salinger's misunderstanding of the form or whether it was a romantic attempt to break the form and let life or something into it is difficult to say.

Second stage. Ulterior imitation. A year later, Salinger, having become a *New Yorker* regular, was using the form in his own special way—not so much modifying it in order to develop its neglected possibilities (though he did thicken the style a little) as exploiting the fact that it *was* set and *was* familiar to the magazine's audience in order to get a certain response from that audience. "The Laughing Man" is ostensibly a grown man's memories of belonging to a boys' recreation group organized by a gentle, homely, plebeian law student from N.Y.U. named John Gedsudski. The central device is a story told by "the Chief" to his young charges, a series of wild installments about a hideously maimed superman and his war against a cruel French detective and his exquisite daughter; contrapuntally, we are given glimpses of Chief Gedsudski's doomed love for a beautiful Wellesley girl of good family; and by implication we are told of the narrator's doomed idolatry for the Chief. The story is, I think, a good one, but it is certainly a much better one for those who, like me, have been brought up on *The New Yorker* and its conventions than for those who have not; its effect depends not only on the "casual" tone but on its departures from the "casual" tone, not only on the adult narrator's apparent condescension toward himself as a child but on his actual shy and mournful tenderness for the child he was and for all childlike souls.

Third stage. Byronic equilibrium between classical form and romantic egoism. A year later, Salinger was able to use the "casual" form with a power and irony he has never exceeded. "For Esmé—with Love and Squalor" is a brilliant story, both technically and spiritually, yet in both technique and mood it foreshadows the obscurities of the latest stories. It begins in the classical "casual" manner: "Just recently, by air mail, I received an invitation to a wedding that will take place in England on April 18th . . ." In the next two sentences, we learn that the narrator is living in the humorous world of the American Matriarchy, the world of Dagwood and Jiggs, the world of generous impractical husbands with strong sensible wives and grim mothers-in-law; he is living in a *New Yorker* neighborhood in that world, but the culture is the same culture: the narrator wants to go to the wedding, "expenses be hanged," but he has "discussed the matter rather extensively" with his wife, "a breathtakingly levelheaded girl," and "we've decided" that he is to stay home and help entertain his mother-in-law ("Mother Grencher") for two weeks.

From this carefully clichéd humor, the narrator slips back to "April of 1944," to a portrait of himself as a glum G.I. training in England for the invasion. In this section the tone is carefully controlled at a somewhat higher level of sophistication: the narrator now appears to be an intellectual of sorts, for his training course is a "rather specialized" one given by British Intelligence ("rather" is a good "casual" adverb) and the trainees are "letter-writing types." Thurberish and Perelmanesque touches are sprinkled through the narration, as when the narrator artfully contrasts the dreary reality of war with its romance by describing a walk in the rain—". . . after synchronizing my wristwatch and the clock in the latrine, I walked down the long, wet cobblestone hill into town. I ignored the flashes of lightning all around me. They either had your number on them or they didn't." We are given hints of the *New Yorker* readers' old sad friend the non-fullback, *l'homme moyen sensible,* the man just a shade too decent and intelligent to go fighting or wenching or succeeding, the *rather* watered-down milksop; but only hints. And even in these hints, continuity with the henpecked husband of the exordium is maintained: the narrator rereads a letter from his wife "telling me how the service at Schrafft's Eighty-eighth Street had fallen off" and one from his mother-in-law "asking me to please send her some cashmere yarn first chance I got away from 'camp.'" When the thirteen-year-old girl, Esmé, makes her appearance, with her enchanting combination of innocence and responsible world-liness, the story still continues to walk along the faint, wan-dering borderline between wistfulness and tragedy. Esmé is the Little Sister, one of the most powerful and unexpected and true of all the figures in Salinger's *commedia;* but she is also the English Child of the *New Yorker's* anglophilia. This section is still cast as a conventional "casual"; the conditioned reader therefore accepts it as authentic autobiography and accepts the narrator as the usual rueful literary-type-in-an-operators'-world.

Then I changes to X, Prufrock to Hamlet, Thurber to—whom? Kafka? Dostoyevsky? "I'm still around," says the nar-rator with a last smirk, "but from here on in, for reasons I'm not at liberty to disclose, I've disguised myself . . ." and Sergeant X, hagridden, shaking, sleepless, is before us. He is in Germany. The war is over. X is just out of the hospital —he has had a "nervous breakdown," as a fellow soldier brightly puts it—and has returned to duty, his duty being to arrest war criminals. In the house of a Nazi spinster he has arrested, he finds a copy of a book, *Die Zeit Ohne Beispiel* ("The Epoch without Precedent") by Hitler's monstrous Minister of Propaganda and Public Enlightenment, Dr. Goeb-bels, and in it the woman has written "in ink, in German, in a small, hopelessly sincere handwriting" the words "Dear God, life is hell." X picks up a pencil stub and writes, in English, a sentence of Father Zossima's from *The Brothers Karamazov:* "Fathers and teachers, I ponder 'What is hell?' I maintain that it is the suffering of being unable to love." Sitting in agony amid unopened mail from home, retching and fainting, Sergeant X comes on a small parcel from Esmé; it is her dead father's watch, which she has sent to this chance acquaintance with a letter in which the clear lilt of her innocence is heard again; and X feels a healing sleep creep over him.

Professors Frederick L. Gwynn and Joseph L. Blotner, in their excellent little handbook on Salinger, say flatly that the incident of the Dostoyevsky inscription is "the high point" of

Salinger's art. To me, Esmé's letter, with its *believable* charisma, is a higher point. After all, the word "love" is easy enough to say—like the word "miracle."

But if one is going to analyze what it is that Salinger has done and how he has done it, then one must observe the immense cleverness of the shift from I to X. It is what authenticates the abyss which opens in the third section of the story. If one could read backwards, of course, the possibility that X was fictitious would contaminate the I of the opening, but readers cannot read backwards; on the other hand, if the third section continued in the first person, it would *feel* wrong, it would *wallow*. The very coyness of the transition from I to X plays its part in assuring that the reader's credence will be transferred from the "casual" to the terrible and piteous. A fellow soldier's cheery observation that X must have been "unstable like" even before the war and this friend's oafish demand that X "be *sincere*" (which causes X to vomit) also play their part. And these likewise are the beginnings of Salinger's morbid game of pseudo-subjectifying. For, once he has implanted in our minds the suggestion of a private origin, the aura of personal tragedy and humiliation becomes so choking at this point in the story that we feel the narrative is indeed the confession, not the creation, of the writer; and the disarming exordium now seems in retrospect to have been the determined lightness of a man who fears a recurrence of horror; in fact, we suspect that all the literary tactics of the story were dictated by that fear; and the precision of clinical detail—X's delayed realization that his hands are shaking, his tic, his bleeding gums, his having to shield his eyes from light, and the rest—makes us mutter, "He didn't just read up on that."

Unnumbered stage. I do not know when "De Daumier-Smith's Blue Period" was written; the piece, never published in a magazine, first appeared in the collection *Nine Stories* in 1953. In it, Salinger uses the "casual" form to authenticate a description of the classical Zen mystical experience of *satori*. Few writers have tried to describe mystical experiences; in fact most mystics regard the attempt as futile. It is interesting that Salinger should have undertaken to do it by means of the "casual" format. The enterprise is not as presumptuous as it might seem, but it reveals a certain peculiarity—I would say a defect—in Salinger's idea of spirituality.

Mystical experiences in general, oriental or Christian, involve a penetration of the mind into some still center of reality, into the eye of the storm of being, where the three laws of rational thought (A is A, Everything is either A or not-A, Nothing can be both A and not-A) are inoperative, and from which all things may be seen together in motionless unity, all boundaries and distinctions themselves being revealed as portions of the One, and all movements and changes revealed as themselves seized in stasis. To the Christian, this is "experimental knowledge of the presence of God"; since love is God's distinctive mode of communication, the Christian mystic feels himself to be in the throes of unrecountable passion. But to the Zen Buddhist, enlightenment is distinguished by less intimate signs: it is irrational, and any attempt to reconcile it with a theology is a mutilation; it is conclusive, and it simply overrules the sights and sounds of the moment and even the ideas that may have prepared for it; it is liberating, and is often preceded by a paralyzing civil war of the conscious mind; it is sudden, and is usually precipitated by a trivial event—even by a nonsense phrase or a blow. Love and lovelike ecstasies have no place in *satori,* and the Zen practitioner finds, sitting in the eye of the storm, not God but the Things-As-They-Are-ness of Things As They Are. Chao-pien, a great bureaucrat of the Sung dynasty, describes his own Zen experience in this poem:

Devoid of thought, I sat quietly by the desk in my official
   room,
With my fountain-mind undisturbed, as serene as water;
A sudden clash of thunder, the mind-doors burst open,
And lo, there sitteth the old man in all his homeliness.

Dr. Suzuki, the well-known interpreter of Zen to the West, comments simply that a Christian would have ended,

And lo, there sitteth God in all His glory!

In "De Daumier-Smith's Blue Period," the narrator, a somewhat disoriented *flaneur* working for a Japanese who runs a correspondence art school, has a mystical experience which is irrational, conclusive, liberating and sudden—he sees a big salesgirl in the window of an orthopedic appliances store, changing the truss on a dummy; she slips on some irrigation basins and falls heavily on her backside, and "Suddenly . . . the sun came up and sped toward the bridge of my nose at the rate of ninety-three million miles a second. . . . The thing lasted for no more than a few seconds. When I got my sight back, the girl had gone from the window, leaving behind her a shimmering field of exquisite, twice-blessed enamel flowers." Although the Zen characteristics of this are obvious, the experience in its context seems somehow suffused with love, and the deliberate frivolity of the narrative seems dictated by an embarrassment alien to *satori* and more appropriate to Christian love. The design of the story is Zen; the feeling of the story is Christian. Salinger has never solved this problem, and as he attacks it again and again, his literary commitment to this sort of narrative seems to have prevailed over his feelings.

The story fails also because it is not morbid enough: remaining safely within the "casual" form, it imparts no sense of troubled depths in the narrator, and for some reason we (at least in the West) cannot accept religious evidence except from palpable human beings who are united with us in a common life of anxiety and pain. Perhaps because of the tradition of the Christian martyrs, who "bore witness to the Faith" by suffering, we in the West cannot take a mystical experience very seriously on the evidence of smiling men, even if we are supplied with copious hints that the smiles are really grimaces of pain. We certainly cannot take mystical experience seriously unless there is a man who seems real to us and who says "*I* had it." Despite the initials, we do not discern Jerome David Salinger the man (or the chimera, either) in Jean de Daumier-Smith. Just as in reading "For Esmé" we say to ourselves that the author could not possibly have gotten Sergeant X's symptoms out of a book, so in reading "Blue Period" we say to ourselves that he could not possibly have gotten Daumier-Smith's symptoms anywhere else. Perhaps it was from a fear of overtaxing the "casual" form that Salinger made Daumier-Smith too cute and too remote. This lack of morbidity and lack of subjectivity were to be corrected in later attempts. But the lack of God (Who is, after all, the only link between love and mysticism) seems difficult for him to do anything about.

Latest phase. In 1955, Salinger returned to the "casual" form in "Raise High the Roofbeam, Carpenters," but with a difference. This was a mutant "casual," an almost frightening case of gigantism. There was no fear now of overtaxing the form; Salinger was no longer writing within (or ostensibly within) the *New Yorker* tradition. He was now explicitly writing in the Salinger tradition.

This narrative recounts Seymour Glass's wedding day; the bridegroom never actually appears, either at the wedding or in the story, though he does elope with the bride afterwards and though excerpts from his diary are reprinted. The power of the narrative derives from the role of the narrator, who is Seymour's brother, Buddy; the bridegroom's absence is all the more rich in comic embarrassment because of his brother's presence. But the narrator's role in "Raise High" is not limited to this function; there is already an implication that the behavior of the opaque Seymour contains philosophic riches beyond the dreams of commonplace men, and that Buddy has the key. Thus Salinger creates not only an apostle but an apostolic succession, and by melding himself with Buddy he acquires a kind of seerlike status of his own. The dual function of the chimera—to support fiction with the authority of the author, and to afford an alternative life for the author himself—is now established.

143063

Buddy is again the narrator of "Zooey" (1957), in which the plausibility of the "casual" form is augmented by the reader's persistent feeling that Buddy Glass is so fantastically cumbersome a device that he must be more than a mere device. By 1959, when "Seymour, an Introduction" appeared in *The New Yorker* Buddy Glass had acquired many of the current biographical particulars (some of them hoaxes) attributed to Jerome David Salinger, while Salinger reciprocally had acquired in the public mind many of the particulars attributed to Buddy Glass (some of them facts). "Seymour, an Introduction" is not really a "casual"; or if it is, the form has been obliterated in its own wild growth; but it is supported by the same technique of authentication.

This sequence of experiments shows, centrally, that Salinger's audience is peculiarly *immediate* to him; he writes to his readers; he takes into account the things they have read, not in the way of myths and classics but in the way of ephemeral magazine sketches; he writes in the context of the particular periodical where his work will appear; I cannot think of any author now living who has written so ambitiously and at the same time so journalistically. It is no accident that we keep speculating as to how much of "Buddy Glass" or "Sergeant X" is really the mysterious Jerome David Salinger; we are meant to speculate about this—probably not because it helps sales (though it does), but perhaps because it helps Salinger (though it does not). A very similar pseudo-subjectivity did not, in my opinion, help Poe; it did not help Gide; it helped establish their reputations among romantically susceptible folk, especially among those who, for reasons of their own, would have liked to think that art releases its votaries from the canons of normality; but pseudo-subjectivity did not help Poe and Gide artistically. (Perhaps in other ways, but not artistically.) In any case, those two, were engaged in a somewhat different enterprise: they were not interested in literary creation, but in becoming men of letters.

Salinger is interested in literary creation, but he is beguiled by being a creator and evidently cannot escape distracting visions of the alternative social Selves offered to him by being the creator of this or of that. In "Seymour, an Introduction," speaking through Buddy, he alludes to "the four dead men, the four variously notorious Sick Men or underadjusted bachelors," including Kafka, Kierkegaard and van Gogh, "whom I most often run to—occasionally in real disasters—when I want any perfectly credible information about modern artistic processes." He goes on to denounce "our busy neo-Freudian Arts and Letters clinics" and their "very young students and greener clinicians, themselves implicitly bursting with good mental health," who seek diagnostically to reduce the aberrations of artists to commonplace complexes such as ordinary folk might have; the artist's disease, he cries, is Art Itself: "However contradictory the coroner's report—whether he pronounces Consumption or Loneliness or Suicide to be the cause of death—isn't it plain how the true artist-seer actually dies?" This is a dangerous frame of mind in which to make art, particularly art that concerns art. It breeds chimeras and men of letters.

So much for publicity and the strange dialectic of publicity and privacy. We can now turn to the fact of Salinger's popularity. Aside from extrinsic publicity, and the commercial benefits of exhibitionistic shyness (or whatever the phenomenon is), and the esteem of the populace for any artist who acts like some kind of nut or something, and the self-romanticizing esteem of the educated for any artist who demonstrates that the artist's eye is a wound, there is still a plain historical basis for Salinger's reputation: it is that *The Catcher in the Rye* has become the testament of a rather discouraged, self-conscious, self-pitying, pharisaical (Do I mean that word? I think I do) generation of youngsters and youngish thirty-five-year-olds. The book, which is, I believe, one of the half-dozen or so best novels ever written by an American, means a good deal more even than its admirers seem to find in it. But they do buy it; they quote its catchwords to their friends; they find themselves whistling its tune, as it were; it seems to speak for them; and so they also bought *Franny and Zooey,* which does *not* speak for them but which does awe them, and valiantly go at *Raise High the Roofbeam.*

That *The Catcher in the Rye* is serviceable as a temporal testament is surprising. Salinger's Holden Caulfield is not really like Goethe's Young Werther, the personified egotism of a generation. He is more like Huck Finn, who is *not* an eponymous figure. In his actions and attitudes and in his style, Holden, like Huck, sums up a rare but permanent kind of boy—a fabulous Boy Errant—a kind of spirit—trying to survive in a particular moral habitat. Holden is neither discouraged nor self-conscious nor self-pitying nor pharisaical; and *Huckleberry Finn* was read not by Huck Finns but by Tom Sawyers.

Why, I wonder, has *The Catcher in the Rye* been received more as a *Sorrows of Werther* than as an *Adventures of Huckleberry Finn?* (Not that *The Catcher* has been quite as epidemic as *Werther* was; it has not inspired countless nervous breakdowns as *Werther* inspired suicides; it is far less gross in affect and effect.) Fifty years after writing *Werther,* Goethe told Eckermann that the book was not a manifesto of one particular generation but a manifesto of *each* generation against the last: "The much-talked-about 'age of Werther' is not strictly speaking a mere historical event. It belongs to the life of every individual who must accommodate himself and his innate and instinctive sense of freedom to the irksome restrictions of an obsolescent world. Happiness unattained, ambition unfulfilled, desires unsatisfied are the defects not of any particular age, but of every individual human being. It would be a pity indeed if everyone had not once in his life known a period when it seemed to him as if *Werther* had been written especially for him." Even if this were true of *Werther,* it is not true of *The Catcher.* Holden stands for something much more important than selfish little grievances against the universe like happiness unattained, ambition unfulfilled, and desires unsatisfied; he stands for something much less numerous and much more enduring than a "generation."

I should like to set down, in no particular order, a few statements about Holden Caulfield:

A teacher tells him that he, Holden, is "confused and frightened and even sickened by human behavior"; but, sick as he becomes, his perceptions are clear and his conduct is gallant.

His ultimate word of condemnation is "phony."

He wants to scrub out all the dirty words scrawled on all the walls of the world, yet his own vocabulary is fairly gamey; his reason is not prudery but the vivid thought of the inroads such language could make in the innocence of children.

He is celibate not by impulse but by compassion: he can do nothing with the prostitute he has hired: "I thought of her going in a store and buying [the dress] and nobody in the store knowing she was a prostitute and all. . . . It made me feel sad as hell—I don't know why exactly."

His anger is formed of twisted compassion: to the pimp who beats him up he cries, "You're a stupid chiseling moron, and in about two years you'll be one of those scraggy guys that come up to you on the street and ask for a dime for coffee. You'll have snot all over your dirty, filthy overcoat, and you'll—"

He feels the injustices done to others as done to himself.

He thinks he is "yellow," but in the hands of bullies he is as steadfast, as humbly unconscious of his spiritual appearance, as a martyr.

What he wants to be is "the catcher in the rye," the only big person in a field of playing children, with the job of catching them and keeping them from falling off "some crazy cliff."

He finds Catholics cliquish, and envies them: "He was enjoying the conversation about tennis and all, but you could tell he would've enjoyed it *more* if I was a Catholic and all. That kind of stuff drives me crazy. . . . I'd be the same way, probably, if I was a Catholic."

He dreams of being a deaf-mute and living as a recluse; but he adds a beautiful deaf-mute girl to his dream.

He wakes up a schoolmate to ask: "What's the routine on joining a monastery?"

The tendency of these statements is obvious. In his relations with "old Sally," who is practicing to be the Beautiful Wrong Girl, Holden is the Absolute Lover. In his relations with the world and the flesh and the devil he is the Hurt Saint. His quixotry is part of his sanctity: Don Quixote, whatever Cervantes may originally have intended, is no mere jape at chivalry; he has escaped from the topical interests of his creator; it is true that the mad Don thinks the windmills are giants, but it is also true that he *fights* the windmills thinking they are giants; his perceptions in the world of the spirit are not faulty, only his perceptions in the world of the flesh; and when we try to think of the Don's gaunt, sad, strangely optimistic countenance, we actually borrow the lineaments of an El Greco saint; because Don Quixote, under the aspect of eternity, is a saint. To say that Holden Caulfield is a finished Christian saint would be saying too much; he is a saint struggling in the toils of sanity. His rhetoric—and in this Salinger towers above a dozen contemporaries equally skilled in "natural" dialogue, and towers far above the redoubtable aesthete Hemingway—Holden's rhetoric is the natural language of this struggle. To the extent that we, the readers, are Holden's tribunal, his command of the three languages —the wild undercurrent of pain beneath the wild tirades and the wild gags—is perfectly effective: Holden excites our deepest pity, he makes us feel ashamed, and he enchants us. But beyond that, his rhetoric has the unearthly effect—the unworldly effect, perhaps—of letting us catch, through the Boy Errant's rapt eyes, glimpses of eternity shining through the phenomenal world. "That killed me," he says. "She scared hell out of me," he says. His particular phrase is "and all"— "She looked so damn *nice,* the way she kept going around and around in her blue coat and all," he says—as if each experience wore a halo. His fallacy is *ab uno disce omnes:*

he abstracts and generalizes wildly, and his closing words are, "It's funny. Don't ever tell anybody anything. If you do, you start missing everybody." Fleetingly, for the duration of a word, Holden sees beyond the solidity of the world that has committed him to a psychiatric ward (the world that also knew Don Quixote was a mad old man) into Mercy, Pity, Peace and Love.

When *The Catcher in the Rye* was published in 1951 and became a Book-of-the-Month-Club selection and a best seller, it was generally mistaken for a clinical study of adolescence. It is strange that William Saroyan's *The Human Comedy*, with its spiritual flat feet, its loose rhetoric and its canting sentimentality, should have passed for some sort of warm, profound affirmation, while *The Catcher in the Rye* (which owes names and incidents to the earlier book but transcends it as *Hamlet* transcends Holinshed) has been mistaken for a document on the neurosis or folly of a boy, or, more recently, for a document on the mere neurosis or folly of our age.

What now?

"Franny," "Raise High the Roofbeam, Carpenters," "Zooey," and "Seymour, an Introduction" together posit what is perhaps the most strenuous universe of discourse in modern fiction, the Glass ménage.

As Salinger, deftly picking up narrative threads from earlier stories, has assembled the family, it consists of Les Glass and Bessie Gallagher Glass, who had been a vaudeville team on the old Pantages circuit. (Salinger himself is the son of a Jewish father and a Scotch-Irish mother.) Les and Bessie had seven children. (Salinger has one older sister.) The oldest was Seymour, who had committed suicide in "A Perfect Day for Bananafish." Next is Buddy, the narrator of "Raise High the Roofbeam, Carpenters," "Zooey" and "Seymour, an Introduction." Next is Boo Boo (Glass) Tannenbaum, who had been the suburban mother of "Down at the Dinghy." Next the twins, Walt and Waker; Walt, who was killed in a

freak G.I. accident in 1945, had been the lover of the now be-
sotted Westport matron in "Uncle Wiggily in Connecticut";
Waker is a Catholic priest, apparently now a cloistered monk.
Next, Zachary, or Zooey, is a youthful television actor. Finally, Frances, or Franny, is a college girl. Most of the
Glass children, when young, were radio quiz kids, and their
erudition, of which copious samples are given, is now so great
as sometimes to provide a little inadvertent comic relief. They
can speak God knows how many languages; they know the
sutras and haiku and Kierkegaard and obscure Russian tracts
and Rilke and W. C. Fields and the Tao; they talk so
learnedly that all Salinger's rhythmic and mimetic gifts are
called into play to transform into dialogue what sometimes
seems a convulsive emptying of the author's notebooks. It is
brave of Salinger to offer encyclopedic knowledge as a heroic
attribute in this frontal fashion, because nothing causes such
widespread resentment nowadays as education. The television
quiz shows of a few years ago were popular for the same
reason that Roman circuses were popular, not because the
gladiators were skilled but because they were killed; and the
undisguised glee with which the public and its press viewed
the later exposure of the "intellectuals" was in no way related to ethical sentiment; in the intricate, expert-run world of
today, men with education are thought to have the same
advantages over plain folk that men with swords had over the
Roman plebs. And so, considering Salinger's own deliberate
involvement with Buddy Glass, his posture is something of a
proclamation in itself. (Salinger's own difficulties in school
have been mentioned.)

But the real question about Salinger's outpouring of information is whether it is fitly related to his spiritual message.
Salinger's spiritual message is, I think, refracted by his eclec-
ticism. On the one side are his acknowledged inclinations toward Zen and the evident quest, in which all the Glass
children are engaged, for some ultimate experience of cen-
trality. On the other side is Salinger's flurried oscillation

between lucubration and the luscious emotions, both of which are repugnant to Zen.

In "Franny" and "Zooey," Franny goes on a college football date with a literary-minded youth, listens distraitly to his attempts to impress her, goes to the ladies' room and cries bitterly, reads from a pea-green Russian mystical tract, returns to her date, tries to explain her state of mind to him and passes out; when she revives slightly she lies murmuring silent ejaculations to Jesus. When she is brought home, she undergoes crying jags, long discussions with Zooey (who emerges from a long conference in the bathroom with mother Glass), a phone conversation with Buddy (acted by Zooey) and at last goes to sleep. We know she is healed. In all this, Salinger avoids any direct description of a mystical experience, substituting a discursive and clinical analysis of what a mystical experience is *not*. But one has the impression of a terrible discontinuity at the heart of Salinger's mysticism. There is Jesus, but Jesus as a compelling man. There is divinity, but it is the remote Godhead of Meister Eckhart; it is not the living God. Mysticism—which violently obliterates the distinction between knower and known, between one and many, between each and all—has the effect of assuaging the primal wound, returning to that first universe in which the Self and the Outside World are undivided. But the religious reconciliation of mysticism and reason—the idea that all souls and all things and all instants of time are part of one existence because together they are supported above the abyss of non-existence by the strong hand of a conscious God—is not in Salinger.

Seymour Glass, whose ghost hangs over the Glass family like an impossible mortgage, began as the Absolute Lover; the Dead Brother followed; the Hurt Saint came later; the Artist-Martyr was a still later emphasis. Many commentators have remarked on the difficulty Salinger has now created for himself in taking this character, who did marry a cold and shallow girl and who did commit suicide, and trying to represent him as a wise and charismatic spiritual master—as a bodhisattva, in fact. The essential problem of deciding what Seymour Glass means is one of deciding what, if anything, the world means. Salinger has not really decided.

"Raise High the Roofbeam, Carpenters" begins with a Chinese tale—very much in the anti-intellectual tradition of Tao and Zen—about a buyer of horses so skillful and so wise that he saw the *essential* horse but failed to notice such distracting accidents of the phenomenal world as the horse's color and gender. Buddy Glass's comment on this is that since Seymour's death "I haven't been able to think of anybody whom I'd care to send out to look for horses in his stead." (For horses, maybe not; but for women, I say to myself, almost anybody else would do.)

Yet in "Seymour, an Introduction" Buddy recalls the time when Seymour and he, eight and six, were allowed to get up and entertain their parents' friends at a party; there were sixty guests, mostly strangers to the children, and when they began to leave at two o'clock in the morning, Seymour asked and received permission to fetch their coats; he retrieved them from all over the apartment and "from watching the guests for some three hours, from grinning at them, from I think, loving them, Seymour—without asking any questions first— brought very nearly all the guests, one or two at a time, and without any mistakes, their own true coats, and all the men . . . their hats." Buddy goes on to assert that this talent (of all talents!) is essential to first-rate achievement in Chinese and Japanese poetry—in which Seymour was, of course, proficient from the age of eleven and which, for some reason, Salinger makes the touchstone of spiritual insight.

This contradiction is symptomatic of Salinger's difficulties in elevating the crumpled Seymour to spiritual mastery. He had not decided whether that small portion of a thing that protrudes into the physical world is or is not the pathway to knowledge of the spiritual remainder of it. Is "loving" a part of Seymour's cognitive processes? If so, Salinger is caught in a predicament from which he can escape only by ambiguity. Seymour loved his Beautiful Wrong Muriel; this at least is a permanent fact in Salinger's universe of discourse. Well, then, did he love *Muriel* or did he *love* Muriel? Did he perceive what spiritual reality lay behind the handsome part of her that protruded into the physical world, and did he (without irony, without self-punishment) find the spirit lovely? Or did he perceive a cold, unlighted vacuity behind the palpable Muriel and did he, from pity or charity—and precisely *because* of the unloveliness of what he found—give of himself in love to fill that insatiable void? In "Raise High the Roofbeam, Carpenters," when Seymour fails to attend his own wedding, Buddy takes the bridegroom's diary into the bathroom (the Glass family do their best thinking in privies) and leafs through it, and what he finds there is a stream of praise for the bride so *continuously* ambiguous that, were it not for the diarist's manifest pain, one would think he was being sarcastic.

Salinger has tried to escape this dilemma, it seems to me, by surreptitiously sawing off both its horns. He has, through Buddy Glass, repudiated Zen: "Seymour's and my roots in Eastern philosophy . . . were, are, planted in the New and Old Testaments, Advaita Vedanta, and classical Taoism." And he has partly shifted his emphasis from Seymour as family Guru ("I want to talk to Seymour," mutters Franny in "Zooey," seven years after Seymour's death) to Seymour as Artist-Martyr ("the artist and Sick Man I've loved most in this world," Buddy calls him in "Seymour, an Introduction").

The next step in the progress of J. D. Salinger's social Self is impossible to predict, but it is impossible to be optimistic about it. In every previous phase of his work, he had a definable audience whose expectations were distinct; and those expectations wrought very powerfully on Salinger's mind, and posed problems for him, and piqued his pride. But for nearly ten years he has been writing for an audience of converts. A cult is not a healthy audience. It can do no work on an author's mind because it is not made up of people who are themselves, who have prejudices, who have stupidities, who have habits of their own.

Has Salinger begun to write fiction for an audience of fictions?

Or will the dynamics of reputation, which have succeeded in making the general public eat the caviar, provide him with a psychological base for a new start—a return to the grief and sternness and joy of *The Catcher in the Rye?*

Who is to be Jerome David Salinger's next Fat Lady?

THE FABULIST'S WORLDS:

VLADIMIR NABOKOV

His tragedy, Vladimir Nabokov has said, is that he cannot write and be read in his native tongue. To American admirers of Nabokov's fiction and poetry, this may seem a sweet sadness, since his English, synthetic like Isak Dinesen's, is enormously elegant and witty. Nabokov was born in St. Petersburg in 1899 to an eminent Russian family. His father was a member of the first Duma; his grandfather was State Minister of Justice under Alexander II; his great-grandfather was president of the Academy of Medicine. In 1919 the family fled from Russia, and Nabokov completed his education at Trinity College, Cambridge. Until 1940, when he came to America, he lived in England, Germany and France, establishing a reputation in *emigré* circles as a novelist and poet. In America he taught at various universities and became professor of Russian literature at Cornell in 1948. Although he was well known to American readers, particularly through his Pnin stories in *The New Yorker,* it was the publication of *Lolita* that made him famous. The book turned the public's attention back to his previous novels and also prepared it for his next and latest novel, *Pale Fire,* one of the most intricate pieces of artifice in literature. Following the publication of *Lolita,* Nabokov gave up teaching and now devotes all his time to writing. He is married and has one son.

THE FABULIST'S WORLDS:

VLADIMIR NABOKOV

by Alan Pryce-Jones

The case of Vladimir Nabokov is an odd one. He can be fitted into no easy category: neither as a part of Russian literary history, nor as an exile. It does not matter that, with a success only surpassed by Conrad, he has forged a new arm for himself out of the English language; no one would ever take him for a writer to whom English comes naturally. It does not matter that he can, at will, shock, enchant, chill, bemuse his readers; he writes, on the evidence, exactly as he feels—and his feelings are like no one else's. With unquenchable volatility he springs from one attitude to the next, content to make his final exit after the fashion of the Commendatore in *Don Giovanni:* with an air of menace, that is, but half hidden by a puff of stage smoke.

He is a moralist. That is one of the reasons why it is absurd that his reputation should rest on a *succès de scandale.* Not that *Lolita* really shocked anyone who read the book with attention. And five minutes of conversation with the author suffice to show that, because he is virtually unshockable, it did not readily occur to him that a hue and cry would be raised by what, in his own eyes, was no more than a private vision of truth. He has himself written, in a postface to the paperback edition of *Lolita,* that "all my Russian readers know that my old worlds—Russian, British, German, French —are just as fantastic and personal as my new one is."

It is of these worlds that I shall try to write. For the art of Nabokov is less a novelist's art than a fabulist's. He does not see people as they are, but as they might have appeared to the medieval constructor of a bestiary. His worlds are static. They may become tense with obsession, but they do not move or expand, or break apart like the worlds of everyday reality.

The first world—the Russian—is perhaps the truest to reality. Since it is the world of Nabokov's childhood, he depicts it—like most writers—with especial zest. Its seeds are planted in the St. Petersburg of 1899, when he was born to a prosperous and consequential household, admirably described in his autobiographical *Conclusive Evidence: A Memoir* (1951). No book better conveys the peculiar charm which veiled the last spasms of the Russian Empire. It is not an easy charm to convey, if only because it carries with it some of the faint air of disgrace which clings also to Edwardian England. Was not there something shady about the kind of Russian life so carefully described by the Edwardian Maurice Baring: the delicious country life which could only be lived at the expense of shutting away the threatening world outside; the luxurious journeys to Paris and Nice on the Nord Express; the furs and the diamonds and the little Fabergé flowers in tourmaline and crystal? A hush before a storm seems to accord with nature. A waltz, a throb of talk, a card-playing winter in Abbazia, make a less satisfactory prelude. By their lightheartedness in the face of danger, these delightful people only stress the inescapability of downfall.

The Nabokovs, however, were made of superior human material. Among his ancestors Vladimir lists "the first caveman who painted a mammoth; Nabok, a medieval Russified Tartar prince. . . . ; a long line of German barons; an obscure Crusader ["after whom the island of Corfu was named," said my informant with a little cough]; a well-known composer, born in Saxony two centuries and a half ago; boyars, landowners, military men; a bearded, fabulously rich Siberian merchant; one the lesser Decembrists. . . . ; Danzas, Pushkin's second in his fatal duel (not in straight line, though, but I must have him all the same); the first President of the Russian Imperial Academy of Medicine (my mother's maternal grandfather); the commander of the fortress where Dostoyevsky was kept before his trial. . . . ; a State Minister of Justice (my father's father); and a famous Russian Liberal (my father)." Some fifty servants saw to the needs of the family, and Nabokov casually records that in 1916, before he was out of his teens, therefore, he was left the equivalent of some two million dollars by an uncle. Alas, not for long. Three years later, in an exile which has now become permanent, he was arriving at Trinity College, Cambridge.

While it lasted, however, the life of Russia made an indelible impression on him. And most beautifully he conveys the flavor of life as it flowed round his adolescence. Again and again, in these autobiographical pages, a familiar experience is caught with wit and precision, as, for one, the sensation of looking with childish fixity of attention out of a train window: "The door of the compartment was open and I could see the corridor window, where the wires—six thin black wires— were doing their best to slant up, to ascend skywards, despite the lightning blows dealt them by one telegraph pole after another; but just as all six, in a triumphant swoop of pathetic elation, were about to reach the top of the window, a particularly vicious blow would bring them down, as low as they had ever been, and they would have to start all over again." In these few lines much of the essential Nabokov resides. He is a nostalgic writer, above all; and he has preserved, even in the unlikeliest contexts, the nostalgia of childhood.

Lolita—when she appears on the scene many years later —is much more than a nymphet: she is a ruthless evocation of childhood, all the crueler for the fact that she is in the past, and thus irrecoverable. The gap of thirty years between herself and Humbert is an essential part of their disaster. To bridge the gap is not merely a fictional device; it is as real an effort for her creator as the swoop and fall of the telegraph wires in recollection: neither more real nor less. The effort of memory is what counts. Humbert works back to the innocence of childhood, even though that involves the destruction of innocence, just as Nabokov works back to the graces of the long-ago past, with a father and a tutor in one compartment of a luxury train, a mother and her maid in another, a brother in a third, and Osip the valet as odd man out. The wires do not really move. Lolita was never really a child. Both illusions belong to a lonely man in exile striving to begin life all over again through the deceptive mirror of art, as if the exile had never happened.

For Nabokov's nostalgia is still an exile's dream, though he has now been an American citizen for nearly twenty years. "My private tragedy," he has written in the *Lolita* postface, "which cannot, and indeed should not, be anybody's concern, is that I had to abandon my natural idiom, my untrammeled, rich, and infinitely docile Russian tongue for a second-rate brand of English." The strain of this abandonment may be responsible for the marked strain of irritability in his work. He has very little patience with the west, and none at all with his countrymen now in power. Not that he objects to being dispossessed; not that he wastes any time mourning the lost millions. What has been stolen from him is an emotional heritage, an interpenetration of landscape and family and personal dignity. In each of his books this theft provides part of the theme, even when, as in the novel *Pnin*, he tempers his nostalgia with humor. The past never ceases to beckon, however possessive the present may become.

More than twenty years ago, Sartre defined Nabokov as *"un enfant de vieux."* He underlined the debt which Nabokov owes to Dostoyevsky, and went on to point an essential difference between them. Dostoyevsky believes in the world he creates: Nabokov does not. He is all the time observing himself at work, knocking down—like a child with a card castle—the very page that he has been at pains to construct. Sartre goes on to a further comparison with Gide. Both, in fiction, play the part of critic as consciously as that of creator. Gide, however—at least in *The Counterfeiters*—experiments, while Nabokov merely mines the procedures of the classical novel from within in order to explode their futility. It is Sartre's contention that everything in Nabokov is preparation for a climax which never occurs. There is literature in whatever he writes, but no life, because Nabokov, driven out of the society he knew as a child, has not been able to attach himself to any other.

These comments were written on the Nabokov of early middle age, who had not yet written the books which have made his reputation in English-speaking countries. In 1939 it was still possible for a stern professional like Sartre to look on Nabokov as an amateur of talent, strayed from some Aksakov country house to London or Berlin and consuming his loneliness in elegant meditation. In fact, however, this is a very partial truth. Nabokov has very little need of a stable society, since his universal subject matter is the disintegration of modern life. He has assumed the role of scapegoat, less in order to make a virtue of necessity than to drain to its utmost an essential experience of the twentieth century. It would be more just to compare him with Valéry Larbaud than with Gide. Both, at heart, are poets laureate of the *wagon-lit*. But whereas Larbaud never had to part with Osip the valet, Nabokov has been forced to accept life on much harsher terms. Objective he cannot be: it is no part of his talent to construct a detached comment on the world around him. And so he has learned the art of the shrug. Permanently a stranger, he picks a way through Europe and America, noting, in the pages of his bestiary, the bizarre animals on his path.

No wonder, then, that he has a special penchant for Gogol. He speaks, in his short book on Gogol (1944), of that writer pottering on the brink of his private abyss in order to become the greatest artist that Russia has yet produced. There is no reason to admit this large claim for Gogol in order to perceive that Nabokov is the right man to make it. He too is a potterer. He too stands by an abyss of his own. His special stance is to be the man of sense in an age of unreason. At the same time, he is perfectly aware that sense is not always sensible. The Albinus of *Laughter in the Dark* (1938) is the first full expression of a Nabokov anti-hero—the men in Nabokov's books are all there for punishment rather than as objective creations—and it is possible to define, through Albinus, the nature of that abyss. It cleaves the twin worlds of reality and dream. Nabokov's protagonists are always slipping from one to the other. Sometimes, as with the Cincinnatus of *Invitation to a Beheading* (originally also published in 1938, in Russian), they acquire a dual personality even though neither can be attached to a "real world." It is as if, having constructed a world of fantasy, Nabokov were trying to project one shadow behind another to infinity.

In Albinus, however, all Nabokov's essential themes are resumed. Albinus is mildly unhappy with his wife. Very well, sense tells him that he must overcome his natural shyness and impress himself upon the cinema usherette who has caught his eye. Almost at once unreason takes over. Albinus's unhappiness had only been relative. He did not wish to lose his wife, but merely to complement a tepid domestic affection by something tenser and more dangerous. What he had not foreseen was that through yielding to this impulse he would fall victim to an obsession. The usherette wants nothing but his money. Through her he loses wife and child, dignity, peace, human stature, and finally life itself.

It is important to the understanding of Nabokov that a train of events such as this is never allowed to reach towards tragedy. He diminishes his characters to the point where they become ciphers in a cosmic farce. Only the cruelty of life stirs in him a sense of relish. There is a scene towards the end of *Laughter in the Dark* which is especially hard to forget. Albinus has lost his sight in a car smash, and is living in Switzerland with Margot—bought out of her cinema—and, unbeknown to him, her lover. With cold amusement, Nabokov recounts in detail the steps by which a lover can insinuate himself into a house without his presence being suspected by his blind rival: how, like a double, he is always there and never perceived by his victim. "Rex seated himself cautiously on the sofa and took Margot on his knees. She spread out the newspaper and, after patting it and poring over it, began to read aloud. Albinus nodded his head now and then and slowly consumed invisible cherries, spitting the invisible stones into his fist. Rex mimicked Margot, pursing his lips and then drawing them in again as she did when she was reading. Or he pretended he was going to let her fall, so that suddenly her voice would jump and she had to search for the end of the snapped sentence." When Albinus is finally rescued, his rescuer finds the two men together. "Rex bent slowly forward and touched Albinus's forehead very gently with the flowering end of the grass stem which he had just been sucking. Albinus sighed strangely and brushed away the imaginary fly. Rex tickled his lips and again Albinus made that helpless movement. This was good fun indeed."

"This was good fun indeed." The comment can be attached to all that is most typical of Nabokov, ferocious though it may sound. Humbert's destruction by Lolita, the interplay of executioner and victim in *Invitation to a Beheading*, the tyrannies of *Bend Sinister*, each have their funny side, presented with bland savagery. Nabokov has a remarkably observant eye, and what he sees is usually deflation, anticlimax, a turning away. There is a short passage in one of his novels which lays down the pattern for any event which he may depict: "I turned on my heel and slammed the door after me —at least, I tried to slam it—it was one of those confounded pneumatic doors which resist." His characters are always turning away, but they never succeed in slamming the door.

From 1922 to 1937, Nabokov lived in Berlin by writing and teaching. It was in the latter years of this period that he wrote his last, and, according to experts, his best novel in Russian, *Dar*, which appeared in English in 1963 under the title, *The Gift*. It contains the germ of much later work, but stands in its own right as an eminent success. Its theme is half-autobiographical, although Nabokov, in a later preface, warns: "I am not, and never was, Fyodor Godunov-Cherdyntsev," the book's literary hero. Nevertheless, its evocations of childhood in Imperial Russia reinforce the memories of *Conclusive Evidence,* and in the person of its author-protagonist there is more than a hint of Pnin, of the John Shade of *Pale Fire,* only set, this time, against the feverish atmosphere of émigré life in Berlin during the 1920s. Again, it describes a book within a book; again, its theme is largely abstract. "Its heroine," Nabokov has written, "is not Zina, but Russian Literature."

The Gift was finished in France, from which, after a brief interlude, Nabokov moved to the United States, where he taught Russian and European literature, first at Wellesley College and later at Cornell University. Since the success of *Lolita* he has traveled in Europe and worked in California on the script of the novel. For over forty years, therefore, he has experienced, on the surface, the kind of *dédoublement* which is commonly undergone by his characters. He has been a Russian Liberal millionaire of the old school, but also a teacher earning a living. He has written in Russian (it is only quite lately that his earlier books have been translated into other languages) but used German or English in everyday speech. He has found old political creeds inoperative without feeling the impulse to adopt new ones. If there is any continuity in his make-up it is apparently due in large part to a lifelong skill in lepidopterology. References to moths and butterflies abound in his writings. And in his approach to characterization there is much of the entomologist: armed with stealthy net and chloroform bottle, Nabokov is stalking us all for the rare victim he needs to enlarge his collection.

If, in these decades, *Lolita* has been his most sensational success, it is not, in my view, his best book. I much prefer to it both *Pnin* and *The Real Life of Sebastian Knight.* This is partly because in the earlier books Nabokov kept in check a penchant for baroque prose which, in *Lolita,* easily slips out of control. Perhaps this is an aspect of Humbert's punishment. He has to be shown up as the man of straw he is. But Nabokov, at all times, uses the English language as an undergraduate uses a sports car. He shifts gear, revs noisily, slams on brakes, just to show he can. And, perhaps inevitably, he has an imperfect ear for speech in a foreign tongue. He uses words like "chappie" and "beastie" at one end of the scale, and like "rufous" or "carrick" (and what *is* a carrick?) at the other, but without quite convincing the reader that this vocabulary is inevitably right. It has been suggested that, in *Lolita*, Nabokov deliberately adjusted his style to Humbert's mentality; and in so far as the novel is written in the first person by a distracted and fanciful vulgarian—as Humbert is at pains to show himself—this is true. It is, however, a manner into which Nabokov easily slips. Like Meredith, he is naturally allusive; like Firbank, he reaches out towards the rococo phrase. And yet he is not "like" anybody except himself, as he points out. That may be why his excursions into modern life read a little like excursions in slumming. Naturally a withdrawn and Olympian talent, he uses the language of twentieth-century democracy with almost too hearty a vivacity.

However, *The Real Life of Sebastian Knight* (1941) is exactly suited to his special gift. It is the story of a Russian not unlike Vladimir Nabokov who attempts to reconstruct the life of a half-brother six years older than himself. Sebastian had adopted his mother's maiden name, and after the Revolution —and a period at Trinity College, Cambridge—he set up as a writer. He died young; and thereafter his half-brother embarked on a long journey of investigation, probing into his past, in order to dig out the real clues to an enigmatic character, in contrast to the false picture put forward in a misleading biography. It will be seen that the two men have a good deal in common with their creator. Nabokov is performing, as it were, a duet with himself. The result is a short book, in appearance desultory and willful. The track is picked up and dropped again. Characters enter the story as essential to it

and disappear again unnoticed. But the whole is far more artful than the parts. It recaptures the movement of life, and it
allows Nabokov to mix reflection and anecdote in the manner
which comes most easily to him.

Yet a devil's advocate might argue that once again Nabokov
has chosen a protagonist with whom he has only an evasive
sympathy. The real Sebastian's reality is, at strongest, wraith-
like, and it is for this that life—or Nabokov—punishes him.
We are told that he was an outstanding writer, but we never
fully believe that his half-brother shares this opinion. When
he falls in love it is the mystery surrounding his loves which
engages our imagination, not its possible solution. Only in
Pnin (1957) does Nabokov offer us a protagonist who is also
a hero.

Pnin has to be punished also. But punished for his innocence, his charm. For these very qualities, too, he is fundamentally invulnerable when the world attacks him. Pnin is a
professor in exile, in his fifties teaching Russian in provincial
America. He has never fully mastered English, never adapted
himself to the exigencies of Waindell College. Misadventure
pursues him whatever he does; yet he is not only touching
and delightfully funny at the same time, but also a heroic
figure. The last glance we have of him is in his little car, sand-
wiched between two trucks, loaded with suitcases. He has lost
his job somewhere in the academic labyrinth of his adopted
country, but he is not downhearted: "Then the little sedan
boldly swung past the front truck and, free at last, spurted
up the shining road, which one could make out narrowing to
a thread of gold in the soft mist where hill after hill made
beauty of distance, and where there was simply no saying
what miracle might happen." The sequence might easily have
been sentimental, but that is not Nabokov's way. Timofey
Pnin may make us laugh out loud, but he remains a professor
of stature and as such he is inured to the blows of fate. He is
the one creation of Nabokov's whom his creator respects
sufficiently to present him naturalistically. Usually he turns
those whom he supports into a symbol or a dream projection.

Cincinnatus and the Krug of *Bend Sinister* are Pnin's only rivals, but from both of them the integument of humanity has been lifted; Pnin alone is accorded the dignity of remaining a man.

Whatever the virtues of his other books, it is unlikely that they will displace *Lolita* (1958)*, and it is ironic that the undeniable merits of *Lolita* should rest on a tissue of irrelevancies. Had it not been given the accolade of a banning, had its publication not been the center of an excited burst of gossip, Nabokov might still be teaching Russian but the public would have gained a much clearer view of his fiction. The news was put about that *Lolita* was a daring novel, and so—by virtue of its theme—it is. But the obsessive love of a middle-aged man for an adolescent girl need only shock if it dares too much: if, that is, the writer has insufficient confidence in his own ability, and so goes too far in whetting the appetite of his readers. This is a fault which Nabokov skillfully avoids. Humbert's obsession has to be depicted as such, but it does not spill over into the desire to shock. Where the book fails is in the total lack of affection shown to everyone in it. Humbert is a sniveler, Lolita a tigress not the less formidable for being only twleve years old; everyone else is more or less ridiculous. And the book itself is designed as a prolonged wail.

Much of it is extremely amusing. The long journey through one motel after another is a wonderful *tour de force* of wry comedy. Much of it is moving. An obsession is not less heartfelt than some nobler emotion. And the moral of it all—if a moral must be dug from it—is admirably cogent: Do not expect to escape the consequence of your actions. But the total effect is curiously chilling. Humbert gives in without a struggle and is punished accordingly. That is all there is to it. In order to provide a truly satisfying fiction there has to be conflict. In *Lolita* both victims acquiesce, and only one even complains.

Lolita is an obsessive book. It marks the central point of a

* Published by Olympia Press in Paris in 1956.

continuing process: as time passes, Nabokov likes his fellow men less and less. I have already mentioned Krug, the philosopher of *Bend Sinister*—a book now fifteen years old. It is significant that Krug has already begun that process of dehumanization which culminates in Dr. Kinbote, the protagonist of *Pale Fire* (1962), Nabokov's most recently written novel.

Reading *Bend Sinister* (1947) is rather like reading an early novel by Iris Murdoch. Each separate page makes easy sense, but precisely what Nabokov is saying over any extended passage is hard to define. When he is in contact with his small son, Krug is delightfully human; at other times he is treated as one element in a set of Chinese boxes. For in this novel Nabokov is writing deliberately as a virtuoso. Although the surface of his prose is pleasantly limpid, he enjoys putting obstacles in the way of understanding by writing such paragraphs as this: he is describing an engraving which "represents a sixteenth-century gentleman in the act of handing a book to a humble fellow who holds a spear and a bay-crowned hat in his left hand. Note the sinistral detail (Why? Ah, 'that is the question,' as Monsieur Homais once remarked, quoting *Le Journal d'Hier;* a question which is answered in a wooden voice by the Portrait on the title page of the First Folio). Note also the legend: 'Ink, a Drug.' Somebody's idle pencil (Ember highly treasures this scholium) has numbered the letters so as to spell *Grudinka* which means 'bacon' in several Slavic languages."

This kind of elliptical writing leads up to the still more extravagant gesture of *Pale Fire*. Here the private joke goes very far indeed. For the structure of *Pale Fire* is that of a long poem with spoof annotations of great length and complexity. The Chinese boxes are multiplied more adroitly than ever, until it is almost impossible to determine whether Nabokov is engineering a manic exposure of bogus scholarship or whether he has been carried away by the eddies of his own bizarre humor.

A main purpose of all this is to make a crushing comment on the personality of Dr. Kinbote, who is first put forward as the reverential friend and admirer of a dead poet, John Shade, and then allowed to reveal his total inadequacy as he adds note to note in an elucidation of Shade's posthumous poem. The notes construct a whole imaginary world, centered on the kingdom of Zembla, its royal family and its way of life. They are extremely ingenious and at times extremely funny. Kinbote himself is soon left behind. Nabokov is far too accomplished a mind to confine himself to the hair-splitting excesses of a pedant. He is always ready to take over from his own characters—at the end of *Bend Sinister,* for instance, he abolishes them altogether and assumes command in his own person. Similarly, in *Pale Fire,* he flashes in and out of the role of Kinbote. Yet somehow the total effect is less brilliant than it ought to be. In this vein, Nabokov draws on his German rather than his American experience. He can crush, or ridicule; he lacks the lucid sense of mockery which illuminates the best American satire.

In general, this obstinate attachment to a European attitude of mind possesses considerable advantages in the kind of book which Nabokov has made his own. For it enables him to keep the detachment which is essential to a satirist. Even when he adopts an American setting—and apart from *Lolita* and one or two short stories in *Nabokov's Dozen* (1958) the occasion is rare—he never makes the mistake of assuming an American viewpoint except with his tongue in his cheek. The switch of attitude otherwise would be too great. For it must always be remembered that he is not simply a European writer who has lived for twenty years in the United States: he is a writer whose imaginative core was formed by a civilization which was scattered into exile forty-five years ago.

Paradoxically, this is what makes him an essential element in American writing today. He is by no means the superior European looking in on American life from the outside and disliking what he finds. He is an insider, a participant. But he applies to what he finds in the United States the same inflexible standards which condition his responses to the Europe he has left behind. It is inevitable that someone who dislikes modern life should dislike it most where it is most modern. It may be the attacks of dictatorship on the free intelligence which he abhors, as in *Bend Sinister;* it may be the pedantry of learned men, as in *Pale Fire,* or the cruelty of man to man, as in *Invitation to a Beheading.* In each instance his satiric wit, his unique savagery of style, are reserved for a typical failure of civilization at the present day.

For good or ill, nevertheless, *Lolita* is likely to remain a landmark in the history of the novel. For a long time to come, critics will be accusing Nabokov of taking his procedures too slavishly from eighteenth-century French sources. They will be dragging in Sade and Laclos, wagging an angry finger, or calling for more. They will be arguing the subtlety of his technique—for, like the engineers of the Trojan horse, Nabokov scores his victory over vulgar feeling by destroying his victims from within. It seems probable that, having so far turned new ground with each new novel, he will continue to surprise these critics if they expect him to repeat his effects. His true flair is for using fiction as a criticism of life. We need not expect success to mellow that criticism: we can legitimately hope that freedom from other cares will allow him to deepen and extend it.

BASIC PATTERNS

Carson McCullers

Although only in her middle forties, Carson McCullers has been around—literarily speaking—a long time, since 1940 to be exact, when at twenty-three, with talent nearly full-blown, she produced her first novel, *The Heart Is a Lonely Hunter.* A year later came a more sophisticated work, *Reflections in a Golden Eye,* and although critics found this novel less palatable, it established her still more firmly as a masterful prose stylist and psychologist of startling intuition. Soon after her initial success her health began to fail, and only a miracle of tenacity and spiritual strength kept her writing through a series of strokes that resulted in partial paralysis before she was thirty. After the publication of her novella *The Member of the Wedding* in 1946 and an omnibus volume of her works including several previously unpublished stories, *The Ballad of the Sad Café* in 1951, she remained silent for nearly a decade. Then, typing one page a day with one hand for a year, she produced another novel, *Clock Without Hands* in 1961. Mrs. McCullers (born Carson Smith) started writing at the age of sixteen, and at seventeen she left her native Columbus, Georgia, to pursue a career as concert pianist in New York. Losing her tuition money for the Juilliard School of Music, she turned back from music to writing, taking odd jobs during the day to study story writing at Columbia at night. For a brief happy period she rented a Brooklyn brownstone with a group of writers and artists, among them Richard Wright, Gypsy Rose Lee and W. H. Auden. She lived in North Carolina for two years after her marriage to Reeves McCullers in 1937, then for a while abroad. Finally she settled in Nyack, N.Y., where, since her husband's death in 1953 she has lived in a large Victorian house with a beloved housekeeper. Because of its dramatic quality her fiction has made good vehicles for the stage; in 1951 she herself dramatized *The Member of the Wedding,* which also became a successful motion picture. Her two early novels, *The Heart Is a Lonely Hunter* and *Reflections in a Golden Eye,* have been sold to the movies; the first is already in production. And Edward Albee's dramatization of *The Ballad of the Sad Café* is scheduled for Broadway production. Though her fiction rarely leaves the bounds of a closed southern world, Mrs. McCullers has steadily acquired an international reputation, with French and English critics ranking her close to Faulkner and Hemingway. (She was one of three Americans represented at the Edinburgh Writers' Conference in 1962.) Still youthful in appearance, with an easy smile and forthright, sometimes brooding look, Mrs. McCullers combines in her person great human warmth and a mystic's serene detachment.

Truman Capote

On a memorable television program of a few years back, Truman Capote compared prose writing to athletics. To write prose, he said, one must stay in training. This meticulous care is plain in all Capote's work. Of *Breakfast at Tiffany's* Norman Mailer—not known for his charity to fellow craftsmen—said he would not change two words in it. Capote was born in New Orleans in 1924, attended schools in New York and Connecticut, and worked for a short while in the art department of *The New Yorker.* His interests and accomplishments seem to have moved steadily from the internal to the external. The early stories, collected under the title *A Tree of Night,* withheld their meanings like dreams, while maintaining the validity dreams have. One would not have suspected either from these or from his first, surreal novel, *Other*

Voices, Other Rooms, Capote's exquisite talent for reportage. *The Muses Are Heard* and a lengthy published interview with Marlon Brando, as well as *Local Color,* a collection of his travel pieces, have the delicate clarity of good photography. Capote wrote the script for the much admired movie, *Beat the Devil,* the book for the musical *House of Flowers,* and the stage adaptation of his novel *The Grass Harp.* Little, if any, of Capote's work has slipped from sight; his reputation from the beginning has been high and steady. For the past several years he has worked on a factual account of a Kansas murder case, *In Cold Blood,* to be published in 1964. Although he continues to travel, he maintains a residence in Brooklyn Heights, New York.

MCCULLERS AND CAPOTE:

BASIC PATTERNS

by Mark Schorer

In one of his fascinating "essays for the left hand" called
"Identity in the Modern Novel," Jerome S. Bruner makes a
distinction between subjectivity and myth, or what he phrases
as "subjectification and the demise of fate." He first speculated
on this subject in an earlier essay, "Myth and Identity,"
which concludes as follows:

> . . . one may ask whether the rise of the novel as an
> art form, and particularly the subjectification of the
> novel since the middle of the nineteenth century,
> whether these do not symbolize the voyage into the in-
> terior that comes with the failure of prevailing myths to
> provide external models toward which one may aspire.
> For when the prevailing myths fail to fit the varieties of
> man's plight, frustration expresses itself first in mytho-
> clasm and then in the lonely search for internal iden-
> tity. . . . Perhaps the modern novel, in contrast to the
> myth, is the response to the internal anguish that can
> find no external constraint in myth, a form of internal
> map. . . . the alternative to externalization in myth ap-

pears to be the internalization of the personal novel, the first a communal effort, the second the long search for identity.

It is this proposal that is then amplified in the following essay, where Dr. Bruner writes that "the psychological novel, in contrast to the myth, exists as a recognition of the distinction between subjective and objective. . . . The myth is objective, transcendental, timeless, moved by impulses beyond man to meet inhuman demands. In the objective verisimilitude of myth lies the triumph of its externalization of man's inner experience. With the novel and its interior monologues, the effort is to save the subjectivity, to use it as cause."

Carson McCullers and Truman Capote are among the most subjective of contemporary novelists, writers for whom the sensibility is almost the entire literary resource. Dr. Bruner's distinction may help us to understand how they use that sensibility, the ends to which they put subjectivity, and it may help us to distinguish in turn between them.

In the fiction of Carson McCullers I believe that we can observe the effort to arrive at the objective externality of myth by placing the most extreme demands on that very subjectivity which is its opposite. The effort is not always successful and sometimes it is only partial, but, except for most of the short stories, her least impressive work, it is almost always there. Of these short stories, many of which abandon that southern setting that is most congenial to her talent and, apparently, necessary to its fullest expression, only one approaches the amplitude of feeling in her longer fiction. That story, "A Tree. A Rock. A Cloud." tells of the early morning meeting in an all night café of an uncomprehending young, newspaper boy and a shabby old transient who tries to describe the "science" of love to him—love, which must begin with the humblest of objects, a tree, a rock, a cloud. That the lesson is not communicated is of the essence. That the old man wanders out alone into the dawn of a loveless world is no less so.

"Why does anyone write at all?" Mrs. McCullers asked in the foreword to her commercially unsuccessful play, *The Square Root of Wonderful* (1958), which is concerned with the same theme of universal love and lovelessness. "Why does anyone write at all? I suppose a writer writes out of some inward compulsion to transform his own experience (much of it unconscious) into the universal and symbolical. The themes the artist chooses are always deeply personal. I suppose my central theme is the theme of spiritual isolation. Certainly I have always felt alone."

To transform the private insight into the universal truth—this is, of course, the axiomatic basis of all creative effort; but cannot it be conceived, too, in more particular terms as the inverse of the mythopoeic effort—where the private impulse finds its satisfying correlatives in the already formed universal statements—and yet conceivably arriving at something like the same end?

Spiritual isolation, universal alienation and loneliness—this is the given condition of the McCullers world. Then the effort to overcome it through communication, through love, and this in spite of the premonition felt from the start that no such resolution is possible. The anxious search for love in a loveless world and the recognition that one cannot hope—even if one wished it—to *be* loved, only *to* love—so that love is at least as much pain as it is benison. It is to do violence to the texture and feeling of Mrs. McCullers' work so to abstract the thematic core, and yet in at least one remarkable passage, itself abstract, she gives us a certain sanction for this procedure. The passage occurs rather early in *The Ballad of the Sad Café* (1951):

> First of all, love is a joint experience between two persons—but the fact that it is a joint experience does not mean that it is a similar experience to the two people involved. There are the lover and the beloved, but these two come from different countries. Often the beloved is only a stimulus for all the stored-up love which

has lain quiet within the lover for a long time hitherto. And somehow every lover knows this. He feels in his soul that his love is a solitary thing. He comes to know a new strange loneliness and it is this knowledge which makes him suffer. So there is only one thing for the lover to do. He must house his love within himself as best he can; he must create for himself a whole new inward world—a world intense and strange, complete in himself. Let it be added here that this lover about whom we speak need not necessarily be a young man saving for a wedding ring—this lover can be man, woman, child, or indeed any human creature on this earth.

Now, the beloved can also be of any description. The most outlandish people can be the stimulus for love. A man may be a doddering great-grandfather and still love only a strange girl he saw in the streets of Cheehaw one afternoon two decades past. The preacher may love a fallen woman. The beloved may be treacherous, greasy-headed, and given to evil habits. Yes, and the lover may see this as clearly as anyone else—but that does not affect the evolution of his love one whit. A most mediocre person can be the object of a love which is wild, extravagant, and beautiful as the poison lilies of the swamp. A good man may be the stimulus for a love both violent and debased, or a jabbering madman may bring about in the soul of someone a tender and simple idyll. Therefore, the value and quality of any love is determined solely by the lover himself.

It is for this reason that most of us would rather love than be loved. Almost everyone wants to be the lover. And the curt truth is that, in a deep secret way, the state of being beloved is intolerable to many. The beloved fears and hates the lover, and with the best of reasons. For the lover is forever trying to strip bare his beloved. The lover craves any possible relation with the beloved, even if this experience can cause him only pain.

It is a long passage, but its quotation here is justified in that it is probably the passage in which Mrs. McCullers comes closest to telling us explicitly what concerns her most.

Written some time after the publication of her first novel, *The Heart Is a Lonely Hunter* (1940), the passage might serve as epigraph for that novel, as its very title suggests. This novel, with its many characters and its full easy evocation of the whole dulled life of a southern town in the years of the Depression, has at its center a small group of characters, only five, who, within the formless flow of the life around them, enact their nearly mathematical parable.

The novel has three parts. The first introduces these five, each with his obsession: the deaf-mute, John Singer, whose entire life exists in its dedication to another mute, a gross Greek named Antonapoulos, a half-wit who is presently incarcerated in an insane asylum where Singer must henceforth visit him; Biff Brannon, a café owner, obsessed with wonder; Jake Blount, a drunken radical, obsessed with the cause of the workers; Dr. Copeland, an educated Negro obsessed with the idea of justice for his people; and Mick Kelly, an adolescent tomboy whose obsession is music. At the end of the first part, each of these four has turned to the first, Singer, a Christ figure, as the object of his love, the source of understanding. Part Two develops this dependence of these four on Singer, as each of them tries to talk himself out of his solitude with the mute, each feeling that "they wanted to tell each other things that had never been told before." At the end of this central and longest part, Antonapoulos has died and Singer, in an empty world, shoots himself. The third part, with Singer gone, shows us each of the other four as he vanishes, so to speak, into his own solitude.

They are all characters doomed by a fated knowledge— "she knew in the beginning that there was no good place" —even though each of them struggles to communicate the burden of his consciousness, wanders feverishly to find the "good place" where isolation ceases. Their sealed fate is apparent in the fact that they all turn to a deaf-mute for communication, and that he in turn finds the meaning of his life in his love for another mute, who cannot understand him. For all the realistic detail of the novel, it is at heart a parable that is suggested at once in the legendary style. "In the town there were two mutes, and they were always together," is the opening sentence. One would probably find, on close examination, that such fairy-tale-like declarative sentences are the most frequently used throughout the book. At any rate, they give it its tone, and the elliptical treatment of time underscores that tone:

> The town was in the middle of the deep South. The summers were long and the months of winter cold were very few. Nearly always the sky was a glassy, brilliant azure and the sun burned down riotously bright. Then the light, chill rains of November would come . . . Often in the faces along the streets there was the desperate look of hunger and loneliness . . .
> Then one day the Greek became ill . . .

It is a tone appropriate to the retelling of an old myth, or to the attempted construction of a new one: man, deranged by a nearly cosmic loneliness, momentarily redeemed by his power to love. "It was some good."

> All right!
> O.K.!
> Some good.

This quotation, the final reflection of Mick Kelly, suggests that Mrs. McCullers infuses the general legendary tone with a good deal of sharply reported vernacular talk and reflection that is entirely appropriate to the social character of her people. In the next novel, *Reflections in a Golden Eye* (1941), there is almost none of this, and the characters are both different and fewer in number. Correspondingly, the story is much more tautly told, the drama much more concentrated; and the quality of fable, in fact, recedes. For here Mrs. McCullers has abandoned her theme of love and loneliness, or rather, she has given us its inversion, writing now of people whose self-engrossment, malice, contempt, or sheer stupidity have for all their desperation, put them outside the possibility of feeling either loneliness or love. Theirs is a world of static rage and drugged destructiveness. Better that other world for all its pain.

This is not at all to say that one does not read this strange short novel with engrossed interest. The setting is a southern army post in peacetime. Leonora Penderton, "a little feeble-minded," feels nothing but contempt for her husband, Captain Penderton, a homosexual in everything but practice, and is having a meaningless sexual relationship with Major Langdon, whose invalid wife, Alison, is "on the verge of actual lunacy" and over the verge before the story ends. These four are set against two young men. One is Anacleto, Alison's Philippine houseboy, fantastic and comically elegant, whose devotion to Alison never in any way qualifies the generally destructive action. The other is Private Williams, who becomes the unwitting center of it. Mindless and unknown to thought, living by animal instinct alone, he is fascinated by the accidental sight of Leonora's naked body, and presently, night after night, he lets himself silently into her house and kneels motionless beside her bed, staring at her sleeping face. By day he serves as her groom, and in the atmosphere of the stables a situation like that in Lawrence's *The Prussian Officer* develops between him and the captain. That unhappy half-man, like Lawrence's Hauptmann, becomes obsessed with the young soldier's wholeness, at once enraged and enraptured, and when, one night, he finds him in his wife's bedroom, he shoots him and is himself thereby at last finished, "a broken and dissipated monk."

The title of the book derives from Anacleto's description of a water color he has been painting, of a peacock with an immense golden eye in which is reflected something tiny and grotesque. If the Lawrentian opposition, apparently intended, between the natural and the corrupt is not realized in this novel, that is perhaps because the static quality of the con-

ception of the peacock's eye dominates the entire imaginative
performance, with the young soldier somehow included in the
grotesquerie. It is a dreadful world because his presence does
not make it less negative: here there is no one to be redeemed,
no love to deepen the loneliness.

We are not in any way echoing the old philistine demand
that literature be "affirmative." At most, Mrs. McCullers'
writing affirms little enough: *All right! O.K.! Some good.* It
is, rather, a slackening of imaginative verve that is in question,
as if the quality of the subject itself had somehow been in-
jected into the presentation, frozen it. Mrs. McCullers once
spoke of the "dimensions of a work of art" as being like "a
flowering dream." That is as good a metaphorical account
of her own successful work as one could find. And the
trouble with *Reflections in a Golden Eye* is that the dream
does not flower; we are trapped within its frightening rigidi-
ties, as we are in a horrid dream, before waking. All that is
changed again in *The Member of the Wedding* (1946).

In some "Notes on Writing" that she published in *Esquire*
a few years ago, Mrs. McCullers began as follows:

> When I was a child of about four, I was walking with
> my nurse past a convent. For once, the convent doors
> were open. And I saw the children eating ice-cream
> cones, playing on iron swings, and I watched, fascinated.
> I wanted to go in, but my nurse said no, I was not
> Catholic. The next day, the gate was shut. But, year by
> year, I thought of what was going on, of this wonderful
> party, where I was shut out. I wanted to climb the wall,
> but I was too little. I beat on the wall once, and I knew
> all the time that there was a marvelous party going on,
> but I couldn't get in.

This is the illusion by which Frankie Addams, the heroine of
The Member of the Wedding, lives, the illusion of a marvelous
party going on somewhere that she must find and join.

Frankie Addams is not four but twelve years old when the
novel opens. For a long time she had been "a member of

nothing in the world," had become "an unjoined person," and in her yearning, pubescent loneliness, she lives in frenzied plans for flight from where she is to the discovery of some membership, some human connection, elsewhere. Then suddenly all her uncertain plans seem to find their actuality in the wedding of her older brother: she will become the *me* of their *we*, and the three of them will never separate. "She knew who she was and how she was going into the world."

So ends the first of the three parts of the book. But now, in fact, she knows less than ever who she is as, in the second part, she ceases to be Frankie and becomes F. Jasmine, or Miss F. Jasmine Addams, Esq. Her intensifying fantasies are always set against the anxious innocence of her six-year-old cousin, John Henry, not yet given to dreams, and the downright wisdom of Berenice, the Negro cook in the motherless household, experienced beyond the state of dreams. It is Berenice who, in this second part of the novel, tries to explain to Frankie how everyone is "caught" in himself, each in his own individuality, and how it is futile to try to break free of it. To that Frankie adds that one could say as well that everyone is "loose," by which she is trying to say that everyone is separate from everyone else, which is, of course, to say the same thing. But she believes that her separateness is about to be overcome and her freedom found.

Part III begins after the disaster of the wedding, and when, on the second page, she is named again, her name is Frances. She has settled at last into her own identity. When the book closes, she is a year older, she has a new best friend, John Henry has died, Berenice is leaving, the Addamses are moving to another house, and presently Frances will discover the nature of her identity. The materials necessary to that discovery she already possesses: the painful inevitability of separateness, the moderate mitigations to be found in love.

Less of a parable than *The Heart Is a Lonely Hunter, The Member of the Wedding* manages, within the realistic tradition of the novel, to explore the same theme, and in doing so, with a quite wonderful blend of pathos and humor, overcomes the limitations of *Reflections in a Golden Eye*. With the novel-ette, *The Ballad of the Sad Café,* the theme remains the same but the method pushes farther away from social realism than anything she had yet written. It is probably her most success-ful work and attains most completely the objectification of myth.

The novelette is most properly named, for it does indeed share in most of the qualities of the traditional ballad except for the fact that it is not written in verse. The whole melo-dramatic action, the somehow depersonalized characters, the objective narration, the indifference to psychological as to so-cial realism, the refusal to comment on even the most mysteri-ous elements in the action, the frame in which the action is set (it begins and ends with a doomed, closed building in-habited by a haunted, crazed, and solitary figure), and by the now well-known legendary style, here much heightened—all this and more detailed matters of stylistic device and texture as well as more general matters such as the brooding, fated at-mosphere of the work are characteristics familiar to us in the ballad form. In the prose version of this form, Mrs. McCul-lers' talent finds its most complete consolidation.

The closed building, with its deranged inhabitant, Miss Amelia Evans, was once the only store in a desolate southern town. Miss Amelia had been a huge, harsh, mannish crea-ture who, at nineteen, married a handsome young man of du-bious character named Marvin Macy, who had fallen hope-lessly (and utterly improbably) in love with her. But she does not love him, refuses to consummate the marriage, and soon expels him from her establishment. For a subsequent crime he is imprisoned for many years. In the meantime, a grotesque hunchback named Lyman, claiming to be Amelia's cousin, has appeared, and he, quite as improbably, becomes the ob-ject of her love. She pampers him and he transforms the store into a café and the dead town into a lively community. This state of things continues happily until Macy returns and Ly-man chooses him as the object of his love. The climax lies in a wrestling match between Amelia and Macy which she has nearly won when Lyman flings himself on her back and gives the advantage to Macy. Then Macy and Lyman destroy the café and flee the town together. Presently Miss Amelia boards the place up and incarcerates herself. The town falls back into its old death. "There is absolutely nothing to do in the town. . . . The soul rots with boredom. You might as well go down to the Forks Falls highway and listen to the chain gang." And so the story ends with an account of the twelve men on the chain gang, seven black and five white, singing. "Just twelve mortal men who are together." Together, of course, in their captivity.

Some good, one might add; but the pain is immeasurably greater. This is the familiar theme, but here it has achieved an aesthetic logic in the presentation that is perhaps unique in Mrs. McCullers' longer work. The array of grotesque characters is perfectly suited to the fantastic action. The lover-beloved interchange is as patterned as a folk dance. The style is that of the fable or folk tale, and it gives universal validity to what is a highly private vision of the world, a vision for which the story itself is an extended metaphor, the symbolic objectification.

Mrs. McCullers' most recent novel is perhaps *too* recent to invite any very confident judgment, yet I believe that it is fair to say that it is a falling away from her best. Like *The Heart Is a Lonely Hunter, Clock Without Hands* (1961) is involved in public issues, but while the desolate sense of waste and human suffering that was evoked by the atmosphere of the Depression in the earlier novel was entirely appropriate to its general theme and, indeed, gave a special resonance to that theme, the public issues that enter *Clock Without Hands* are of a more specific and therefore more refractory kind.

Once more, the characters are few. There is J. F. Malone, an ordinary man, a pharmacist in a southern town, who, at the age of forty, suddenly learns that he has only a short time to live. He is man, alone, confronting his final destiny, and his story is moving. But it is ill-joined with the story of the second major character, a fanatical ex-congressman named

Judge Fox Clane who is obsessed with the wild notion of redeeming Confederate currency and thus restoring the prestige and grandeur of the old South. This is the sort of grotesque character that Mrs. McCullers in earlier work had created with masterly authority, but here, where this absurd fanaticism is juxtaposed with the moral realities that suddenly confront Malone, and where the fanaticism itself is based on concrete contemporary social realities with which we are most seriously concerned, the incongruities cannot be overcome. Nor are they much modified by the presence of two other characters, young boys both, one of them, Jester, the Judge's grandson, sensitive and sensible and, in his loneliness, reaching out for friendship with the other, a blue-eyed Negro, Sherman Pew, the Judge's amanuensis, so thwarted that he cannot accept friendship and lives in fantasy. Jester defies his grandfather and the town destroys Sherman with the Judge's support. The book ends as the Judge topples into final senility and Malone, after a redeeming act of conscience, falls into death. But somehow all these pieces have not fallen into the kind of meaningful pattern that is evident in almost everything else that Mrs. McCullers has written.

She has, except in rather oblique ways, abandoned the theme of love and loneliness, and the novel is therefore without the kind of lyric expansiveness with which that theme imbued her earlier work. Rather than pushing her materials in the direction of fable, she seems here to have attempted some sort of allegory, at once over-rational and not at all clear, of the old and the new South. It is impossible for her not to interest us with anything she writes, and to charm us with her deft management of the comic-pathetic, which she does in this novel as in the others; yet there remains this disturbing disjunction between the half of her novel that is moving and the half that confuses us and seems to belong somewhere else.

Truman Capote's talent is more urbane, more various, and more extravagant than Carson McCullers', and his work has always seemed in danger of being overwhelmed by the stylish and the chic in a way that hers never has. Rereading his work, one must conclude that this is a matter of personal reputation rather than of actual achievement. The fact is that they are simply two different writers. Although their names are frequently coupled, the differences are greater than the similarities.

Both were born in the South—she in Columbus, Georgia, in 1917, he in New Orleans in 1924; she remained there until 1935, he until 1942. Both make occasional returns to the South, but Mrs. McCullers now lives most of her life, her activities limited by a painful illness, in a large Victorian house in Nyack, New York, while Capote, who has an elegant establishment in Brooklyn Heights, is always traveling and seems now to do most of his writing abroad. Capote began to publish at seventeen, Mrs. McCullers at nineteen. Both have made successful adaptations for the stage from some of their fiction. Both write slowly, Mrs. McCullers almost always in pain. Some similarities appear in this catalogue, but in temperament, as in the whole history of their writing, they are very different persons.

If Truman Capote is a writer who comes from the South, he is not a "southern writer" in the sense that Mrs. McCullers is: he is equally at home and perhaps even more at home in very different settings. The doctrine of love, as we have cited it in Mrs. McCullers' "A Tree. A Rock. A Cloud." and as we have quoted it from "The Ballad of the Sad Café," may seem alike, but they are given different interpretations. In Capote's *The Grass Harp* (1953), the Judge speaks as follows:

> "We are speaking of love. A leaf, a handful of seed—
> begin with these, learn a little what it is to love. First,
> a leaf, a fall of rain, then someone to receive what a leaf
> has taught you, what a fall of rain has ripened. No easy
> process, understand; it could take a lifetime, it has mine,
> and still I've never mastered it—I only know how true

it is: that love is a chain of love, as nature is a chain of life."

And later in the novel, Dolly recalls this speech:

"Charlie said that love is a chain of love. I hoped you listened and understood him. Because when you love one thing," she held the blue egg as preciously as the Judge had held a leaf, "you can love another, and that is owning, that is something to live with. You can forgive everything."

The difference is that in the Capote world, love does make for communion and even community in a way that Mrs. McCullers can rarely permit. His is the gentler view, hers the more disabused. And if both like to write about children and grotesques, freaks and cripples and perverts, Mrs. McCullers seems to view them as representative of the human race whereas for Capote they are exemplars of a private world within the world at large, and of a private view. And finally, if both are novelists of sensibility, Mrs. McCullers' sensibility, as we have observed, expresses itself most fully in the objective forms of parable and fable, Capote's sensibility moves in two different directions—into the most subjective drama of all, the psychic drama far below the level of reason, on the one hand, and, on the other, into objective social drama, often fanciful, and always indifferent to "social problems" in the usual sense. Close readers could probably find many minor similarities of detail (the crossed eyes of Miss Amelia Evans, for example, "exchanging with each other one long and secret gaze of grief," and the crossed eyes of Verena in *The Grass Harp,* peering "inward upon a stony vista"), but these make for no important similarity: in the end they are two quite different writers.

Rereading all of Truman Capote's writing, we are perhaps surprised by the range of his volatile gift, thinking of him still, as most readers do, as the strangely precocious youth

from New Orleans, author of *Other Voices, Other Rooms.*
His is, in fact, a various prose, equally at ease—to name the
extremes—in situations of dark and frightful nightmare, and
of extravagant comedy. Perhaps the single constant in his
prose is style, and the emphasis that he himself places upon
the importance of style. By style one means, of course, not
only the language as such but the observed physical detail and
the varieties of the precisely overheard human voices. (Here
Capote's range is greater than Mrs. McCullers': she is marvelous with the vernacular of children and of Negroes, but not
particularly remarkable in reporting the speech of adult white
urban characters; Capote, one feels, does not let any character
talk unless he knows precisely *how* he talks, the very individual and individuating accents.) Capote's style changes, of
course, with his changing moods and modes, so that the variety is multiplied.

His earliest stories, the products of the motherless boy not
yet out of his teens and then hardly out of them, were written
in what is frequently called the "Gothic" tradition or in the
tradition of what Hawthorne meant by the word "romance"
("Hawthorne got us off to a fine start," Capote has said of
style in the American short story), a tradition in which the
subject matter is freed from the limits of recognizable social
experience, is free to shift continually and without bridge sign
or traffic signal from fact into fantasy, from the real into the
surreal, from the daily into the dream, from the natural into
the supernatural.

Over and over in these stories the central thematic concern
shows itself to be with the idea of the *Doppelgänger,* the alter
ego, and the supernatural is, in fact, symbolic of the psychic
world in which that other self, which we never meet in our
active, diligent, and brightly lit social lives, has its being. In
general, these are stories about people who are alone and without love, who are alone *because* they are without love, and
who, in their isolate, alienated condition, come upon sinister,
usually grotesque, often disgusting creatures with whom they
are imprisoned and whom they are unable and usually disin-

clined to elude: these creatures are their primary selves, discovered at last, and therefore their destiny, which, once they
have recognized it, they are necessarily committed to. And
then, perhaps, they are free to love.

These stories, one may be certain, are written out of no
systematic familiarity with modern psychological theories ("I
would not know a Freudian symbol as such," Capote has said,
"if you put it to me") but immediately out of the author's
own experience of the irrational, his clutch on the remembered body of his own dreams and psychic frights. With a
sometimes alarming immediacy they produce the most awful
nighttime horrors of childhood, the hopelessness, the will-less-
ness, the ghastly mechanical compulsion of nightmare. One
thinks sometimes almost entirely in pictorial terms when reading these stories, of some of the paintings of Fuseli, of Bosch,
later, perhaps, of Max Ernst.

The analogy with such painters is useful only in that it is
meant to suggest Capote's imaginative habit, in these stories,
of direct presentation. Here there is no comment and, one feels,
no previous speculation: these horrors are simply *there:* this
is *it,* the stories say. In one of the earliest, "A Tree of Night,"
Kay, a pretty, ordinary girl on her way back to college after
a distant funeral, is compelled by two monsters (who earn
their living by re-enacting in public the burial and resurrection of Lazarus) with whom she is isolated on a train into a
confrontation with her own unconscious life to which at last
she yields:

> Staring up into his hairless, vapid face, flushed brilliant
> by the lantern light, Kay knew of what she was afraid:
> it was a memory, a childish memory of terrors that once,
> long ago, had hovered above her like haunted limbs on
> a tree of night. Aunts, cooks, strangers—each eager to
> spin a tale or teach a rhyme of spooks and death, omens,
> spirits, demons. And always there had been the unfail-
> ing threat of the wizard man: stay close to the house,
> child, else a wizard man will snatch you and eat you

alive! He lived everywhere, the wizard man, and everywhere was danger. At night, in bed, hear him tapping
at the window? Listen!

The "wizard man," the bogeyman of every childhood, that
formless embodiment of every formless fear, the animated
threat to every assumption of security—he takes many forms
and, in these stories, is everywhere. He is that Mr. Revercomb
in "Master Misery," who sucks the life out of others by seizing
upon their dreams, and he is that Mr. Destronelli of "The
Headless Hawk," masked in nearly all the characters, none of
whom he really is, and his is the voice on the telephone in
"Shut a Final Door," that voice of fate and dread which is also
the hero's voice, Walter Ranney's, fleeing and unable to flee,
as in the paralysis that overtakes us in our most wretched
dreams.

"The Headless Hawk," the story that depends most completely on the nightmare mood and that explores it not only
in a dream and in a fit of fever but also in strange dislocations
that overtake the objective action, uses as its epigraph a passage from the Book of Job:

> They are of those that rebel against the light; they know
> not the ways thereof, nor abide in the paths thereof. In
> the dark they dig through houses, which they had
> marked for themselves in the daytime: they know not
> the light . . .

The central character is a young man named Vincent who, in
his closest associations, can turn to maimed people alone, and
these he must maim further if he is to preserve that self from
the recognition of which, paradoxically, he is at the same time
always fleeing. Now it is a deranged young girl known to him
only by the initials D.J., who pursues him mutely; he accepts
her, rejects her, and is pursued still. She in turn is haunted
by Mr. Destronelli, who appears in many guises, finally in
Vincent himself. Presenting these mirrored and distorted relationships that evade all logic, the story depends probably

more than any other on the dissheveled imagery of tortured dream and hallucination, and by these means explores most explicitly the *Doppelgänger* theme. In the climactic scene Vincent finds his other self, "old and horrid," clinging "spider-like onto his back," and then, in a grisly Mardi gras throng, he sees "that many are also saddled with malevolent semblances of themselves, outward embodiments of inner decay."

This is the major and compulsive theme of these early stories—the despairing attempt to escape identity and the ultimate, desperate acceptance of it in the exposed dark night of the soul. It appears, in reverse, in "Master Misery," where another young girl, Sylvia, is systematically deprived of her dreams, and so is deprived finally of her own self. ". . . there was nothing left to steal." At the same time the sinister figure who buys these dreams, a figure we are never permitted to see in this story that appears to be a kind of diabolic *Sacred Fount*, presumably enriches and even creates his self, and re-creates it.

The mood and method of these stories, if not so explicitly the alter-ego theme, find their fullest treatment in Capote's first novel, *Other Voices, Other Rooms* (1948). Like a number of the stories, it begins in circumstances that are mundane enough as young Joel Knox is trying to get to an isolated place in the South where his father is; but very soon, as Joel finds himself in increasingly eerie circumstances, these enter the narrative method itself and more and more frantically he is spun about in the kaleidescope of hallucination, and the reader with him. In search of his father, he is searching no less for someone who will love him: "Only how, how, could you say something so indefinite, so meaningless as this: God, let me be loved." (This is in rather sharp difference from Mrs. McCullers' characters, who are searching rather for someone to whom they can give their love.) Joel's father, when Joel is finally permitted to see him, is a paralyzed lunatic, and it is the decayed and elegantly sinister Cousin Randolph (the wizard of the novel) who will love him in his fashion, and force him to know himself. Thrust suddenly into this world of the sinister, the perverse, the lunatic, and the horrible, Joel makes an attempt to escape back into the sunnier world that he had left. But a deeper regression is in store for him. In the weird decay of the Cloud Hotel, in the final act of his initiation, he becomes at last what he is, and in this recognition there is relief and exhilaration and no regret.

Eight years after the publication of *Other Voices, Other Rooms,* having reread the novel, Capote said to an interviewer for the *Paris Review,* "I am a stranger to that book; the person who wrote it seems to have so little in common with my present self. Our mentalities, our interior temperatures are entirely different." That "interior temperature" was presumably already preparing for its alteration even when the nightmare mood most intensely commanded his imagination; for in such an early story as "Children on Their Birthdays" as well as in such later stories as "House of Flowers" and "A Christmas Memory," both the tone and the technique are quite different.

In these gentler stories we are asked to enter a world of private love, not madness, a world in which the characters live in relative peace with others and in considerable peace with themselves. Through love they are able—Miss Bobbit of "Children on Their Birthdays" is the best example—to metamorphose that other life which they have almost, as it seems, inadvertently entered. The plot now is no longer concerned with thrusting a character down into the deep putrescent well of his self but rather with his lifting others up into the air of day, out of the well of derision and shame. In these stories the characters are freed from nightmare but are still possessed by dreams. ". . . a man who doesn't dream is like a man who doesn't sweat: he stores up a lot of poison," says the Judge in *The Grass Harp* (1953), the novel that is most intent on the examination of this mood of love. Here hate and anger, self-hate and self-pity, the cancer of pride, the disease of advantage and profit still all enter the plot; but these are now peripheral, no longer the positives. And the dreams of the good are gentle, happy, hardly more than benign reveries, with none of the turbulent assault upon the feelings that is the intent of the nightmare stories.

The material of these stories is drawn from the realities of a recognizable social world, but because the stories themselves are not concerned with "social problems" in any direct way and because the characters are, in one way or another, set apart from social realities, they are not bound by the limits of ordinary realism and maintain some of that freedom of fantasy and romance that is Capote's métier. Vehemence yields here to pity, to pathos, even to sentiment, and "Gothic" melodrama to humor. In this mood, where pity and humor are conjoined, even nature is altered. A story like "The Headless Hawk" ends with nature violently awry: ". . . it was as if the sky were a thunder-cracked mirror, for the rain fell between them like a curtain of splintered glass"; and this clattering image of sky and rain is characteristic of the treatment of nature in the earlier stories, where all is defaced, crippled, knotted, harsh, lunar, lunatic. But in "Children on Their Birthdays," for example, "it has been raining buoyant summer rain shot through with sun," and when the sun emerges again at the end of the story, it brings "with it into the air all the sweetness of wisteria." For this propitious climate, this beneficent world, Royal's "house of flowers" is the metaphor, or the tree house in *The Grass Harp.*

This short novel has an air of the legendary which derives from at least two sources. One is the frame of the story, the idea of the harp, a field of dry grass over which the wind passes and speaks, "gathering, telling, a harp of voices remembering a story." The other is the remembered quality of the narrative, for the story is cast in the form of nostalgic reminiscence of a lost childhood, and the frequent interruptions of present time remind us over and over that Collin, the narrator, is reliving an idyll, or what, in retrospect, seems to have been idyllic.

> Those famous landscapes of youth and woodland water
> —in after years how often, trailing through the cold

rooms of museums, I stopped before such a picture, stood long haunted moments having it recall that gone scene, not as it was, a band of goose-fleshed children dabbling in an autumn creek but as the painting presented it, husky youths and wading water-diamonded girls; and I've wondered then, wonder now, how they fared, where they went in this world, that extraordinary family.

But the core of the story is real enough and not without a certain harshness.

A young boy—eleven when he arrives, sixteen when the story opens—comes to live with his father's two sisters, Verena and Dolly. Verena is hard, practical, loveless, formidably organized; Dolly is soft, gentle, affectionate, and a little dotty. The boy is, of course, attracted to Dollyheart, as she is called by her devoted friend, a Negro servant named Catherine; and the three of them work contentedly collecting herbs and roots for Dolly's secret remedy for dropsy. When Verena discovers that Dolly is, in fact, managing a considerably successful enterprise she decides to take it over and put it on a sound commercial basis, and she enlists the help of a sharp city character named Morris Ritz. Dolly stubbornly refuses to yield up her secret formula and, when she is reproached for her general uselessness, she packs a few things together and, with Collin and Catherine, takes up her abode in a tree house on the edge of the field, the grass harp. There they are joined by two other dissident spirits, Judge Charlie Cool, retired and more or less expelled from his own house by his daughters-in-law, and an eighteen-year-old "loner" named Riley Henderson.

The rest of the novel has to do with the efforts of the conventional and indignant townspeople, under the leadership of Verena and a brutal sheriff, to force these five idiots back into sanity. When it develops that Morris Ritz has fleeced Verena and fled the town, she collapses, and so does the comic war that the village has been waging on the inhabitants of the tree. In a rainstorm, the broken Verena herself climbs into the tree, laments the perfidious Morris, and concludes: "It's too long to be alone, a lifetime. I walk through the house, nothing is mine: your pink room, your kitchen, the house is yours, and Catherine's too, I think. Only don't leave me, let me live with you. I'm feeling old, I want my sister." And they return to the house in the town.

But the tree house episode has been the major demarcation in the lives of them all, and the events of their lives are thought of as happening either before or after it. "Those few autumn days were a monument and a signpost." Their lives continue. Dolly does not marry the Judge, who has come to love her in the tree, but devotes herself to Verena and dies of a stroke.

> If in other ways he was a disappointed man, it was not because of Dolly, for I believe she became what he'd wanted, the one person in the world—to whom, as he'd described it, everything can be said. But when everything can be said perhaps there is nothing more to say.

Riley Henderson marries and becomes an industrious and respected citizen. Collin leaves the town to take up the study of law. Verena dies. But the grass harp goes on telling its story, and what it tells is that each of those eccentrics in the tree discovered there what he really was in himself. They discovered their separateness and their communion. "You're not yourself," Verena tells Dolly toward the end of the story, and Dolly replies, "You'd best look again: I am myself." The Judge has discovered what she is in herself and what he is when he calls her a "pagan," a "spirit"—

> someone not to be calculated by the eye alone. Spirits are accepters of life, they grant its differences—and consequently are always in trouble. Myself, I should never have been a Judge; as such, I was too often on the wrong side: the law doesn't admit differences. . . . But ah, the energy we spend hiding from one another, afraid as we are of being identified. But here we are, identified: five

fools in a tree. A great piece of luck provided we know how to use it: no longer any need to worry about the picture we present—free to find out who we truly are.

And if, as Collin later thinks, "No matter what passions compose them, all private worlds are good," it is because in the private world we find out who we truly are, and once we find that out, the novel seems to say, we can make the vulgar public world meet us on our own terms—or, if it will not, feel indifferent in our difference.

Capote's progression from the wholly private psychic world into the world of objective social realities continues. Isolating his characters still, but in a different way, and transforming the dulcet humor and the sentiment of the gentler stories and of *The Grass Harp* into high impertinent comedy, he moves into yet another area of experience and feeling, and perhaps the most suitable. Holly Golightly of *Breakfast at Tiffany's* (1958) seems to be an eccentric fraud, as anyone must who lives only by his own sense of the independence of the self; she is committed to nothing whatever except her sense of her own freedom; she will not give even a stray cat a name until she, a stray herself, must have one and then must name herself; a "wild thing."

> "Never love a wild thing, Mr. Bell," Holly advised him. "That was Doc's mistake. He was always lugging home wild things. A hawk with a hurt wing. One time it was a full-grown bobcat with a broken leg. But you can't give your heart to a wild thing: the more you do, the stronger they get. Until they're strong enough to run into the woods. Or fly into a tree. Then a taller tree. Then the sky. That's how you'll end up, Mr. Bell. If you let yourself love a wild thing. You'll end up looking at the sky . . . Good luck: and believe me, dearest Doc—it's better to look at the sky than live there. Such an empty place; so vague. Just a country where the thunder goes and things disappear."

This passage is not only the clue to the story and to Holly's character, but it is also the prediction of the end of the story and of her end, as she too disappears in, as it were, the sky. There is pathos still, then, but Holly's final choice is *her* choice, and that fact modifies the pathos, as, throughout the story, it is modified by the rowdy stylishness, the randy chic, the lacquered, the enameled, the rhinestoned and beplumed conduct of the inhabitants of Capote's crazy caravansary, these self-possessed madmen and modish eccentrics.

With this progression from the drama of the innermost terrors to what is basically a comedy of very special manners, and with his true gift for the observation of manners, it is not surprising that during almost all the time that he has been a writer of fiction, Capote has also been a reporter. His first attempts, quite simple but effective accounts of places and getting to places, appeared in the collection called *Local Color* (1950). From these travel sketches he proceeded to characterizations of persons, mainly glamorous, of public prominence. The most effective, probably, is an interview with Marlon Brando in Japan—"just a young man sitting on a pile of candy"—called "The Duke in his Domain." In this modest piece, Capote takes us at the outset into the best known Kyoto hotel late in an afternoon, and leads us out of it into the streets of the city early in the morning; between these parentheses, Marlon Brando talks, talks for hours, muses, remembers, makes the gestures of a host while recalling the horrors of home, rambles, ruminates, inspects his past, himself, almost discovers himself, and reveals himself to us. It is one of the most brilliant pieces of reporting in our time.

The most sustained piece of reporting that Truman Capote has published until now is *The Muses Are Heard* (1956), his account of the tour of Russia made by the American company presenting *Porgy and Bess* under State Department auspices. Its deadpan observation of another collection of very funny people in situations which, when they are not alarming, are wacky beyond mere lunacy surely constitutes a considerable piece of modern satire. So the reportage, like the fiction, has moved, too, from places to people in places, from the poetic to the social, from the solemn to the comic.

In *Breakfast at Tiffany's,* the narrator makes this observation: "the average personality reshapes frequently, every few years even our bodies undergo a complete overhaul—desirable or not, it is a natural thing that we should change."

It is demonstrably natural for Capote. His is hardly an average personality, whatever that may be. His literary personality, however, the mind and the work behind the books, has changed all the time that the mind has been working at them. Their substance, as the social texture has grown denser, has become more and more solid. The next change will become evident when Capote publishes the book which he is now writing—*In Cold Blood,* the detailed and immensely compelling account ("a cliff-hanger" without question) of a calculated, meaningless, multiple murder in the state of Kansas. It is still another kind of subject, another kind of writing for him; and it may prove to be the most remarkable.

Capote's experience and discipline as a writer of fiction help, of course, to make him the superb reporter that he is; one wonders now how his reporting will in turn modify his fiction when he takes that up again. Until then, we must rest with the observation of the way in which, beginning as an extreme example of the novelist of isolated sensibility, he has set that sensibility to work in the objective if off-beat, of course, materials of social actuality. Inversely, Carson McCullers has found the means to give her sensibility objective expression in literary forms that transcend social realities in approximations of myth.

These two writers seem to have moved in quite opposite directions from beginnings that were only superficially alike.

THE AMERICAN

INDIVIDUALIST TRADITION

SAUL BELLOW

Saul Bellow, born in Quebec in 1915 of Russian parents, spent most of his childhood and youth in Chicago. After beginning his education at the University of Chicago, he was graduated from Northwestern University in 1937 with honors in anthropology and sociology, two disciplines whose concerns one can see in his fiction. Like many serious writers of the postwar era Bellow frequently takes on teaching assignments. He has lectured at the University of Minnesota, Princeton, New York University, Bard College and the University of Chicago. Not until his current work in progress, *Herzog,* part of which has appeared in *Esquire,* have his characters been teachers, however. They have been drifters, paralyzed incompetents, or adventurers. Bellow's first novel, *Dangling Man,* was received with quiet but firm appreciation, as perhaps befits the book's tightly controlled effects. Neither *Dangling Man* nor his second novel, *The Victim,* prepared critics for the virtuosity of style and episode in *The Adventures of Augie March,* which won the National Book Award for fiction in 1953. Bellow is *engagé;* the engagement shows not only in his fiction and the fact that he teaches, but in the vivid and witty articles he writes about life and letters. He is also an active patron of young writers and was the guiding spirit of the influential little magazine, *The*

Noble Savage, which went through five issues before folding. Bellow has been married twice, has two sons, and makes his home in Tivoli, New York.

WILLIAM STYRON

William Styron has written two large books and one small one. The large books, *Lie Down in Darkness* and *Set This House on Fire,* were published nine years apart. In the interim considerable critical tension built up, since *Lie Down in Darkness* had been an ambitious and accomplished book for a man of twenty-six to have written. The tension, as so often happens, broke in two directions. *Set This House on Fire* was received as a brilliantly written work of great and realized intentions; it was also criticized as an unduly long, overdone novel, the last half of which wandered into pretentiousness. But whatever the reaction, no responsible critic was willing to write Styron off, as Jones and Mailer have been written off at various points in their careers. A manifest, if traditional, narrative skill in all of Styron's work immediately re-establishes the tension, setting up expectations for the future. Styron was born in Newport News, Virginia, in 1925. During World War II he interrupted his education at Duke University to serve in the Marine Corps. After the success of his first book he lived abroad for a number of years, and now resides in Roxbury, Connecticut, with his wife and children.

THE AMERICAN

INDIVIDUALIST TRADITION:

BELLOW AND STYRON

by Robert Gorham Davis

At a time when politics and the national mood hardly encouraged confident expansiveness, Saul Bellow and William Styron brought the literary fifties to a close with two quite unpredictable works, *Henderson the Rain King* and *Set This House on Fire*. Affirmative in tone, exuberant in style, free and ambitious in dramatic invention, these novels are unlike the other American fiction of the decade. And yet they represent a kind of philanthropic fantasy, of moral make-believe, conceivable only in America.

What went into these vigorous, talented fictions? How much truth have they? What sources of energy have their authors been able to tap at a time when most serious novelists are so negative or self-restrictive?

Some of these questions the authors themselves try to answer. Very conscious of being Americans, they allude freely and wittily to the culture that nurtured them. More revealing, however, are the less conscious patterns that become evident if all their novels are considered together. Bellow expresses the sense of alienation common enough in our time, but it is combined in a peculiar way with a passionate concern for being helpful to others. His novels abound in test cases of altruism, both positive and negative. Styron's first novel, *Lie Down in Darkness,* describes people doomed by selfishness and alienation, unable to help themselves or others. But in *Set This House on Fire* he goes even further than Bellow by making the melodramatic conclusion center on a spectacular act of gratuitous mercy.

Dangling Man, Saul Bellow's first novel, appeared in 1944, during the war, and at once attracted attention. It is in the form of a diary, a rather Kafkaesque diary, kept by a young man living in Chicago, identified only as Joseph. (In Kafka's *The Trial,* the hero is Joseph K.) Bellow's Joseph, like Bellow himself, was born in 1915 and spent his boyhood in Montreal. The diary entries run from December 15, 1942, to April 9, 1943.

Sometimes they are brief:

> December 28
>
> What would Goethe say to the view from this window, the wintry ill-lit street, he with his recurring pleasures, fruits, and flowers.
>
> January 31
>
> Slight let up in the cold. The fury of cleanliness. One of my shirts came back from the laundry without a single button. I must complain.

More often they are accounts, running to six or seven pages, of some stormy incident in which Joseph got involved the day before.

Expecting to go into the Army, Joseph had given up his job in a travel bureau and moved with his wife Eva into supposedly temporary lodgings. But red tape over his Canadian citizenship causes endless exasperating delays.

The dangling makes Joseph feel impotent. Because he is not playing any interesting social role at a time of change and excitement, people forget him or condescend to him. When he demands recognition simply as a human being, and his motives are not understood, he loses control of himself; the incidents end in humiliating defeats. He fights with his spoiled niece because she won't let him use her phonograph, with a bank officer who won't cash his wife's pay check for him, with a former mistress who won't return a book, with a boozy, thieving old tenant of the lodging house who doesn't shut the door when he uses the hall toilet. After a squabble has started, the most trivial details take on malign significance.

Since his wife is silently reproachful on such occasions, Joseph has to express himself in writing. A diary is the ideal form for a sensitive man living from day to day, whose life conspicuously lacks the grand pattern of change which gives shape to a novel. In the journal entries at the end of Joyce's *A Portrait of the Artist as a Young Man,* we find the same mixture of undignified domestic circumstances and bold, eloquently stated ideas. Bellow also had as examples Rilke's *The Notebooks of Malte Laurids Brigge,* Auden's *The Orators* and the real diaries of Kafka and Gide.

Nevertheless, *Dangling Man* is clearly the work of a novelist. Only a masochist or a man very eager to understand experience, to make art of it, could bring himself to describe in such dramatic detail scene after scene of frustration and defeat.

For instance, to make up for a previous misunderstanding, Joseph goes to give his father-in-law, home sick in bed, a friendly massage. His mother-in-law, who has been cleaning a chicken, pours Joseph a glass of orange juice. He expected to be asked to stay for lunch, but orange juice is better than nothing. At the sink, where the glass has been left for him, entrails of chicken ravel over the sopping drain board, and the white enamel is spattered with blood. In the orange juice floats a brown feather. With quiet distaste Joseph pours the drink down the drain.

In a time of universal disaster, what importance has a feather floating in orange juice? It is the mother-in-law's way of saying that Joseph is not writing the essays on history which he had planned for this brief period of respite, that he is living on his wife's slender earnings and not making her happy.

With hat and scarf on, Joseph wanders into the living room of his parents-in-law's flat and stares out at the ugliness of culverts, tracks, houses, billboards, electric signs, chimneys. "Was there a particle of what, elsewhere or in the past, had spoken in man's favor?" Before, he had sorrowed for men condemned to live amidst such ugliness and squalor. Now he sees all these uglinesses as symptoms, expressions. "What men created they also were."

Joseph is struggling hard to preserve his faith in a common humanity, a common goodness that lies behind and somehow denies what he reads in the newspapers. Is everything, for instance, determined by money? To assert his own freedom, Joseph tries privately and tactfully to return a hundred-dollar bill that his prospering older brother hands him. Characteristically he has to rummage in a bureau drawer for a pin with which to attach it to his brother's pillow. This leads to accusations by his angry niece and awkward explanations which make him feel anything but free. In Bellow's novels there is often the problem that unequal wealth creates between persons united by love or kinship.

Even more fundamental is the effect of history on personal identity. Joseph is a former communist left dangling politically by the Nazi-Soviet pact. Though he spends much of his day reading newspapers, his diary never mentions Hitler and Stalin, or Roosevelt and Churchill. He prefers "our imperialism to theirs," and is willing to fight the Germans, yet says "I would rather die in the war than consume its benefits . . . of course, I hope to survive. But I would rather be a victim than a beneficiary." His determinedly non-political, non-historical attitude would have been inconceivable for a person of his kind five years earlier, at the time of the Spanish Civil War. Now, with others of his generation, he tries to find in personal integrity and in purely personal relationships a substitute for politics.

The uncertain nature of the shift is dramatized by an incident in a restaurant where Joseph has gone with a friend who may have a job for him. There he discovers a former communist associate who seems deliberately to be ignoring his presence. Though the man lunching with him protests, "I came here to talk to you about a job, not to see you throw a fit," Joseph works himself into a rage, confronts the party member, makes a scene.

He justifies this on the highest grounds. People must be recognized as individuals; communication must be kept open despite differences of opinion. What Joseph—and perhaps his author—does not recognize is that he has transferred his communist dogmatism to the new personalist philosophy which came into favor after the Hitler-Stalin pact and the invasion of Poland. Joseph's approach to the communist is still the willful, stubborn confrontation of one ideology with another. He does not go to the communist in a spirit of love. On the contrary, he exclaims that he despises him. Nor does he really care about being persuasive intellectually. Out of frustration and his egotistic need to be recognized, yet offering nothing in return, Joseph irrationally demands from a political enemy what the other has no reason to give.

Nor had Joseph valued his mother-in-law, even before he faced the feather in his orange juice. He thought her a stupid, self-satisfied bore. It is not clear even that he loves his wife. Though the diary deals intimately enough with other aspects of his life, there is no hint of what goes on in his marriage sexually.

Considering the repeated failures of Joseph's attempts to find sources of dignity outside social status and organized activity, it is not surprising that he greets induction, when it finally comes, with a welcome cry of relief that is only partly ironic: "I am no longer to be held accountable for myself. . . . I am in other hands, relieved of self-determination, freedom cancelled. Hurray for regular hours! And for the supervision of the spirit! Long live regimentation!" Like the novels to follow, *Dangling Man* ends in a way that is only apparently decisive or conclusive. The stated themes have not been resolved nor the questions answered.

The Victim (1947) develops directly out of the *Dangling Man*. Written in conventional novel form, in the past tense and third person, it takes a single embarrassing involvement, of the kind described in Joseph's journal, and gives it full, sustained development.

Emotionally Asa Leventhal's situation is very like Joseph's. He has a sympathetic wife, but all through a stifling New York summer, she is off in the South taking care of her mother. He has work on a trade publication to occupy him, but it is not work that he particularly likes, and his relations with his superiors are uncomfortable. Asa is a burly man with a large head, large nose and a mat of curly hair. That his mother died insane has never ceased to trouble him. Though he seems solemnly impassive, he is easily obsessed, and needs the correction of his wife's graceful good sense.

Asa's brother is also away, in the West, looking for a better job. His younger son, Asa's nephew, is ill with a high, inexplicable fever. The sister-in-law, an excitable Italian woman dominated by her mother, summons Asa to Staten Island at unreasonable hours, when he can be of no real help. He patiently goes and tries to act also as a substitute father to his older nephew.

Though his sister-in-law is terrified of hospitals, Asa forces her to send the sick boy to one, under the care of a specialist whom he has found. But the boy dies, just before his father returns, and Asa knows that in the minds of the family he is associated with—or even blamed for—the death.

This is not all that is happening to Asa during the hot, lonely summer. Even harder to deal with psychologically is the reappearance in his life of a strange character named Kirby Allbee.

Some years back, before the happiness of his marriage, Asa had been through a period of unemployment when, like the diarist Joseph, he kept making scenes. He thought unjustly that his friends were not doing enough for him, yet his fits of

anger made him so difficult that they could hardly have been
blamed if they avoided him.

One of the most consequential of these incidents he had
completely forgotten. He had gone to interview a possible em-
ployer named Rudiger, at the suggestion of a casual acquaintance, Kirby Allbee, who worked for Rudiger. Rudiger was
clearly in a bad mood, and dismissed Asa with provocative
rudeness. Asa refused to take such treatment, denounced Rudiger with a violence which left that usually imperious man
gasping for words, and departed.

Now suddenly in the sultry summer, in the midst of Asa's
loneliness and worry about his brother's family, Allbee not
only re-enters but takes over Asa's life.

Where Asa had been angry at Allbee for sending him to a
man who had no interest in hiring him, Allbee's boss had been
furious with Allbee for exposing him to Asa's wrath. This was
one cause, if not the determining cause, of Allbee's dismissal.
Other firms in the same line of business would not hire him,
he drifted lower, began drinking, was utterly shattered when
his wife, who had left him, died in an accident. In his rather
irrational despair he becomes obsessed by the notion that Asa
is responsible for all his woes, and seeks him out, intent on
some sort of recompense or retribution. There are late-at-
night visits to Asa's apartment, telephone calls to the firm
where Asa works, strange encounters on the streets and in
restaurants.

Since Allbee, of an old New England family, is an anti-
Semite, Asa assumes his accusations are purely pathological.
When Asa seeks reassurance, however, from friends and former business associates acquainted with Allbee and Rudiger,
he is troubled by the way they respond. They had heard at
the time about Asa's fracas with Rudiger, and knowing Rudiger, could well believe that it led him to fire Allbee, with
whom he was already at odds. It was also known that at a
party Asa had resented the way Allbee had talked about Jews.
This resentment could have made Asa careless of consequences when he got angry with Allbee's boss, just as the

mother-in-law in *Dangling Man,* not consciously intending a slur, was careless about the feather in the orange juice.

As he painfully reconstructs a forgotten past, Asa realizes that there is something to all this, but not nearly enough to justify Allbee in his demented attempt to saddle Asa with blame for disasters which he clearly has brought upon himself. But when Asa, in the same spirit as the diarist Joseph, tries to convince others of this, it has the opposite effect. They suspect that he protests too much. It makes them recall how difficult he used to be. Above all they simply don't want to have to think about it. They resent his forcing his problems on them, intimate problems of a kind better left undiscussed, just as Asa resents having to live with Allbee's degeneration and despair.

Like *Dangling Man,* but more profoundly, *The Victim* faces the question of our responsibility, simply as human beings, for other individuals who are imposed on us by circumstances, whom we do not particularly value or respect, and with whom we are not engaged in any meaningful creative or social activities.

Out of mingled compassion, weakness, fear and guilt, Asa lets Allbee intrude more and more into his life, lets him stay at the apartment, though his distaste for him steadily increases. Apart from this distaste, the relationship is reminiscent of Conrad's *The Secret Sharer.* Asa sees that perhaps only luck kept him from going under as Allbee did, and that deep down he is not so different from Allbee as he should like to believe. And yet both toward his brother's family and toward Allbee, Asa's intentions are genuinely good.

Bellow brilliantly characterizes Allbee, whose name suggests universality. Allbee is arrogant, wheedling, confessional, maudlin and hardest to take, especially on the subject of Jews, when he is trying to be agreeable. The physical aspects of the intimacy are the most difficult to bear. Longing for his wife, her delicacy, her sex, Asa is given Allbee instead, with his aggressive masculine untidiness. He surprises Allbee in the apartment with a woman; he has to take care of Allbee drunk;

Allbee asks to touch Asa's thickly curling and "Jewish" hair. Their living together ends with a suicide gesture on Allbee's part as dangerous to Asa as to himself.

Even more than in *Dangling Man,* scenes and objects have an "intentionality" which carries us beyond ordinary realism. The same sultry, threatening oppressiveness is found in the weather, in the realm of physical action and in the depths of the psyche. Staten Island is not merely Staten Island, but the place where Asa's nephew lies ill with a stubborn fever. In any night street Allbee may be lurking, every ring of the phone is a threat.

The style is richer and more homogeneous, too, though it seems a little studied and academic compared to the easy wit and figurative precision of Bellow's later work. "The clouds were heavily suspended and slow. To the south and east, the air was brassy, the factories were beginning to smolder and faced massively, India red, brown, into the sun and across the hot green netting of the bridges." Or at a birthday party: "The child lowered her face to the clear ring of candles. Leventhal saw the liquid image of them in her eyes and on her white forehead. She blew, and the whitish odorous smoke drifted over the table."

The Victim ends as inconclusively as *Dangling Man.* Some years later at the theater Asa and his wife encounter Allbee, squiring an aging, once famous actress. Allbee hasn't changed much. Though he has pulled himself together, he is obviously leading a corrupt and unvaluable life. In his brief talk in the foyer with Asa he says, "I'm the type that comes to terms with whoever runs things." Too late, after the bell has rung for the final act, Asa calls out, "Wait a minute, what's your idea of who runs things?" but his question goes unanswered.

This is not, however, the real theme of the book. What remains unexplained is the meaning and use of Asa's summer of suffering. At the theater, in his rude, overfamiliar manner, Allbee expresses genuine appreciation for what Asa did. Asa undoubtedly helped a man who hardly deserved helping, and who is now putting his partly restored self-confidence to

purely selfish uses. But what of those who were not saved—
the feverish child and Allbee's wife? The encounter at the theater endows the earlier events of the novel with the same
ironic pointlessness that disappearance into the Army gave to
all Joseph's quarrelsome efforts in *Dangling Man*. Whether
something does remain from acts of goodness, some residue
of value or meaning, will perhaps be answered in two future
novels, *The Adventures of Augie March* and *Henderson the
Rain King*.

Where *Dangling Man* and *The Victim* are closed and re-
stricted books, limited in space and time, *The Adventures of
Augie March* (1953) is open and expansive, with a huge cast
of highly individualized characters, and rapid movement
through time and space, through decades and across conti-
nents. No American novel since Dos Passos' *U.S.A.* has given
such a vividly immediate sense of widely ranging scenes and
occupations, of experiences in all sorts of moods and aspects.
Augie steals books in Chicago, runs a coalyard, helps a girl
get an abortion and then tries to cure her of blood poisoning,
manages a prize fighter, attempts smuggling, trains an eagle
to hunt iguanas in Mexico, is secretary to a millionaire, finds
himself alone with a lunatic in a lifeboat after his ship is tor-
pedoed. He alternates unpredictably between poverty and
riches.

All this is told in a style beautifully adapted to content, a
style that is packed, nervous, witty, observant. Sometimes too
much is observed, the sentences strain with lists of things remembered. Riding in the Chicago City Hall elevator of a
winter afternoon, Augie feels "hothouse and arctic drafts
mixed up, brute things and airs of sex, evidence of heavy
feeding and systematic shaving, of calculations, grief, not-
caring, and hopes of tremendous millions in concrete." Taking his grandmother to an old folks' home, he is appalled by
the "terrible appearances of white hair and rashy, vessel-
busted hands holding canes, fans, newspapers in all languages
and alphabets, faces gone in the under-surface flues and in
the eyes, of these people sitting in the sunshine and leaf-

burning outside or in the mealy moldiness and gravy acids in the house." He remembers working in Woolworth's basement "hearing how the floor bore up under the ambling weight of hundreds, with the fanning, breathing movie organ next door and the rumble descending from the trolleys on Chicago Avenue—the bloody-rinded Saturday gloom of wind-borne ash and blackened forms of five-story buildings rising up to a blind Northern dimness from the Christmas blaze of shops."

In the diary entries of *Dangling Man,* passages of theoretic reflection and of particular reporting remain more or less separate. In *Augie March* they fuse, become one in the individual sentences, even in the phrases. The strength of Bellow's later writing derives from the simultaneity of evocation and analysis, impression and idea. Things strike him sharply in all their thingness, their uniqueness and temporality, and yet at the same time, in the medieval scholastic phrase, he sees the *universalia in res.* And he sees them in the light of his own being and moods also, for this, like *Dangling Man,* is first-person narrative; Augie is telling his own story.

Since the story covers decades, it is a story of changes. Grandma Lausch, the family autocrat of Augie's earliest years, goes in dazed proud defeat to an old folks' home. With his mother becoming blind, his feeble-minded brother has to be sent to an institution. Commissioner Einhorn, crippled, flamboyant, the great man of affairs of Augie's youth, loses all his money in the depression, yields place to an inferior son. Augie's brother Simon, on the other hand, marries a wealthy girl and makes a lot of money on his own. Augie himself, who had once supported himself by stealing books and had experimented twice with really serious criminality, keeps finding himself in situations in which he can have all that he wants simply for the asking.

And yet *Augie March* is not so different from the two earlier novels as all this would suggest. True, Augie is attractive to others as Joseph and Asa Leventhal were not. Powerful people seek him out, fall in love with him, place confidence in him. They, not he, however, are the goal-setters, the purposive ones. On ill-fated prize-fighting and smuggling trips, he simply goes along, sharing the risks, but not deciding what shall happen. In the matter of an equally ill-fated abortion, though Augie has to pay a high price for his assistance, it is the girl who makes all the decisions. Augie admires her, but he has not made her pregnant, and does not wish to marry her. For a brief time he manages a coalyard, but he has been set up in this business by his brother, so that Augie can demonstrate to prospective parents-in-law that he is capable of managing things. An expedition to Mexico to train an eagle and make wild-life movies is entirely his rich wife's idea. When he is asked in Mexico to do an important service for Trotsky, though he has no real interest in Left politics, he exclaims, "Please God! keep me from being sucked into another of those great currents where I can't be myself."

The great currents are currents in the lives of other people, people who do have strong wills and goals, and who, appealed to by Augie, want to take him along. "There was something adoptional about me." His principal way of asserting himself is to say "No" to people. "I have said 'No' to Joe Gorman, too. To Grandma. To Jimmy. To lots of people." Augie does not break with them out of selfishness or unwillingness to take risks. He tries to help people, and suffers a good many beatings, literal or figurative, in the course of it. No, he breaks with them in the interest of what he thinks is freedom, the right to be himself.

His definition of freedom is basically negative. Augie thinks that specializing, settling down to one job that he cares about, would be against freedom. It is a madman in a lifeboat—and not Augie—who talks eloquently about "the shriek of unused capacities, the doom of serving no great end or design, or contributing to no master force." This murderous sage contends that boredom is a sign of harmony not accomplished, of "the obedience that is not willingly given because nobody knows how to request it." All that Augie can see is "endless vistas."

At one point Augie does think of settling down. He is having an affair with an affectionate girl who is ready to merge her life positively with his. He talks of going to a small town, becoming a teacher. But after Pearl Harbor he is in a frenzy to enlist, everything else forgotten. The novel ends in the post-war period. Augie is engaged in illicit international trade, a higher level of the dishonesties which had troubled his youth in Chicago. He is married to a restless, handsome, flamboyant, dishonest woman. The novel concludes inconclusively as *Dangling Man* did, with wry irony, with uncertain laughter. For all his mobility, his constantly reasserted freedom, where has Augie got? "I may well be a flop at this line of endeavor. Columbus too thought he was a flop, probably, when they sent him back in chains. Which didn't prove there was no America."

Augie is a dangling man, too. He is attracted to people and ideas, has dreams of self-realization, but his temperament and his—or his author's—idea of freedom make impossible the kind of committed attachment to people, places, work and institutions on which self-realization and community depend. Much of the intensity which gives vividness to this and other novels by Bellow is the intensity of unsatisfied desire. Adequate ends for desires are never as clearly imagined as the desires themselves, nor, so far as work is concerned, are adequate goals or purposes to work toward. Bellow himself has his writing, his reputation, his art to live for. In *Augie March,* as in so many novels, a falsifying transference occurs. The central character is endowed with the temperament of a novelist, moves about freely, observing kinds of work from the outside, as a novelist must, and yet is not permitted to write novels. His author writes them for him.

The people Augie knows are mostly marginal operators, swindlers, parasites. Though the last word of this marvelously rich and exciting book is "America," we get no direct sense of what sustains America, its schools, churches, businesses, political and cultural institutions, and of what goes on in the minds of the people, good and bad, who are really running things in America. These are the people whom Asa Leventhal asked about so plaintively in the last moment of *The Victim.*

Such marginality would not matter if the novel were more purely comic and picaresque. But Augie, or his master, genuinely seeks self-fulfillment, genuinely recognizes the need to serve "a great end or design," find harmony, contribute to a "master force." And yet in a novel which permits itself great imaginative scope, as in the episode of the sinking ship or of the relationship with Trotskyists in Mexico, we do not directly enter areas of experience in America itself where meaningful design and devotion may still be possible. The experiences of the book are not of a kind to answer the questions Augie and the author keep asking. And, as at the end of *The Victim,* it is not clear what all the intense activity has actually taught or produced.

The Adventures of Augie March is an ebullient book. Its people are emphatic, resourceful, full of ideas, sexually charged. One may ask, however, whether there is not too much freedom of invention, whether Augie, for all the knocks he takes, does not keep changing his mode of life a little too easily, whether the failure of his search for design is not ultimately reflected in a lack of governing design in the book itself.

As if in reaction to the exuberances of *Augie March,* Bellow's next significant fiction, the one-hundred-page *Seize the Day* (1956), observes the classic unities even more strictly than did *Dangling Man* or *The Victim.* It covers only a few hours in the life of one Tommy Wilhelm, temporarily resident in the Hotel Gloriana in New York. Like Asa Leventhal, he is a heavy-set, brooding man. Once handsome, he is now a blond hippopotamus, increasingly slovenly in his habits as he grows older and more discouraged. Like Joseph, when trying too self-consciously to show more character than he really possesses, he becomes emotional and loses even what power he might have over the people whom he confronts. Like Augie March he too readily lets other people deflect the course of his life, but lacking Augie's charm and intelligence, he has no way of breaking free again.

When Tommy Wilhelm, born Wilky Adler, was in college, his published photograph attracted the attention of a movie agent, the unsuccessful relative of some powerful people in Hollywood. Unable to judge the man or his promise to make a star of him, Tommy gave up college, quarreled with his family, but then, when a screen test turned out badly, went to Hollywood anyway. "This was typical of Wilhelm. After much thought and hesitation and debate, he invariably took the course he had rejected innumerable times. Ten such decisions made up the history of his life. He had decided that it would be a bad mistake to go to Hollywood, and then he went. He had made up his mind not to marry his wife, but ran off and got married. He had resolved not to invest money with Tamkin, and then had given him a check."

Seven bad years in Hollywood ended when Wilhelm entered the Army. After the war he got a well-paying job as a salesman, but quarreled and quit the firm or was forced out —it is not clear which—when he resisted dividing his sales territory with the president's nephew. Now, as with Allbee in *The Victim,* everything is spiraling rapidly downward. Wilhelm loves his two boys, but, involved with another woman, he unwisely left his wife under circumstances that gave her great legal advantage. Because she is twisting the screws hard to get more money for the boys' education and medical expenses, Wilhelm has sunk all his remaining funds in a margin speculation in lard futures. It is a joint venture with a very questionable psychologist named Tamkin. Like so many characters in *Augie March,* Tamkin is a great talker, full of genuinely interesting ideas.

Wilhelm sees no way out of his difficulties because he sees no way out of himself. His father, a well-to-do retired physician living in the same hotel, refuses to help on the grounds that once he starts doling out money to Wilhelm and Wilhelm's sister and their families, they will drain away all that he has and still be no better off themselves. It is the same problem as in *The Victim.* In purely private situations in which no communal rules of justice obtain or are enforced, how responsible are we for other people? When is help actually help, and what does it do for giver as well as receiver?

Though he knows that it will accomplish nothing, the miserable Wilhelm persists in telling his father his troubles. Like the characters whom Joseph and Asa approached in the earlier novels, Dr. Adler simply does not want to have to listen. The old people who fill the Gloriana like to boast about their children, but Wilhelm's presence makes it embarrassing for Dr. Adler. He has never quite forgiven his son for the pathetic attempt at independence signaled by his change of name. When Wilhelm pleads with him, the neat, angry doctor tells him some home truths and warns him against Dr. Tamkin. This lecture angers Wilhelm both because it is unanswerable and because it is unsoftened by an offer to help financially. "You hate me," he tells his father. "And if I had money you wouldn't." In the world of the Gloriana respect depends on money.

The price of lard futures plummets and Tamkin disappears. Wilhelm wonders if Tamkin had actually put up any money of his own. Perhaps he had used Wilhelm's money for other purposes. Pursuing as in a nightmare a man who looks like Tamkin, Wilhelm finds himself in a funeral parlor, staring down at the corpse. His misery overwhelms him, and he weeps both for himself and the dead man, who represents all humanity. "The source of all tears had suddenly sprung open within him, black, deep and hot . . . the heavy sea-like music came up to his ears . . . He heard it and sank deeper than sorrow, through torn sobs and cries toward the consummation of his heart's ultimate need." The source and consummation are both within himself, apparently, but this is the last sentence of the book and the author does not explain further.

Seize the Day is Bellow's one exercise in pure naturalism. He takes a character ill-equipped for life, whose mistakes become more and more unredeemable as he grows older, and lets him sink under their weight. But is this really the end for Tommy? It was not for Allbee. Is the consummation referred to in the last sentence some kind of new beginning spiritually? What is the "heart's ultimate need" referred to so cryptically?

Bellow's following book, *Henderson the Rain King* (1958), seems to pick up where *Seize the Day* ended, and certainly suggests that no end is final while life remains in the body. Henderson, now aged fifty-five, has made as many mistakes as Wilhelm, Augie and Joseph put together. He has advantages that they did not have. He comes of an old family, is not Jewish, has inherited both wealth and bookishness, is very strong, but describes his life as one long litany of blundering and inner anguish. "I am to suffering what Gary is to smoke. One of the world's biggest operations." Like the earlier Bellow heroes, Henderson, "a monster of grief," is easily angered, easily made indignant, by wives, children, mistresses, servants, tenants and unprepared strangers who happen to encounter him in a bad mood. Because of his strength, his money, his background, his bull-headedness, he can act outrageously and survive—so far as external consequences are concerned. It is within himself that he has to pay. He really doesn't mean ill; he just gets carried away. Later he regrets, but is too clumsy and proud to make amends properly. "The confusing thing is that I always have some real basic motivation, and how I go so wrong I can never understand."

To escape himself or recreate himself, Henderson departs on a photographing trip to Africa with a friend of his own age who has just remarried. Characteristically he finds it impossible to travel with the newlyweds, and sets off by himself with a single native guide. Here the narrative of *Henderson the Rain King* enters a realm of fantasy far exceeding anything in *The Adventures of Augie March*. It is not by any means free fantasy, however. This is the anthropological world of Frazer and Lord Raglan, of temporary kings, totem and taboo. The symbolism is also controlled, as Marcus Klein has shown, by the first parable of *Thus Spake Zara-*

thustra, with its references to frogs, lions and a child. If in *Henderson* the various relations of men and animals are not quite so inclusive as in Ovid's *Metamorphoses,* they have the same mythic character. In America Henderson has been involved with pigs, cats, a chimpanzee, an octopus, a seal and an old brown bear in a roller coaster. In Africa he encounters cows, frogs and then lions.

Among Africans Henderson proves as "adoptive" as Augie. In the first tribe he lives with, after he has proved himself in a ceremonial wrestling match with the prince, he sets himself with characteristic energy to relieve the community of a plague of frogs. Unfortunately, trying to get quick results, he destroys the water supply on which both people and cattle depend. In a second community he becomes even more fantastically involved in tribal politics based on magic, totemism and belief in the transmigration of souls. Henderson ends up by being made king himself.

In both tribes he finds men and women he can love and respect; they seem to him founts of the wisdom he has always sought. Henderson's experiences in Africa combine the Peace Corps' kind of mission—he admires Schweitzer and Grenfell—and the attempt of the postwar generation to discover outside the West (in Zen Buddhism, for instance) access to kinds of reality which American or Western culture ignores because it hasn't learned, really, "to encounter death."

When his faithful interpreter demurs at the risks they are taking, Henderson explains, "Millions of Americans have gone forth since the war to redeem the present and discover the future. I can swear to you, Romilayu, there are guys exactly like me in India and in China and South America and all over the place . . . It's the destiny of my generation of Americans to go out in the world and try to find the wisdom of life."

Seize the Day ended when Tommy Wilhelm confronted death, his own death, on the face of a strange corpse. Henderson discovers forces stronger than death in nature, in animals and in man himself. Prince Dahfu, who has studied medicine and knows the cultures both of Europe—or at least the Middle East—and Africa, gives Henderson a carefully organized course intended to produce the changes in self which Tommy Wilhelm had despairingly prayed for. The course is extremely demanding; such change does not come easily. Beginning with morality, the conception of "high conduct," it reaches down into the physical and even the animal. A lioness plays a principal part. So does imagination. "Imagination is a force of nature," the prince says. "Is this not enough to make a person full of ecstasy? Imagination, imagination, imagination! It converts to actual. It sustains, it alters, it redeems!"

Henderson itself is a triumph of the imagination, with its marvelous descriptions of a purely fictive Africa, an Africa of the soul. For all the exoticism of the events, the writing is as tough and witty as in the earlier books. Henderson, who tells his own story as Augie did, uses an even more flavorful language. Despite his comic blunderings and bull-headedness, he is an appealing figure. And despite the fantastic setting, the central character is capable of deeper emotional attachment to people and objects than has been true in the preceding books. The death of the prince is a great blow to Henderson, but it makes him cling fast to the redeeming fact of greatness. For all his suffering in Africa he loves life, loves people. The sight of the stewardess on the plane reminds him that, "Every twenty years or so the earth renews itself in young maidens . . . Blessings on her thighs."

But the end is still not satisfying. Henderson's bullying impatience with the American consular authorities while trying to arrange passage for the sacred lion cub suggests that he has not changed so greatly after all. How much of what he learned in Africa can be exported? Henderson returns full of good intentions. His love for his wife is strong again. He is going to train to become a doctor. He will adopt the homeless boy whom he has befriended on the plane. But these purposes, though worthy, are the kinds of good works beloved of television serials. Does the ending, set symbolically in a cold, windswept field in Newfoundland, quite convince the reader that Henderson, back in America, will not blunder into his old ways again? But perhaps the reader has profited, if Henderson has not. This brilliant, comic, imaginative fantasy is very American, its hero full of good intentions that others do not appreciate; of striving, of belief that one can always start over again if only one wants to enough.

At first, William Styron's *Lie Down in Darkness* seems very different from anything written by Bellow. Styron, ten years younger than Bellow, published his first novel in 1951. It is a long, highly concentrated book which begins and ends on the funeral day of a beautiful young southern girl, Peyton Loftis, who committed suicide in New York and whose body has been brought back for burial to a city like Norfolk, Virginia. Through the memories of the unhappy group of people waiting at the station, and the recreated consciousness of Peyton herself, the past twenty years are reviewed thematically, symphonically to discover what went wrong or what was irremediably wrong to begin with.

The dead girl, beautiful, talented, restless, is the daughter of a well-connected lawyer, Milton Loftis, who had no need to practice his profession because of his wife Helen's wealth. Milton has indulged or spoiled his daughter to try to make sure that his more or less incestuous love for her is returned. His wife, in reaction, becomes more and more preoccupied by their other daughter, Maudie, who is physically and mentally defective. After Maudie's death, under circumstances which lead to a good deal of recrimination, Helen comes to hate Milton and Peyton, and the silly woman, Dolly, with whom Milton, still handsome, is having a prolonged affair.

As Malcolm Cowley showed in some detail when the novel was first published, *Lie Down in Darkness* is based directly on Faulkner's *The Sound and the Fury*. Styron's Peyton resembles Faulkner's Quentin in more than name. Not only does each commit suicide, but the suicides are preceded by the same thought and symbolic actions. Both have weak fathers with similar philosophies of life. In both families there are mentally defective siblings and a loyal Negro female servant. Both end to the refrains of a Negro gospel meeting. Both are naturalistic accounts of a doomed family. As the clergyman, Carey Carr, waits for Peyton's body, he thinks that this family "has succeeded—almost effortlessly, it seemed —in destroying itself."

What saves the novel—makes it, indeed, one of the most imaginative novels of the postwar period—is Styron's ability to experience the doom as a moral fact. Though he has borrowed his form, his themes and much of the pattern of his action from others, (especially from Faulkner and Fitzgerald) there is for him nothing mechanical or abstract about the downfall of the Loftis family. It is lived out in the anguished, crowded consciousness of characters in whom Styron really believes or who re-enact what he himself has obviously deeply felt. Every moment is a living present in places which for that moment are the world—a hospital waiting room, a football game at the University of Virginia, a fashionable wedding, an open grave in potter's field. For the characters what is happening is not something literary but the only life they will ever have, a life in which there is no turning back or undoing the past.

Milton Loftis is even more of a dangling man, and over a longer period of time—his whole life, in fact—than Bellow's Joseph. Superficially his situation seems quite different. Milton has money, a big house, a family, an assured social position in a moderately large Virginia city. But the money came from his wife's mother, and after the inheritance he let his small law practice dwindle away. Because he lacks energy and intelligence, his vague political ambitions come to nothing. The most significant events of the novel take place during the war. Businessmen whom he knows put on uniforms, try to act soldierly. Milton has only an air-raid warden's helmet.

No strength or meaning abides in his social role, which is essentially a passive and feminine one. His egotism has to depend on fading good looks and a certain courtly charm which is attractive to women. He is chiefly engaged by golf and his relationships with his wife Helen, his mistress Dolly, his daughter Peyton. All three relationships he manages very badly.

In character—or lack of it—in soft indeterminateness, Milton is like Tommy Wilhelm. Both come of fathers with a selfish philosophy of life, but with more assurance than their sons. Both are in the habit of deciding not to do things which are wrong and unwise, and then of going ahead and doing them anyway.

When Maudie, the defective child, is dangerously ill and Helen needs Milton's support, he gets drunk, though he had resolved not to, and exposes himself to nightmare scenes of public degradation during a football weekend. After Maudie's death he pulls himself together, gives up his mistress and patiently rebuilds a relationship with Helen, who has been close to insanity.

Then, at the carefully arranged wedding for Peyton, he brings the structure of all their lives crashing down in irretrievable ruin. It is a little like the scene of the closing of the safe in *Sister Carrie,* when Hurstwood's moment of weakness assures his doom. Peyton, waiting alone and nervously for the ceremony to begin, asks her father for a drink. He refuses. Drinking has made trouble for Peyton, and Milton has been partly responsible for this. Both know also that when Milton is drunk he shows sexual feelings for his daughter. She pleads, however, and the old habit of indulgence returns. When he goes to where he has a bottle stashed away, he decides to be firm and returns the bottle to its place. But when he hears in the distance the boastful voice of Helen's brother, old resentments revive and make Milton feel allied with Peyton against Helen and her family, and the world. He decides to permit one ceremonial parting drink. It leads to others of course, and to disastrous embarrassments at the wedding. The door is closed finally on the kind of social and family life which might conceivably have saved Peyton from the self-punishing abasement so brilliantly described in the last part of the novel.

Milton's producing the whisky is sheer weakness, as are all his indulgences of himself and Peyton. The novel does not dramatize a conflict of equal values or forces between which the reader himself would find it difficult to choose. Nor is it clear just what causes Milton's weakness. Peyton says of her father and the so-called Lost Generation, "They weren't lost. What they were doing was losing us." But Milton himself had begun drinking excessively in college, perhaps because *his* father had been lost another generation earlier.

How can a strong novel be written about weakness, when the causes of the weakness are so ill-defined, and when the weak character is undistinguished in sensibility or ideas? Peyton, it is true, is described as a bright girl who likes to read, but we get to know her well only after she has gone to pieces.

Styron solves this difficulty in his material by filling the vacuum with his own imaginative strengths. But the contrast with *Augie March* is striking. Most of Bellow's characters vibrate with ideas, however mistaken. They reach out to life experimentally, eagerly, and their varied encounters with the social world are highly educational. This is not true of Milton Loftis, of Helen, Dolly and Carey Carr. The felt experience which their author gives them, as he enters their separate consciousnesses, exceeds in language and probably in sensitivity what they are capable of feeling. The rhetoric which Styron learned from Faulkner and Fitzgerald and which they in turn learned from Conrad, Joyce and Flaubert gives a false portentousness, an eloquent fervor to the inner life of some extremely limited, self-centered and basically uninteresting people.

F. R. Leavis shows how even Conrad, in *Heart of Darkness,* with a genuinely horrifying story to tell, overburdens his rhetoric with pseudo-philosophic and religious abstractions, "unspeakable rites," "monstrous passions," "inconceivable mysteries" and other inscrutable and unfathomable profundities which he never demonstrated or found adequate symbols for.

When Milton makes drunken love to silly Dolly at a club-house dance, she has an unlikely vision of "shells, rocks and sea things, sad as the universe, drowsing beneath the summer moon." When Milton goes to his wife's room after a telephone call from his mistress has broken up a party, "red fire, reflected from the snow, the sinking sun, had fallen upon the bed, and her folded arms seemed to gather this light to her breast like roses." When Peyton and a boy lie entwined after drunken love-making, "Twilight fell over their bodies. They were painted with fire, like those fallen children who live and breathe and soundlessly scream, and whose souls blaze forever."

Styron's next work, *The Long March* (1952), a novella, does describe an action which requires will power and courage, but which socially still remains almost devoid of meaning. It is the story of a reserve officer, Captain Mannix, called back into the marines at the time of the Korean War. Out of stubbornness and hatred for his superior officer, Mannix insists, despite a badly injured foot, on finishing an excessively long practice march after his colonel has ordered him back to camp in a truck.

The language is even more charged with hyperbole than in *Lie Down in Darkness*. In the field tent one could see "Mannix's huge distorted shadow cast brutishly against the impermeable walls by a lantern so sinister that its raging noise had the sound of a typhoon at sea." It is hard to conceive even a sinister lantern as being quite so loud as a typhoon. A single sentence of less than seventy words contains the words "misery," "passionate," "prayerfully," "feverishly," "pain," "agony," "rapture," "desire."

In *Lie Down in Darkness*, drunkenness caused a nightmare effect of unreality. When Milton Loftis, drunk, wandered away from the football game to end up bleeding in a ditch, he was "possessed by the belief that all this was a dream: his search, Peyton, even his fear and agony were all part of an impossible illusion." In *The Long March* physical suffering causes impressions to be projected on the brain "in a scattered, disordered riot, like a movie film pieced together by an idiot." Confronting the forced march, the character from whose point of view the story is told "felt suddenly unreal and disoriented," shifted into another dimension of space and time. Wife, child and home "seemed to have existed in the infinite past or, dreamlike again, never at all. . . ."

In *Set This House on Fire* (1960) illness, fatigue and intoxication combine to maintain a high pitch of delirious intensity. The narrator, Peter Leverett, has been working for the government in Rome, and decides, before sailing for America, to visit a wealthy friend who has rented a large house in a beautiful place called Sambuco. Though there is no real need for it, he wears himself out driving all night, and runs into an accident-prone Italian on a scooter. He reaches Sambuco so shaken up emotionally as a result of his collision that three gulps of beer "rocked me like dynamite, brought new lunatic dimensions to my exhaustion."

In Sambuco Peter finds two dangling men, his host, Mason Flagg, who devotes his energies to lechery and telling lies, and a young painter, Cass Kinsolving, blind drunk most of the time and inhibited from painting. Sambuco has been taken over by an American movie company in a state of shattered morale because the picture they are shooting, principally to use up lire credits, has been so frequently and pointlessly revised. The movie makers are in the novel to provide a suitable audience for Cass's degradation, to strew equipment around for Peter Leverett to trip over, and to provide stars, à la Scott Fitzgerald, to impress him with. "I had an awe of these people almost teen-age in its dazzlement, and the hope now of some actual fellowship—no matter how fugitive—colored my imagination with a sudden iridescent allure."

Mason, whom Peter had known at school in the South, leads as soft, corrupt and pointless a life as Milton Loftis, though he is more worldly and intelligent, energetically evil

and tirelessly articulate. Cass Kinsolving, who plays Trilby
to Mason's Svengali, is also southern, but of a poor family.
He takes with him through Europe a charming, simple-
minded, loyal wife named Poppy, and a whole brood of children. Like Loftis, he makes life miserable for his family by
getting drunk all the time. In Paris, in a fit of frustrated rage,
he sends them fleeing from him into the streets. When he
impulsively carries them off to Italy third-class on the train,
one of the children nearly dies. In Rome he gambles away the
last of Poppy's inheritance. In Sambuco, entirely dependent
on Flagg for food and liquor, Cass produces for his patron
an elaborate pornographic painting, the first painting he has
completed for months, and is forced into obscene displays for
the movie group, of a sort that Nero or Caligula might have
devised. But though he pours incredible amounts of whisky
into an ulcerated stomach, Cass is still capable of great physical strength and bursts of southern eloquence.

Everything in the story is larger than life. When Cass ends
his drunken speech on Sophoclean tragedy to the guests at
the party, he pitches forward onto a piano "in a thunderous
uproar of flats and sharps." Flagg's father confronts in his
own house two oystermen come to avenge the feeble-minded
teen-ager whom Mason has made pregnant. When the
father imperiously orders them from the house, "the two
men seemed to shrivel and bend before his fury like willows
in a gale." When Cass happens to meet Mason's mistress on
the stairs, she suddenly lunges at him, and is "all over me
like glue. One great big shuddering Ingres odalisque, eight
feet tall, all pelvis and groin."

Inner life is as extreme. Added to the deliriums of illness
and intoxication are sexual and destructive fantasies which
occasionally are really carried out. Twice Cass plans to kill
Poppy and all the children. He actually does kill Flagg in a
cliff-edge fight straight from Western movies. What sustains
him in the degradation of his life in Sambuco is a lyrical,
never-consummated love for a beautiful peasant girl, Francesca.

When he watches Francesca caring for her father, whose body is bursting with tuberculosis germs, "all her beauty seemed enhanced and brightened by this desperate, gentle devotion. An angel, by God, he had thought, an angel. . . ." Like Bellow's heroes, Cass throws himself impulsively into trying to do good. He determines to help the peasant family, and cure the father. He submits to Flagg's abuses partly so that he can get American medicines for the dying man. As with Bellow's heroes, his efforts fail. The old peasant dies in a spectacularly horrible way, the girl is murdered equally horribly, and Cass kills Flagg on the mistaken assumption that Flagg was her murderer. For years Peter Leverett guiltily supports the accident-prone Italian he collided with, only to learn that his supposed victim had another bad accident as soon as he was out of the hospital.

Like Bellow's novels—and especially *Henderson the Rain King*—*Set This House on Fire* is a comedy of errors. The well-intentioned, impulsive efforts do not turn out any better than the selfish ones. Like Henderson, Cass is an American in a strange land, who doesn't really understand the people he is trying to help. Nor does he understand the complication of guilt and longing which has blocked his creativity and made him an obsessive drinker. In the Navy he had been treated by a psychiatrist whom he liked and admired, but as with Milton Loftis, the roots of his trouble spread out too far to be traced. Now at the end of the novel Cass is cured by the talk of an Italian policeman, a philosophical fascist, who recognizes in Cass both natural goodness and a masochistic, inverted pride in his own faults.

Faced with Hamlet's existential choice, Cass elects to "be." He goes back to America and lives as Augie March once planned to live. In a small town on the James River he fishes, teaches art, works part-time in a factory, provides a healthy, normal American life for Poppy and the now even more numerous kids. Like the life Henderson looks forward to, it is the idealized dream life of popular art and advertising.

Cass's recovery seems arbitrary moreover. Why can Cass

make it when Peyton could not? His degradation and self-destructiveness are as great as hers. Why could she not have been saved by her decent and loving husband, also a painter, as Cass is saved by the policeman? Is it because she originated in the suicidal Quentin of *The Sound and the Fury* where Cass is more like Dick Diver in *Tender is the Night?* Can we believe that Cass, for all his misery, his ulcers, his delirium tremens, his subjugation by Flagg, could love the peasant girl so joyfully and strive so heroically to help her father? Psychic resources were available for this, but not for his painting or for his wife and children. His acts of mercy, carried out by extreme effort of will, seem more like the benevolence, the *noblesse oblige* of daydreams and daydreaming romantic literature. It is not the kind of difficult disinterestedness and self-denying altruism that most of us are actually given the opportunity of exerting—and all too often prove incapable of exerting—in normal social circumstances.

The unreality of the affair with the peasants is emphasized by the rather breathless style in which Styron describes it, a style reminiscent of Landor, Newman, the early Joyce. Seeing in a dream the image of the dead Francesca, Cass "half-rose, in an agony of longing, calling out to her with lips and tongue which, strive as they might, could utter not even the whisper of a sound." Though Styron is a talented raconteur, most of the action has a worked-up, unbelievable quality. Mason Flagg loves to tell—and tells very well—about his experiences in Yugoslavia during the war. The revelation that this is pure lying is one more evidence of his falsity and corruption. But what he tells is no more romantic or incredible than the melodramatic violence described by Cass and Peter, whom we are supposed to believe. Is Mason Flagg's tale within a tale a symbol of the unreality of the book as a whole?

Cass and Mason are Americans leading pointless, unproductive lives in an Italian resort town. Society is represented by disillusioned movie makers, a fawning hotel proprietor and a philosophic policeman. Mason, very rich, hating Italians, lives on his income, buys at the nearest PX. Cass lives on Mason. Anything which they do, whether good or bad, is arbitrary, gratuitous, invented by the author rather than required by circumstances. This is also true of the rich eccentric, Henderson, set down in an imaginary Africa.

In *Seize the Day* and *Lie Down in Darkness,* social circumstances and the past are too much for the characters. In other novels by Bellow and Styron, the characters have a great deal of freedom of a somewhat unlikely kind. Actually this is the author's own freedom to invent. What keeps such freedom from being meaningless is the fact that it symbolizes, more or less unconsciously, important American traits not otherwise represented in what the novels offer socially.

Both Bellow and Styron have been called existentialists. Like the European existentialists, they make life seem empty by removing their characters from ordinary society with its ordinary responsibilities, and by suggesting that significant decisions are made only in extreme circumstances and under extreme pressures. Yet society continues to exist, and the specific vocational acts of athletes, soldiers, scientists, judges, artists, scholars, engineers, administrators and statesmen are not meaningless, whatever one thinks of the basic values of the society in which they operate. Such acts are public, moreover, and can be judged both by the standards of the vocation in question, and by extrinsic standards of an ultimate kind.

Milton Loftis, however, no longer practices a profession. Cass Kinsolving is a painter, but except for the details of his pornographic masterpiece, hardly half a page is devoted to the craft of painting as such, or to the way a talented painter sees and thinks. Bellow's characters hold a variety of jobs, but only once, in a scene in a coalyard, does Bellow deal seriously with a demanding crisis within an occupation itself. He usually describes at length only bizarre undertakings, like Augie's experiences with the eagle, and Henderson's with lions.

Family relationships do count, but this is a realm in which

the significant acts are less public and less easily judged. Usually things go badly, both between husbands and wives and members of different generations. Some marriages are said to be good but this is not demonstrated directly. Crucially significant for both writers are the relationships of individuals brought together more or less by chance. Into these affairs more real effort is poured than into the marriages, but communion is nearly always frustrated or has evil consequences. The operations are successful as self-education, but the patients die.

How then, in the face of all this negativism, can Bellow's and Styron's novels be so positive? It is because the authors are writing consciously as Americans in the distinctive period after the Second World War. For most intellectuals it was a not especially-political period; hence they do not criticize the structure of society or imagine political alternatives. Yet despite McCarthyism and the cold war, their work derives strength from the country's increasing prosperity and material power. There is great social mobility in their novels, and a sense of the accessibility of wealth, even though the means of obtaining it are often dubious.

Above all, both authors display strong and explicit faith in the American individualist tradition. Mostly it is shown operating outside major American institutions, but this has always been true of our best fiction. Since maturity is a matter of self-disciplined and principled conduct within defined social situations, such marginality gives fiction a rather adolescent tone. One of Styron's characters remarks "how stupidly and impossibly and absurdly young we remain in this land." Youthfulness is responsible for the daydream quality of many imagined exploits, but it also gives a sense of optimism, of eagerness, the conviction that one can always—as Henderson believed at fifty-three—start over again. Finally, there is the American belief in goodness, in good intention, manifested so strongly both in *Henderson* and *Set This House on Fire*. It may not work out in individual cases—which explains both the anguish and the comedy—but the country created by this faith is still very demonstrably there, still trying, still convinced by its own rhetoric. Though unacknowledged and largely unexamined, America itself remains the hero of these novels.

THE RADICAL MORALISM OF

NORMAN MAILER

NORMAN MAILER

Norman Mailer was born in New Jersey in 1923, raised in Brook-lyn and educated at Harvard. After serving in the South Pacific he wrote *The Naked and the Dead,* a big book both in size and in-tent, which is widely considered to be the best American novel about World War II. Each of his two subsequent novels, *Barbary Shore* and *The Deer Park,* had a bad press at publication, but today each is read and defended. *Advertisements for Myself,* a kind of Mailer Reader he fashioned from mostly old but some new work, outraged many critics with its egocentricity and preoccupa-tion with sex, but it amused others, and struck still others as an important document of the times. Neither Mailer's book of verse, *Deaths for the Ladies (and Other Disasters)* (1962), nor the magazine articles which have appeared since the publication of *Advertisements* in 1959 are included in the following survey of his work, which attempts to bring some order into the confusion that surrounds Mailer's present reputation by examining the major body of his writing apart from the public image of the author. Mailer now makes his residence in Brooklyn Heights, New York.

THE RADICAL MORALISM OF

NORMAN MAILER

by Diana Trilling

In 1959, at the not very advanced age of thirty-six, Norman Mailer published what amounted to a grand view of his literary lifetime. In a single big volume, *Advertisements for Myself,* he not only reprinted virtually everything he had written except his three novels—and there are even excerpts from these—but also prefaced, or connected, his stories, essays and journalism with an extended commentary in which he reported on his states of mind at various stages of his development as an author and public figure, on the reception given his work in the press and by his publishers, and on his present estimate of his earlier performances. A retrospective enterprise of such proportions is bound to tax the generosity of the public. It assumes, for one thing, that its audience shares the writer's own sense of his importance in the record of his period—which indeed it may, but no public likes to have this certification demanded of it. It also presents its author as if in the absolving perspective of history. And it requires of its readers enough grace to forgive, if they cannot welcome, the persistent self-reference inevitable in such a sustained task of self-evaluation. For someone of Mailer's age and present uncertain place in the American literary scene, the undertaking was perhaps ill-advised. By most of its reviewers, *Advertisements* was received reservedly, or with condescension, or irony. The compelling force of the volume, its demonstration of the courage and complexity of Mailer's talent, was slighted in the apparent desire of its critics to separate themselves from his recent questionable, even distressing, moral positions.

This is unfortunate, and it perhaps constitutes one of those occasions when criticism has failed to live up to its responsibility of open-mindedness and has not met its claim of being able to adjudicate between the valuable and the inconsequent, or shoddy, or even out-and-out wrong in a man's work. But one cannot overlook Mailer's share in confounding criticism, even before the publication of *Advertisements*. We live of course in a period in which precocity is no longer regarded as it was in, say, Dickens' time, as the sign of a genius so deep-rooted and natural that it must surely augur long years of fulfillment. Instead, we take it as the portent of imminent extinction. While Mailer has neither stopped writing nor succumbed to the temptations of Hollywood, he has had his own gifted way of co-operating in our more cynical expectations for him as a novelist and of obstructing the development that might once have followed upon the early flowering of so much talent. After the intolerable triumph of *The Naked and the Dead* (1948), he not only deserted the "naturalism" of his first novel but more and more moved from fiction to nonfiction, and of a polemical sort. And increasingly he has enforced upon the public the myth of the man rather than the work of the writer. When we add to this the nature of his present doctrine and the degree to which he has met the challenge of modernity by disavowing that considerable part of his sense of life which is traditional in favor of the more subversive aspects of his thought, it is scarcely surprising that his career is now shadowed in dubiety.

And yet, whatever Mailer's truancy from the novel, or his

self-mythologizing impulse, or the violence he does to our traditional moral values, perhaps it is none of these but only the paradoxical character of his talent that finally creates his present equivocal situation. Where a writer exists in this much contradiction, the realization of his possibilities is always chancier than it would be in a more unitary talent, and it would be hard to name a writer of our or any time whose work reveals a more abundant or urgent endowment which is yet so little consistent with itself—so much moral affirmation coupled with so much moral anarchism; so much innocence yet so much guile; so much defensive caution but such headlong recklessness; so much despair together with so imperious a demand for salvation; so strong a charismatic charge but also so much that offends or even repels; so much intellection but such a frequency of unsound thinking; such a grand and manly impulse to heroism but so inadequate a capacity for self-discipline; so much sensitiveness and so little sensibility; so much imagination and such insufficient art. Contradictions like these no doubt contribute to Mailer's appeal; but they also make for his limitations. And they describe a talent which necessarily lives on the sharp edge of uncertainty.

Yet to trace the paradoxes in Mailer is not to figure an unknown constellation. It is to experience the shock of recognition, for in the sum of his contradictions he bears a striking resemblance to present-day America. What distinguishes him, however, from other contemporary American writers who also express their culture even while they reject it is the depth to which he is shaken by the crash of modernity against the poor bulwarks of Western tradition and, even more, his driving need to turn this experience to social use.

For the advanced writer of our time, the self is his supreme, even sole, referent. Society has no texture or business worth bothering about; it exists because it weighs upon us and because it conditions us so absolutely. The diverse social scene is homogenized into a force we feel only grossly, as a source of our horror or terror or emptiness. The job of literature in our period is thus more poetical than novelistic—our advanced fiction neither anatomizes the society that is nor conceives the society that might be; it deals merely with the massive brute social fact in its impress upon the individual consciousness. Where the novelist of an earlier day helped us to understand and master a mysterious or recalcitrant environment, the present-day novelist undertakes only to help us define the self in relation to the world that surrounds and threatens to overwhelm it. And this search for self-definition proceeds by sensibility, by the choice of a personal style or stance which will differentiate the self from, or within, its undifferentiated social context.

Mailer is no Balzac of the twentieth century. And he is engrossed in his own grim effort of self-validation. But he conceives society as being quite as actual as the self, and as much to be addressed. It is not so much that he thinks of the modern world as a world of negotiable particulars. But he believes the social totality generates a dialectic between itself and the individual; it is therefore not merely to be endured in self-pity, it must be faced up to and changed. For instance, in his fine story, "The Man Who Studied Yoga"—it is, I think, one of the best stories of our time and aesthetically Mailer's best-integrated piece of fiction—he has a would-be novelist protest to a friend that he "does not want to write a realistic novel, because reality is no longer realistic"; but Mailer's immediate riposte to this familiar statement is a description of the boring "petulance of their small voices" as the two young men luxuriate in their dreariness. Or, typically, he remarks of Beckett's *Waiting for Godot*—which, typically, he had not yet seen—"I doubt if I will like it, because finally not everyone is impotent, nor is our final fate, our human condition, necessarily doomed to impotence, as old Joyce knew, and Beckett I suspect does not." And in *The Deer Park,* where he momentarily borrows Hemingway's symbol of sexual impotence for his narrator, Sergius O'Shaugnessy, he has this passivity predate the opening of the story; once the novel begins, O'Shaugnessy is active enough.

Mailer's temperament, in other words, is adversary not

fugitive, hortatory not seismographic. Even his Hipsterism, concerned as it is with styles of personal being, rejects the premise of a self at the mercy of society, and refuses the sanctuary of sensibility. And no doubt this has much to do with the striking fact that, big as Mailer looms as a personality of the literary Left, one can name only a single serious critic of his general cultural persuasion, Norman Podhoretz in *Partisan Review* (Summer, 1959), who has written about him without embarrassment, as an author of stature. While he outrages conservative opinion by the ultimateness of his judgment upon modern life, he equally alienates radical literary opinion by his offense against the reality it is most disposed to acknowledge—that of our helplessness before Conditions.

"Hip is not totally negative," Mailer declares, "and has a view of life which is predicated on growth." And in the figure of the cool cat he projects an image of man as someone who, far from being inert before danger, is precisely poised for action against the enemy—it is a posture without great appeal to our contemporary distaste for "hostility." And despite Hipsterism's emphasis upon the self, it places on the self the largest possible responsibility for the "collective creation" (as Mailer calls it) which is our culture. "If society was so murderous," he asks us, "then who could ignore the most hideous of questions about his own nature?" There is of course menace in so primary an inquiry, and Mailer has himself been badly scarred in its pursuit. The question nevertheless carries us a salutary distance beyond our modern view of the individual as victim of a world he never made and cannot remake.

Mailer's adversary disposition recalls D. H. Lawrence, his predecessor in the line of literary minds dedicated to the renovation of society by means of a revolution in the individual consciousness. But of the two, Lawrence is actually closer to our present literary spirit, for he is not only the more subjective writer but also the more abstract. Society exists in his novels only as an aggregate of unspecified destructive conditions. The most poetical of social revolutionaries, he scorned politics in their troublesome concreteness. But Mailer has always carried the burden of social actuality of the intellectual thirties. He has engaged in politics—the politics of literary intellectuals—throughout his career, even in years when it has not been the literary fashion. At the time of the publication of his first novel, he became a communist sympathizer and campaigned vigorously for Henry Wallace in that same year. Then, when Stalinism failed him, he turned to Trotskyism, and even today he still professes a modified allegiance to Marxism. For instance, in an interview with Mr. Richard Wollheim in England as recently as September 1961, Mailer describes the socialist preference which has remained to him from his old communist commitment as now only a choice made *faute de mieux,* certainly with no passion of conviction. Of Marxism, however, he speaks like a man of honor who would not disavow a once precious love. By and large, his criticism of socialism is much the same as his criticism of modern civilization: just as it is the ugliness and minimalism of modern life that make him dissent from civilization and wish to prod it into a more conscious barbarism from which he can hope there will arise a revitalized way of personal being, just so he dissents from the ungenerosity, the uncourageousness, the lack of elegance and wit and charm, the personally minimal quality which he finds in socialism. Yet despite his belief that the Marxist economic emphasis is not adequate to the present crisis in world affairs, he still calls himself a Marxist, albeit in the tone of someone submitting to a rather tedious test of his integrity. What Mailer implies is that in a world as ripe for reaction as he thinks ours is, a man sticks to his guns even though they are obsolete.

This is a far cry from Mailer's younger Marxism. In fact, the single live line of connection between the monolithic doctrine of a book like *Barbary Shore,* which came out in 1951, three years after *The Naked and the Dead,* and his present merely vestigial Marxism is Mailer's continuing fear of political reaction in the democracies. For Mailer, as for so many Western intellectuals, political probity rests essentially in demonstrating one's anxiety about the threat from the Right; the abrogation of human rights under the dictatorship of the Left is allowed to disappear in a generalized disapprobation of communism; or another way to put it is that the threat of armed conflict between the democracies and the Soviet Union overrides the principled opposition to communist totalitarianism which, for the sake of convenience, as it were, is presumed to exist in a different moral context from any totalitarianism which might appear in the West. Even before the height of McCarthyism, as far back as his first novels, Mailer had arrived at this conviction that fascism is not merely a potential in America as in any modern capitalism but, what is quite another order of political hypothesis, that it is the most coherent and dominant force in American society. And this fear is apparently no less compelling in Mailer today than it ever was: as late as the spring of 1961, he published an open letter to Fidel Castro in which he addressed the Cuban dictator as "Brother" and elevated him to the rank of a born Hipster in order to sanctify his role as savior of the Cuban workers and peasants from American fascism. But then we must remember, of course, that John F. Kennedy also figures in Mailer's pantheon as a natural Hipster; at least he did at the time of his nomination.

Whatever our evaluation of Mailer's political predictions for America, the important point is that his work is not properly to be understood apart from his profound preoccupation with the idea that modern democratic man is about to yield his dignity, his freedom, his very manhood before the onslaught of political reaction. Second only to his religious zeal, it is Mailer's sense of himself as the heroic antagonist of a malevolent reactionary authority that has powered his fictional imagination.

The Naked and the Dead (1948), published when Mailer was twenty-five, two years after his separation from the Army in which he served with credit in Leyte, Luzon and Japan, was everywhere acclaimed as the best novel of World War II. And even as we read it today, knowing what the war brought as its aftermath of futility and desperation, it remains a re-markable document of the defeat inherent in any modern vic-tory in war. Technically, his first novel advances no farther than Dos Passos, whose influence Mailer acknowledges in *Ad-vertisements*. And in the main it relies on fictional materials which were well-exploited in the first war. But it brings to a familiar subject the informing view of a new and radically al-tered generation. Our present-day belief that we stand outside the ordinary movements of historical evolution, our loss of faith in both the orderly and the revolutionary processes of social development, our always increasing social fragmenta-tion and our always diminishing trust in our individual possi-bility—it is these changes in consciousness that separate Mail-er's war novel from the novels that followed World War I, as does, too, its drastically accelerated sense of time. Time is al-ways running out on a soldier, in the midst of the inexorable tedium of his days, but this fact of experience is raised to a principle for Mailer's G.I.s. The hot breath of the future— one might better say, the hot breath of our own expiring day —broods over the pages of *The Naked and the Dead* as foul and stifling as the surrounding jungle air.

Although even before Tolstoy, literature had of course rep-resented the common soldier as the victim of a force he could neither understand nor control, it is only in our time that the Army has become identified with the irrational and destructive authority of society itself. *The Naked and the Dead* incorpo-rates this death-dealing power in two characters, General Cummings and Sergeant Croft. Cummings is a man of the ris-ing middle classes whose overweening personal ambition, bolstered by great gifts for organization and by an imagination which knows no restraints of human feeling, leads him, for private reasons, to order a reconnaissance platoon on a tour of duty which must inevitably end in catastrophe. Croft is an illiterate army regular, brave, skillful and cunning, for whom the hieratical sanctions of war provide a nice measure of sat-isfaction of an unquenchable lust for conquest and blood. Cummings is sufficiently educated to bring the historical process and his own ambitions into working conjunction with each other; he has announced himself on the side of the future. He thinks of his men as the instruments of history and his own will—the two are synonymous. In Mailer's political scheme he is, simply, fascism, and Croft is his eager though unconscious collaborator. The suffering men in Croft's platoon, who endure unspeakable torments as they struggle through swamp and jungle on Cummings' order and who, without voice in their fate, stumble mindlessly in their sergeant's footsteps as he pits himself against the unscaleable heights of Mount Anaka, are the masses of mankind who lack the individual or collective will to resist being propelled to annihilation. This army which, in the name of historical necessity, captures, rules and destroys the common life of humanity, is modern society as Mailer sees it, and the presentiment of worse to come. And his introduction of Lieutenant Hearn, the intelligent, decent liberal whom Cummings cannot quite seduce and must therefore kill, completes his political indictment and prophecy.

The influence of Dos Passos' *U.S.A.* is obvious in Mailer's management of his fictional forces in *The Naked and the Dead* —his crowded canvas of G.I.s together with their officers, and behind them their families, their wives, their girl friends. Where his own young genius announces itself is in his dramatic inventiveness and, even more, in his feeling—unmatched in our time, even by Hemingway in *For Whom The Bell Tolls*—for topography, for the look of the natural scene. As a matter of fact, the two gifts are associated: the most dramatic moments in *The Naked and the Dead* are precipitated by intensities in nature. Indeed, this loyal delight in physical truth is what gives *The Naked and the Dead* its extraordinary distinction. It is therefore of some interest that Mailer's first novel is, so far, his last to be set outdoors—it would seem that his fiction must now be enclosed in walls in order to reproduce the strangling effects of modern life.

The bald schematic structure of Mailer's novels, starting with the first, suggests a paraphrase of T. S. Eliot's comment on Henry James, that James had a mind so pure that no idea could violate it: of Mailer we can say that his novelist's mind is peculiarly violable by idea, even by ideology. In *The Naked and the Dead* there was at least the battle of man against nature to excite the artist in Mailer; but even here the contest between man and society had already begun to make him its ideological prisoner. Despite its brilliant evocation of atmosphere, and its integrity as a story of war, *The Naked and the Dead* takes its ultimate stand, not in art, but in doctrine. As much as it is a drama of human motives, Mailer's first novel is a political document—the testimony of a young Marxist, or proto-Marxist, whose experience of war confirms his worst reading of history. If, however, *The Naked and the Dead* is to be understood as Mailer's forecast of the dreaded victory of fascism, we are bound to balk at the moral as well as political ascendancy of Croft at the end of the book. In Mailer's reading of the future, Croft is clearly the coadjutor of ruthless reactionary assertion. And yet, as the novel draws to its conclusion, he ceases to be one of its villains and usurps the place in his author's sympathies which we had thought was Hearn's. This curious shift in the moral focus of *The Naked and the Dead* perhaps adds to its fictional interest, but it remains unexplained in Mailer's system of thought until some years later in his career, when we meet Marion Faye, the Hipster hero of Mailer's third novel, *The Deer Park,* in whose resemblance to Croft we discover the ominous political implications of Mailer's criteria for heroism.

Mailer's disillusionment with communism followed rapidly on the publication of *The Naked and the Dead* but it was a break only with Stalinism, from which he moved to the Trotskyite Marxism of his second novel. In *Barbary Shore* (1951) Mailer attempted a new literary manner, and he paid dearly in popular success for disappointing a public eager for more of the seen and felt life of his first book. But as doctrine his second novel took up virtually where its predecessor left off—with liberalism dead and with the confusion and despair of the working classes sounding their dull prelude to the victory of the Right; the fact that, between 1948 and 1951, Mailer had himself lost faith in the communism of Soviet Russia simply reinforced his earlier hopelessness for America. What had happened to Mailer's politics in the three years between his first and second novels shows itself, in fact, chiefly in the changed perspective of the two books. Whereas in *The Naked and the Dead* the historical process is viewed in terms of its effect upon the general run of mankind, in *Barbary Shore* Mailer writes out of the dilemma of the defeated radical intellectual. The great battle of history is now fought out, not on the wide "proletarian" front where his first novel had located it, but on the intellectual left flank where Mailer had been isolated by his inability to maintain his trust in Stalin's revolution.

In Mailer's second novel, fascism again trumpets its advance, but now it is personified in an FBI agent named Hollingsworth—the collocation is not absurd to Mailer nor, presumably, to his putative readers. As befits the representative of a social force that is already licensed to execute the political dreams of a Cummings, Hollingsworth has none of the human attributes of a mere novice in tyranny like Mailer's general; for all his shrewdness and sharp-wittedness, Hollingsworth moves through *Barbary Shore* robot-like, directed by a power remote from the scene of his activities. His assignment in the novel is to track down a "little object" stolen from the State Department by a man named McLeod who had come to work for the government after a considerable period as a communist leader and then as a member of the communist opposition. When we meet McLeod in the surrealist Brooklyn boardinghouse which is the setting of *Barbary Shore,* even this recourse has failed him; he has nothing to which to dedicate himself except an intensive study of Marxism and the preservation of the communist ideal which, detached from the Soviet reality which has betrayed it, persists in the form of a symbol—the stolen token he has stashed away for use in an improbable future. As Mailer's highly allegorical story progresses, it turns out that this secret of our future rehabilitation is never recaptured by Hollingsworth, but the dark powers of reaction are nonetheless triumphant—the novel ends with Hollingsworth stealing, if not McLeod's key to the salvation of mankind, then at least his wife who, in *Barbary Shore*, stands for pretty much what Mailer's G.I.s did in *The Naked and the Dead:* the common life of humanity but grown distinctly less human and more sinister with the passage of the years. McLeod commits suicide—we are reminded of Hearn's suicidal conspiracy with his murderers in Mailer's first novel —and the young narrator of the book, an amnesiac writer who has wandered by historical "accident" into this epochal war and been cast as McLeod's confidante and disciple, is left the guardian of our small unpromising legacy of political hope.

In spite of its many funny passages, most of which center around McLeod's mad wife, Guinevere, *Barbary Shore* is a web of fine-spun fantasies, as obscure as they are frightening, allowing us no connection with any recognizable world of feeling. Even Guinevere is drawn so outrageously and abstrusely that we can never be certain of the meaning Mailer attaches to this sharp, slobby lady who is always bartering or withholding her fly-blown sexuality in some strange, awful enterprise of personal advantage. It is only at the last, when McLeod's wife chooses to run off with Hollingsworth, that we begin to understand her place in the ideological scheme of the novel. Greed, cupidity, sloth, a sporadic and wildly misdirected energy, spiritless lust, stupidity and mean ambition— these, Mailer is telling us, are what today define democratic man, or woman; and in a society in which the masculine principle is reduced to an automaton like Hollingsworth, a woman perhaps best symbolizes our deteriorated situation. Guinevere is the civilization—or, if you will, the American masses—with whom the revolutionary idealist has perforce had to align himself, and to whose partnership with fascism his death must be witness.

McLeod dead, it is to a writer and intellectual—or Mailer's rather shadowy version of one—who has lost his memory except for vagrant recollections of having once been close to the radical movement that our decent social values are bequeathed. Lovett, the amnesiac narrator of *Barbary Shore,* is of course the precursor of the orphaned Sergius O'Shaugnessy, Mailer's spokesman in *The Deer Park* and again in his most recent story, "Time of Her Time." Both men are without tie to the past; both inhabit a universe without historical precedent or direction. Both of them announce, that is, Mailer's own thoroughly democratic stance of the self-made man, and his detachment from cultural tradition—Harvard to the contrary notwithstanding. Certainly in view of Mailer's obsessive interest in history, it is remarkable how little reference there is in his work to anything—political, philosophical or literary —that happened day before yesterday; there is only now and tomorrow. Even when Mailer alludes to such towering figures as Hemingway or Faulkner in the generation before his own, they are introduced like parents into a gathering of contemporaries and friends. It is only when he writes about his literary siblings—Bellow, Styron, Jones, Capote, Vidal, Baldwin—that we feel the direct fire of his personal and literary judgment. Mailer's concern with history, in other words, is a concern with history in the making. It is the Marxist's preoccupation with present-day action in the light of future necessity.

Implicit in Marxism as a method of historical analysis there is always this assumption that if we correctly track the movements of history we can foretell future developments and put ourselves in accord with them; we can then aid prophecy in fulfilling itself. But in Mailer there is an unusual collaboration between the higher and lower arts of prognostication: the Marxist's prophetic faculty can regularly call upon the assistance of irrational intuition and even downright superstition. For example, in the early pages of *The Naked and the Dead,* when we first meet Sergeant Croft, he is playing poker and has had a run of bad hands. But firm in his belief that "whatever made things happen was on his side," he awaits the better luck that he is certain is in store for him, and soon he is the winner. Then, later the same day, Croft correctly predicts that before nightfall a boy named Hennessey will be dead, and Mailer tells us of this accurate prevision that it fills the sergeant with a sense "of such omnipotence" and "such portents of power" that his life is as if magically altered. What happens, obviously, is that, by imagining himself in allegiance with fate, Croft marshals a will he otherwise lacks, which does indeed alter his fate. General Cummings, too, exemplifies Mailer's providential view of the relation between destiny and perspicuity: "The fact that you're holding the gun and the other man is not," Cummings explains to Hearn, "is no accident. If you're aware enough, you have the gun when you need it." Thus the rationalistic Marxist, the wily general, and the ignorant superstitious sergeant are all blood brothers in their ability to envision and foster what anyway lies ahead. The Marxist determinist who charts the inevitable course of events so that we can put ourselves on the side of history is of the same family with the military tactician or the gambler whose correct hunch puts him on the winning side of fate.

The fate Mailer's Marxism foretold with the completion of *Barbary Shore* was of a society whose determining forces produced only its dissolution, never its reconstruction along the hoped-for revolutionary lines, and the publication of his second book therefore marked a turning point in Mailer's career. If the alternative to a fascist triumph was so remote from political actuality that it could be represented in an unnamed little lost object, then clearly the political solution had failed. From this point forward, Mailer has sought salvation elsewhere than in politics—in Hipsterism, a mode of being that will re-energize a worn and perverted civilization irresistibly drawn toward reaction.

Hipsterism—or Hip, as Mailer sometimes calls it in a discrimination whose meaning is uncertain—is, we are told, an American existentialism designed to return man to the center of the universe and to bring the individual into direct and vital communication with the self and its needs. It is the doctrine which, enshrined in the place that Marxism once had in his system of thought, allows Mailer to probe modern society on a level deeper than that of political and economic determinism. Since it is manifestly man's destiny in our century to live with death and destruction, then "the only life-giving answer," Mailer says, "is to accept the terms of death, to live with death as immediate danger, to divorce oneself from society, to exist without roots, to set out on that uncharted journey into the rebellious imperatives of the self." God is in danger of dying—this, in fact, is the "single burning pinpoint of the vision in Hip." Because God is no longer all-powerful, man must take His place at the center of the universe and become the embodiment of His embattled vision.

The original settler in this terrain which lies beyond the demands of society, the guide Mailer offers us in our unmapped journey of self-exploration, is not the dark primitive of Lawrence, but he is similarly alien to a white Protestant middle-class culture. He is the Negro, and Mailer makes his most complete statement of the meaning of Hipsterism in his essay, "The White Negro." The Negro, says Mailer, "has the simplest of alternatives: live a life of constant humility or ever-threatening danger. In such a pass where paranoia is as vital to survival as blood, the Negro has stayed alive and begun to grow by following the need of his body where he could." So we too must know our impulse as it speaks to us of a true need of the self. "One must know one's desires, one's rages, one's anguish, one must be aware of the character of one's frustrations." And we must be prepared to act on the mandate of the self. "Whether the life is criminal or not," Mailer sums up, "the decision is to encourage the psychopath in oneself, to explore that domain of experience where society is boredom and therefore sickness, and one exists in the present. . . . One is Hip or one is Square . . . One is a rebel or one conforms."

Although "The White Negro" appeared in 1957, two years after *The Deer Park,* Mailer's third novel already contained in embryo the chief ideas Mailer would develop in his famous essay. Among the rebellious imperatives of the self, none is more exigent than sex, and surely the novelist who would treat this aspect of the modern consciousness not, like Lawrence, as a sacred lost essence but as existential fact cannot do better than to turn to Hollywood. But Mailer would seem to have come to the sexual theme of *The Deer Park* only secondarily, or even incidentally, while embarked upon a political novel along familiar simplistic lines, about a liberal movie director, one Eitel, who is blacklisted in the studios for his refusal to talk before a Congressional investigating committee but who then capitulates to the joint pressures of authoritarian government and ruthless finance and is reinstated in his job. It would appear, that is, that the sexual life of the movie colony originally served somewhat the same function as the tropical setting of *The Naked and the Dead,* of providing the context of a political drama. But by the time Mailer was fully launched in his story, he realized that politics was failing him as the material of fiction, as it had failed him as a means of saving the world; Eitel's crisis of political conscience had turned out to be but a dim counterpoint to the larger crises of personal feeling in which he and the people around him were involved. The sexuality of Hollywood, once intended as merely the ambience in which political hope is defeated, became then the drama itself—the account of a last-ditch fight on behalf of a personal destiny that could no longer be sought in politics.

Considering his sensational material, Mailer is notably neutral in his report of the Hollywood sexual scene. This neutrality of voice must be understood, however, as an aspect of his aesthetic procedure rather than of his moral judgment. Although nothing could be less conventionally censorious than Mailer's investigation of the diverse sexual tastes and deportment of his stars and their hangers-on, of his movie moguls and their call girls, *The Deer Park* is finally as charged with morality as *Lady Chatterley's Lover.* For Mailer, as for Lawrence, sexual activity is never its own justification; its good is measured by the quality of the emotions it produces or expresses. The moral platform of Mailer's Hollywood novel an-

nounces itself from behind the apparent irony of its epigraph
—a quotation from a shocked description of the sexual life
in the Deer Park of Louis XV—and is clearly argued in every
line of Mailer's portrait of a society which manufactures the
American mass sexual dream. Here is truly our jungle within
walls, a miasma of desire fulfilled and yet always unfulfilled
as torturing as the burning, tangled, insect-infested jungle of
The Naked and the Dead. The inhabitants of Mailer's Hollywood are wracked by a fever without cure; in their freedom
from conventional sexual restraint there sounds the rattling of
the chains of a bondage as grinding as that of the Army. Only
love and tenderness, only the terrible self-denying imperatives
of feeling can release these victims from the tyranny of their
unimpeded sexual compulsions—and their search for feeling
is their futile struggle toward the unattainable heights of an
emotional Mount Anaka.

"The only revolution which will be meaningful and natural for the twentieth century," Mailer has said, "is the sexual
revolution one senses everywhere." And as one reads his account of the free sexual life of Hollywood, one might perhaps be misled into thinking that this is the revolution to
which he is referring. But Mailer is more complex than this.
While he recognizes that the Hollywood life of free sexual impulse does indeed constitute a major rebellion against traditional sexual morality, his novelist's eye for truth has searched
out the frenzy and emptiness in the lives of his sexual free-
booters. Mailer has a predilection for last-minute heroes; just
as Croft's sudden triumph at the end of *The Naked and the
Dead* suggests the changes in feeling that Mailer was experi-
encing in the course of composing his first novel, so the re-
placement of Eitel by Faye as the most significant figure in
The Deer Park indicates the dramatic evolution of Mailer's
thought while writing his Hollywood novel. In Marion Faye
we discover the distinction Mailer makes between a sexuality
which, like that of the movie colony, appears to be free but is
really an enslavement, and the sexuality of Hipsterism which
expresses a new, radical principle of selfhood. The difference

is not so much one of behavior as of intention; it is a difference in consciousness. Whereas all the other characters in the
novel, whether in their political decisions or their sexual conduct follow the worn paths of consciousness laid out for them
by an exhausted civilization, Mailer's incipient Hipster hero
has settled the new direction the world must take to save itself: it is the direction of purposeful, as opposed to purposeless, death. Faye is not God the Father, but he is unmistak-
ably in training to be God the Son. Dying for us, the Hipster
becomes our savior; he is the resurrection and the life in a
society of Eitels and call girls who, will-lessly submitting to
their poor destinies, can promise us nothing but further desperation and enervation.

Faye is a young, elaborately sadistic pimp who closely conforms to Mailer's anatomy of the white Negro several years
later. He is totally bored by society, paranoically alert to danger, and he lives in an acute intimacy with the criminal and
the psychopath in himself. This intimacy has, in fact, the
charge of a mystical fulfillment: it is when Faye is most
wholly possessed by his psychopathic needs that he achieves
his strongest sense of spiritual exaltation. As jealous of his
freedom of will as Dostoevski's Underground Man, he finds
the assurance of his autonomy in a strenuous rationalism—
his reiterative reminder to himself that he is master of his fate,
unconditioned by the moral values of his culture. And the
question seems never to enter his or his author's mind whether
a man is any the less a victim for being at the mercy of his
own psychopathology rather than that of his society.

In Faye, then, we are introduced to the new hero of Hip.
And yet he is of course not a wholly new figure in Mailer's
work: he has made a premonitory appearance as Sergeant
Croft in *The Naked and the Dead*. The single indispensable
ingredient Mailer has added to Croft in creating Faye is the
consciousness that his program of cruelty and self-imposition
has a large social and spiritual purpose. The passage of nearly
a decade, in other words, has brought Mailer full circle to the
exposure of the unresolved conflict which already existed in

his first novel—between his overriding fear, in politics, of an authority which makes its law in defiance of the decent social values and his powerful attraction to the same authority in the personal or spiritual realm.

The conflict is not without literary precedent: the modern imagination would seem to take the heroic leap only at some cost in moral logic. But writers like Lawrence or Yeats had the advantage, we now see, of living in a time when they were not required to give public account of their political preferences, and we can suppose that had Mailer been of their period instead of ours, he would have similarly avoided the predicament of presenting us with a hero not easily distinguishable from his named political enemy. He would have been able to evade the political consequences of consigning the future of civilization to a personal authority morally identical with the dark reaction from which it is supposed to rescue us. Or, to put the matter in even cruder terms, he would not have exposed himself to our ridicule for offering us a God who is a fascist.

But the situation has changed: today Mailer is guilty of a mortal fallacy in his moral-political thought. And yet, even as we trap him, we realize that our whole "enlightened" culture is caught in the same inconsistency. No less than Mailer, we all of us who accede in the moral implications of modern literature but continue to make our political choices on the basis of traditional moral values exist in ambiguity. It is quite a long time now since Conrad asked us to choose between his Kurtz and his "Pilgrims" in *Heart of Darkness,* between an heroic principle of evil and a seedy, hypocritical bourgeoisie that lacks the courage of its inherent malevolence. And once we received such an alternative as really our only option, we accepted the premise of a civilization intolerable to itself; we concurred in the negation of the moral values on which we had established our enlightened political ideals. The very notion of a hero of liberalism, or a hero of anti-dictatorship, or a hero of social justice becomes absurd, even unimaginable, in a literature whose moral habitude it is to assign personal grandeur to the demonic and destructive. If Mailer's dual wish —to preserve us from the malign forces of political reaction but also to give civilization another push toward the extinction to which it seems so inexorably drawn—leads him into moral and political self-contradiction, he is not alone in this dilemma. It is the dilemma of anyone of high political seriousness who also identifies himself with the characteristic moral tendency of our literature.

And the moral tendency of contemporary art is not isolate in our culture. Everywhere in Western society there is an erosion, if not an entire sweeping away, of assumptions we once thought secure, which takes place not at the behest of reason but by an undirected tide of feeling, by what almost seems to be a psychological mutation. The psychologists may not be noting the change but the novelists record it even when they are not always aware of the significance in what they so circumstantially bear witness to. Where do we, where shall we, where can we derive our moral sanctions: from a failing tradition or from the wild, free impulses of our racial infancy, from the ego or the id? This is the ultimate pressing question of our time, separating our historical period from any that came before it. And because Mailer not only knows the full force of the question but passionately dedicates himself to its answer, he transcends the follies and excesses which attend Hipsterism and claims his place in the forefront of modern writers.

Obviously in Mailer's application to this ultimate issue, far more than in his politics, we discover his radicalism, just as it is in their deep involvement with this large moral-cultural tendency of our period rather than in their newly fervid socialism or their disenchantment with democracies that we locate the radicalism of his literary contemporaries. For Mailer, as for the whole of a new literary generation, politics is today the least revolutionary aspect of social protest.

That, despite the political struggles which fed his moral imagination, Mailer's present moral radicalism came to him only gradually and from such emotional sources as have always nourished the traditional novelist is plainly indicated in his story, "The Man Who Studied Yoga," written in 1952, shortly after the political disillusionment of *Barbary Shore* but well before the appearance of Marion Faye. Product of a moment of suspension between ideological engagements, this superb long story is singularly free of the restrictions imposed upon Mailer's fiction by his usual systematic thought. And it is also the warmest and most domestic of his fictional works, his sole excursion into the middle-class "normality" in which he too, like the characters in his story, might have entrenched himself against the dangerous next steps in his development. In Mailer's brilliant description of Sam and Eleanor Slovoda we can examine the supposedly "mature" alternative our civilization offers those of us who scorn "regression" to the barbarism of infancy. Sam, an ex-radical and novelist *manqué* who earns his living writing continuities for comics; Eleanor, a painter *manqué,* is a suburban housewife and the dutiful jargon-driven mother of two fine modern-reared children. The course of their lives of quiet desperation-cum-psychoanalysis is interrupted (but only for a day while the children visit their grandmother) by the showing of a pornographic film at a party. After ten years of marriage the Slovodas and their friends are responsible citizens and parents, responsible matrimonial partners, responsible and tender, even humorous social companions. But they ache with the sexual longings that are never to be satisfied, and with the frustration of their dreams for themselves. They are the human counterparts of the charmless rational housing development their culture has provided for them. If this is what it means—and who can argue the flawless truth of what Mailer shows us?—to take our due place in society without violating the established decencies, then Mailer is surely right that conformity is purposeless death; but at this point in his career Mailer himself has no taste for pressing the polemical issue. The story delivers its message without preachment and this is its triumph.

Sam Slovoda has turned to psychoanalysis for the deliverance that will never come, and from Mailer's subtly satiric references we can take it that the therapy is orthodox. In later essays, Mailer goes on to make Freudianism the target of some of his sharpest attacks on the modern dispensation; himself, expectably enough, he by and large lines up with the Reichians. Jung, Fromm, Reich: it is among these analytical dissidents that protest now regularly seeks the psychology with which to replace the Freudian psychology which it believes lives too cozily with the traditional attitudes of our society. Like Reich, Mailer rejects the idea of a self obedient to social law, and from Reich he takes his measure of instinctual gratification, the orgasm; it is in his orgasmic potency that the Hipster finds the best test of his capacity for self-realization. As a matter of fact, Mailer's most recent story, "Time of Her Time," carries this criterion of personal release to the amusing point where, notwithstanding the ingenious twists Mailer makes on his sexual theme, the orgasm plays the same tyrannous role in assessing psychic well-being that sexual "adjustment" does in the mental-health culture that has sprung from Freudianism. In "Time of Her Time," O'Shaugnessy is returned to New York from Hollywood and Mexico. By day he teaches bullfighting; his nights are for love-making with an endless series of Greenwich Village girls who prey upon his swaggering maleness. The epitome of these predators is a graceless, tight-knit Jewish college student who defies him to give her the sexual satisfaction she has not yet experienced. Challenged, O'Shaugnessy finally accomplishes his grim mission by fiercely forcing upon her a reversion to a more primitive zone of feeling than the female genital; stripped of her defenses, the girl attains to womanliness—and she is not grateful. She must hit back at her despised master, or savior, with her own bleak ugly attempt to rob him of his masculine pride. The story ends with both partners in this loveless battle worn and battered, both equally the victims of their excoriated egotism—and with the girl bound for the Freudian couch where, so Mailer has it, she has learned the tactics of assault which are her civilized protection.

"Time of Her Time" is the crudest of Mailer's attacks upon

Freudianism, and it is peculiarly anomalous that Mailer should deal with Freud this unworthily. For, although he is himself not aware of it, the fortitude which is implicit in the demand he makes upon the self is much closer to the Freudian than the Reichian temperament. Mailer's heroic assertion and his insistence upon the controlling power of man's consciousness have their antecedents not in the psychoanalysis that has diverged from Freud but in Freud himself; the Reichian psychology proposes a character considerably less valorous and self-contained. The heroism of Freud, however, was the heroism of endurance; he knew better than most the price that civilization exacts in denied instinct, and tragically, resentfully, he was prepared to pay it. Mailer's is the courage of non-acceptance; he refuses to sacrifice instinct to a civilization which is itself so little removed from savagery. But perhaps because of Freud's readiness to face into the issue as between civilization and instinct, Mailer does, in fact, direct his criticisms not so much to Freud himself as to his disciples today, where he stands on firmer territory. The unwillingness of contemporary orthodox analysis to take account of the actualities of a culture in significant transition, its acknowledged acquiescence in a moribund middle-class morality, its reluctance to treat with the human personality apart from the limitations of social imperatives—these are the grounds of Mailer's adverse judgment upon present-day Freudianism. One could fairly put it that what Mailer attacks in Freud's followers is their passive or neutral assent in a choice which, as Freud made it, had such harsh resonances.

Naturally enough, of the various excesses into which Mailer is led by his own option against civilization, the most disturbing is his expressed tolerance of, even his partisanship with, extreme personal violence. And he is not speaking metaphorically; here as elsewhere he is announcing a program of action. What is worse, he speaks of violence in a language of love learned in the moral culture he undertakes to dismiss in its entirety. For example, in a statement which he made in the course of an interview in *Mademoiselle* (February 1961), he has this to say about a brutal gratuitous murder:

> Let's use our imaginations. It means that one human be-
> ing has determined to extinguish the life of another hu-
> man being. It means that two people are engaging in a
> dialogue with eternity. Now if the brute does it and at
> the last moment likes the man he is extinguishing then
> perhaps the victim did not die in vain. If there is an
> eternity with souls in that eternity, if one is able to be
> born again, the victim may get his reward. At least it
> seems possible that the quality of one being passes into
> the other, and this altogether hate-filled human, grind-
> ing his boot into the face of someone . . . in the act of
> killing, in this terribly private moment, the brute feels a
> moment of tenderness, for the first time perhaps in all of
> his experience. What has happened is that the killer is
> becoming a little more possible, a little bit more ready
> to love someone.

This is of course monstrous and intolerable. We recall, however, that the statement was made at a time of great personal
stress, and we are relieved to counter to its enormity the modified terms in which Mailer, but a few months later, discussed
the violence of Hipsterism with Richard Wollheim in England. "I don't," said Mailer, "see the real choice as one between violence and non-violence. It's rather between the violence of the individual and collective violence. . . . [Whether
or not protest needs to take such a total form as that of Hip-
sterism] depends on whether one thinks a society can solve its
problems rationally. If one thinks it can, then hip will go nowhere. But if one thinks it can't, and that barbarism is closer,
and that violence is in the seed, then at least hip introduces
the notion of art into barbary." We might reply to a formula-
tion like this that barbary is precisely where art is not and
never can be; that art and civilization are genetically inseparable. But no one who admits into the record of contemporary
civilization the savagery of nazism, or the spiraling success of

communist totalitarianism or, at a perhaps absurd extreme, even the gruesome spectacle of professional wrestling, can evade the validity of the problem Mailer poses for us when he asks that we look at the collective violence we call our moral order and, in the light of what we see, decide whether we can exempt the individual of responsibility for our degradation, and continue, as a culture, to feel morally superior to our collective conduct. While Hipsterism's conspiracy with the vicious in man's nature suggests a "cure" which certainly is little better than the disease for which it is prescribed, Mailer at least presses upon us an effort of honesty without which we live in moral delusion.

And yet is it not enough that he tell us what we must learn instead of telling us what we must do? Clearly, this is the chief pitfall Mailer has contrived for himself as a writer—his neglect of the metaphoric character of the literary endeavor. For it is here that his espousal of violence ceases to be a strategy by which we are shorn of the hypocrisies and self-delusions with which we surround our participation in a violent civilization and becomes so gross an offense against the decency we still cherish both in our personal and in our collective lives. But if Mailer's actualization, even in his own conduct, of ideas that, for another writer, would remain simply figures of speech has had its inevitable effect of nullifying some of the difficult truth with which he is dealing, it may also in the long run protect his radical insights from being so quickly and easily absorbed that we make no use of them. "The world doesn't fear a new idea. It can pigeon-hole any idea. But it can't pigeon-hole a real new experience." This is D. H. Lawrence speaking, who produced a body of work which is entirely metaphoric. And Lawrence left the world, certainly not untouched by his urgent insights, but sadly unaltered in its main course.

But Mailer's impulse to break the metaphor barrier and himself act out, or ask that we act out, his ideas would now appear to have another, much deeper source than his impatience with the ability of art to achieve its tangible miracle of renovation. Intense as his, literary dedication unquestionably is, his religious mission is now infinitely more compelling. Just as he writes in order to preach the word of God, he acts in order to attain to God, by whatever thorny path. And when he invites us to follow his example he literally means us to join a religious crusade.

Even as a young writer and young Marxist, Mailer's vision carried him beyond a world of simply defined or materially determined notions of good and evil. We look back upon his first novel from our present vantage to see that Sergeant Croft's ascent of Mount Anaka must be interpreted as the ascent of the Cross, and that Croft's triumph at the end of *The Naked and the Dead* represents a transcendence not merely over his own poor character, as we would judge it, but over an inglorious mankind which presumes to pass moral judgment and which fails to realize that God may appear to us in the strangest of disguises. And similarly with Marion Faye: while so far we see only the stigmata, we can suppose that in the big novel on which Mailer is now working, in which Faye will have a leading part, Mailer's Hipster will come into the full light of his spiritual blessedness, for God may as easily be a pimp as a fascist; it is ourselves who are in error if we fail to know Him. Nor is Mailer's invitation to sin so that we may find grace an unfamiliar heresy. If there has always been missing from Mailer's writing any true perception of the mysterious circuitous paths by which literature accomplishes its improving work, undoubtedly this is because he has always been occupied with the mysterious circuitous ways in which God performs His work. His moral imagination is the imagination not of art but of theology, theology in action.

This defect in Mailer's artistic imagination has many corollaries, of which the most obvious are his small fictional concern with the complexity and variety of human responses and, even more disabling, the absence of a prose adequate to the larger intentions of literature. If we were to conceive of Hemingway offering us his heroic choice and his disenchantment with the hollow idealisms of modern life in a language which was sufficient to propagate a doctrine but no more than that; which failed to be its own quintessential comment on the modern world and which exposed us to the crude manipulations of ideology, without those areas of retirement and indecision and even discordance which are so perfectly re-created for us in the subtle tones and rhythms of Hemingway's best writing—this would approximate Mailer's situation as a novelist. For the life-giving subtleties of style, Mailer substitutes a generosity of words. Like Thomas Wolfe before him, like Saul Bellow in his own generation, he has a giant energy of vocabulary with which he undertakes to make his discriminations of meaning. But his taut strings of noun upon noun, adjective upon adjective, intended to sharpen our response to reality, in fact sharpen only his own act of assertion.

Of some (superficial) aspects of his stylistic problem, Mailer is himself aware. Often in *Advertisements* he refers to his continuing effort to achieve a prose which will support his vision of modernity and forbid us our easy evasions and falsifications. But if, so far, his endeavor has largely missed its goal and indeed has had the perverse effect of reinforcing Mailer's rhetoric of will, this is by no means an inappropriate outcome. To a greater extent than he perhaps recognizes, Mailer is an anti-artist, deeply distrustful of art if only because it puts a shield between the perception and the act. His writer's role, as he conceives it, is much more messianic than creative. While it was in the very nature of Hemingway's literary vocation that even in moments of the most urgent masculine assertion he was able to keep in abeyance the impositions of the merely personal masculine will, it is in the nature of Mailer's social and spiritual vocation that he should wish to challenge, even personally dominate, his reader. And if we listen closely, we perhaps hear his insistence as less the expression of personal authority than as a call to a time when religion was still a masculine discipline—a call, that is, to an Hebraic world, still molded in the image of the stern father, Moses. From Moses to Marion Faye, with a stopover at Marx: Mailer's religious route is surely a strange one. But the braver efforts of culture are not always straightaway and simple.

THE WORLD OF LOVE

Eudora Welty

For the past twenty-two years since the publication of her first
book of stories, *A Curtain of Green,* Eudora Welty has modestly
taken a back seat to her fellow Mississippian, William Faulkner,
but her excellence has never been doubted and it is not unlikely
that future historians will make a place for her very close to him.
Born in Jackson, Mississippi, in 1909, of a West Virginian mother
and Ohioan father (president of an insurance company), Miss
Welty was brought up in Jackson where she still lives with her
widowed mother, making occasional trips East and abroad. As a
young girl her ambition was to be a painter, but she was also an
avid reader, and in school and later at college, she pursued her
literary bent. She attended Mississippi State College for Women
(1925–27) and earned a B.A. two years later at the University
of Wisconsin. Coming East to earn a living, she studied advertising at Columbia, but the depression having made jobs scarce, she
soon returned South. During the next eight years, she held various
jobs in advertising and publicity and for a short while wrote a
society column for the Memphis *Commercial Appeal.* In the meantime, she had begun writing short stories and found a useful ap-
prenticeship in her job with the W.P.A., interviewing and photographing people throughout her native state. In 1936, an obscure

magazine, *Manuscript,* published her first short story, "The Death of a Traveling Salesman." Later, Albert Erskine invited her to write for the *Southern Review* and subsequently her stories appeared in the *Atlantic Monthly* and *The New Yorker.* Critical acclaim greeted her first volume of short stories, for which Katherine Anne Porter wrote a glowing preface. Since then her writing has won her many literary awards and two Guggenheim Fellowships. She was honorary consultant to the Library of Congress from 1958–61 and William Allan Neilson Professor at Smith College in 1962. Periodically, Miss Welty interrupts her fiction writing to comment on contemporary literature and her illuminating pieces have appeared in *The New York Times Book Review* and various literary magazines. Unassuming, simple in her tastes, she shuns "the literary life" while cultivating real literary friendships. Her warmth, her infectious humor, her vivid response to life make her beloved both as an artist and as a person. At present, Miss Welty is completing a long short story.

THE WORLD OF LOVE:

THE FICTION OF EUDORA WELTY

by Alun R. Jones

There has been no doubt of Eudora Welty's standing as a writer since her first collection of stories, *A Curtain of Green,* was published in 1941. Since that time she has consolidated her reputation and confirmed the uniqueness of her achievement by writing two further collections of short stories, *The Wide Net* (1943) and *The Bride of the Innisfallen* (1955), and four longer works of fiction, *The Robber Bridegroom* (1942), *Delta Wedding* (1946), *The Golden Apples* (1949) and *The Ponder Heart* (1956).

Inevitably she has become associated with William Faulkner, Robert Penn Warren, John Crowe Ransom, Allen Tate and that distinguished company of writers who, like Katherine Anne Porter, "have blood knowledge of what life can be in a defeated country on the bare bones of privation." Although she claims Yankee blood on her father's side, she was born in Jackson, Mississippi, not far from the borders of Yoknapatawphaw County, and belongs there in the way that Emily Brontë belongs to the Yorkshire moors. Her close association with the South as a traditional way of life, under pressure and, perhaps, in decay, has been felt to confer on her as a writer special advantages and peculiar limitations, as if she were both the beneficiary and the victim of her background. No one, and certainly not Miss Welty herself, would wish to deny the importance of "place" to a writer, although it could be argued that it is the writers of the South who have made it a place, rather than a point on the compass, just as frontier legend made the West.

Naturally, in her work Miss Welty draws for her material largely on the world of the South, familiar and immediately to hand, but it is human nature and the human dilemma that are explored, and her art is distinctive. Only the most provincial reader confuses the writer with the raw material of his art. Certainly the South seems to lend her an assured sense of personal identity—because you know where you are, you know who you are—and this assurance has, in a sense, enabled her to pursue her art with a freedom and single-mindedness rare among those writers with apparently more fluid, less stable social backgrounds. But indeed, even among the writers of the South, she is the only one to have acknowledged the autonomy of the imagination. Behind her work there lies a fragile, profound and essentially lyrical imagination strengthened by characteristic wit and shrewdness. Thus her art brings together the delicate, introspective refinement of Chekhov, Katherine Mansfield, and Virginia Woolf and the tough, American know-how of Mark Twain, Stephen Crane and Ring Lardner.

The sheer variety of *A Curtain of Green* is immediately impressive. The stories vary in tone from broad and sometimes grotesque farce to delicate melancholy; there are stories of fairy-tale simplicity and fantasies of nightmare complexity, stories of greed, and pride, and horror, and of innocence and love. Yet above all else they portray a wide variety of attitudes and peoples living in a recognizably human world of beauty and corruption, tenderness and hate, wonder and boredom. The stories are concerned largely with single moments of personal crisis and move towards and explore the nature of conflict as the characters struggle to clarify their choices, to come to terms with themselves and the world around them. Although a strong sense of an ordered community binds the settings of the stories together, it is the dark, inner lives of the characters that interest her more than their public faces. She is more concerned with individual self-deception than with social hypocrisy.

She has, too, the storyteller's gift of compelling attention, of capturing her reader's interest in what happens and, more particularly, in what happens next. Moreover, although her subject is often fabulous, bizarre and in itself improbable, she has the unfailing ability to maintain what she has called "believability"—to establish that imaginative confidence between reader and writer which constitutes a mutual act of poetic faith.

Stories such as "Death of a Traveling Salesman" and "The Hitchhikers" contrast the settled life of traditional values and the restless commercial world, a contrast between love and loneliness. In "Death of a Traveling Salesman," R. J. Bowman, forced by illness to recognize the restlessness and futility of his life is brought by accident into contact with a couple whose life is slow, intimate and secure. It is the meeting of two worlds, the past and the present, the simple and the complex, the loved and the loveless. Bowman is overwhelmed by the realization of his own emptiness and horrified by his utter inability to communicate at a profound and simple level:

> But he wanted to leap up, to say to her, I have been sick and I found out then, only then, how lonely I am. Is it too late? My heart puts up a struggle inside me, and you may have heard it, protesting against emptiness . . . It should be full, he would rush on to tell her, thinking of his heart now as a deep lake, it should be holding love like other hearts. It should be flooded with love . . .

The couple receive Bowman with kindness, hospitality and warmth and without ceremony. He knows he has nothing to offer in return, except money, and in desperation he tries to

escape back to the emptiness of his life. His need for love—
the struggle his heart puts up inside him—betrays him:

> Just as he reached the road, where his car seemed to
> sit in the moonlight like a boat, his heart began to give
> off tremendous explosions like a rifle, bang, bang, bang.
> He sank in fright on to the road, his bags falling about
> him. He felt as if all this had happened before. He cov-
> ered his heart with both hands to keep anyone from
> hearing the noise it made.
> But nobody heard it.

The symbolism in this story (the first to be published) is more
direct than in her later stories, but it states the theme that is
in so many ways fundamental to an understanding of her fiction: man's loneliness and his search for a world of love.

"The Hitchhikers," for instance, is a more complex and
more oblique treatment of a similar theme. A commercial
traveler and the two hitchhikers to whom he gives a lift form
a community of drifters. Because they exist on the surface of
life they are trivial and superficial, unable to give or receive
love, unable to realize themselves except as travelers to whom
movement from one town to another has become an escape
from life. The gratuitousness with which one hitchhiker kills
the other, brings home to the commercial traveler an awareness of the rootlessness of his own life. The commercial traveler's ambition is to be "somewhere on a good gravelled road,
driving his car past things that happened to people, quicker
than their happening." He wants life to be ordered and
straightforward and without ties, but life, Miss Welty insists,
is a matter of strong roots and slow growth.

Miss Welty reserves her deepest compassion for those who
recognize their need for love but are refused—as in the pathetic story of Clytie in *A Curtain of Green*, trapped in a
house of lonely and demanding selfishness, who finds release
from the sufferings of her absurd, unlovely and unloved life
in the companionship of death. Clytie lives in a mysterious
world of her own. Aware of the potentiality of wonder and

beauty in the world around her, she meets at every turn only horror and brutality. Her spirit is wild and demented with half-understood longings. She is the pathetic victim of her family's selfishness, of a bullying sister, her drunken brother and invalid father. The house is a prison in which the family has interned itself so as to prevent any contact between the Farr family and the villagers of Farr's Gin. Only Clytie goes out, pathetically wandering in the rain and searching for a world of love which she associates faintly with her youth. Later, when the barber is summoned from the village to attend her father, she reaches out "with breath-taking gentleness" towards him only to be rejected in fear. Automatically she obeys her sister's command:

> "Clytie! Clytie! The water! The water!" came Octavia's monumental voice.
> Clytie did the only thing she could think of to do. She bent her angular body further, and thrust her head into the barrel, under the water, through its glittering surface into the kind, featureless depth, and held it there.
> When Old Lethy found her, she had fallen forward into the barrel, with her poor ladylike black-stockinged legs upended and hung apart like a pair of tongs.

Clytie, a curious kind of Narcissus, has been horrified by the reflection of her own ugly, suffering face. She is shocked into an awareness of how life has perverted and deformed her vision. She is found, significantly, by her father's devoted nurse whom her sister would not allow into the house. Old Lethy represents childhood and affection trying to re-enter the family but her name suggests death and oblivion. (Frequently in her stories Miss Welty uses classical references. In this particular story the sister is called Octavia, which suggests the cold, Roman matron; and the barber is seen, for a moment, standing "like the statue of Hermes," which wonderfully conveys both his physical attitude and the fact that Clytie mistakenly took him to be a messenger from the better world outside.)

Miss Welty moves with assurance through those worlds of feeling where comedy and pathos meet and become insepa- rable. "Clytie" is both grimly comic and profoundly moving. There is in the character of Clytie herself a tragic incongruity between the wonder of what we know to be her inner life and the pathetic figure she cuts in her public actions. In the final line when she describes Clytie's legs upended, she shocks us into an awareness of the casual way that life has picked up Miss Clytie and put her down again as if she were quite trivial and dispensable. By reconciling incongruities in this way, Miss Welty shows how tragic feeling can be expressed in laughter, and laughter in her work is often the release of otherwise unbearable pathos.

The stories are often concerned with those who are in some way deprived and living on the very edge of life but they see deprivation not as a social question but as a human one, a matter not of income and status but of love and loneliness. They cover the social range from faded gentry to sharecrop- pers and Negroes, yet their concern is always with the human dilemma, with man's failure or success in dealing with his own nature, with the realities of the life within him and the needs of those around him.

Each of the stories in *A Curtain of Green* is very different, yet in all of them incident and speech are observed and re- ported with dispassionate fidelity and patterned with unob- trusive artistry. In "Lily Daw and the Three Ladies," three old spinsters cluck and fuss over their irresponsible charge, desperately trying to reduce her wayward life to some sem- blance of ordered dignity. The world of Lily Daw is hugely comic and contrasts violently with that of "The Petrified Man" which is fraught with hypocrisy, petty spite, greed and shallow ambitions. The world of the hairdresser and her client in "The Petrified Man" is exposed relentlessly in the course of two conversations between the women. The story has a bit- ing satiric edge that cuts deeply into the vulgar triviality of commercial, small-town life. It is a world both cheap and sinister, in which human relationships have been grotesquely perverted, a world ruthlessly dominated by women who are themselves dominated by spite, cheap sensation and material possessions. The beauty salon is seen as a cave of primeval tortures producing a succession of Medusa-like creatures who turn their men to stone at a glance. The men are impotent before this monstrous regiment of women. The petrified man of the title is an exhibit at a freak show. The discovery that he is "not really petrified at all," but was, in fact, wanted by the police for raping four women provides the story with its climax and with its central symbol. It is a kind of poetic justice to learn that subjugated man has reasserted himself even if in a violent way against this monstrous regiment. The conversation of the women is recorded with amazing fidelity as relentlessly they expose the shallowness and perversity of their own attitudes. The story, emerging casually out of the conversation, is a shrewd and incisive comment on the social scene and shows a complete mastery of the comedy of manners.

"Why I Live at the P.O." is the indignant and gushing monologue—Katherine Anne Porter describes it as a "terrifying case of dementia praecox"—in which the heroine describes how her sister, separated from her husband, comes back home and turns the family against her, forcing her out of the house. The sheer technical skill involved would seem to mark each of these stories as a tour de force, and yet more significant than this is the way in which each, while maintaining a convincing illusion of reality, creates its own world, with its own distinct logic, language and being. Each creates an immediate sense of actuality, of people talking and things happening before the reader's eyes, and this powerful, almost tactual illusion of reality is strongest when the stories themselves are closest to pure fantasy.

Indeed, one of Miss Welty's outstanding characteristics as a writer is her Tennysonian ability to sustain an atmospheric mood. The world of the imagination is so fully realized in terms of the sensuous and ordinary that it is accepted without question. Although these stories are clearly informed by compassionate intelligence and shaped by an acute feeling for artistic form, we are aware that for the author life continually moves towards the fabulous, sometimes—as in "The Petrified Man"—towards the perverse, just as magic shades off into witchcraft. She is conscious of mythical and imaginative reality impinging on and informing the trivial and the banal.

As her stories become longer, her texture richer and more complex in effect, she increasingly explores in depth the world in which the significant and the mythical lie thinly disguised beneath the everyday world around us. In her next collection, *The Wide Net,* she begins to build with gathering assurance on the territory already cleared and charted in her early stories. For, like all great writers, she is continually in competition with herself. In a story such as "First Love" the myth is embodied in the past and is associated particularly with the way in which the past impresses itself on and enriches the present. There is a strong feeling of the organic unity of life, of tradition as a creative, positive force shaping the present and lending individual lives a general validity.

Her imagination is essentially poetic; her fiction is clearly centripetal, structured like poetry with an intuited center and everything subdued to the demands of this central insight. As her art develops, so her fiction accumulates a more profound sense of human suffering and dignity and it covers a wider area of human activity without losing any of its original power. She continues to affirm the beauties and terrors inherent in the human situation while asserting the right to love and the need to dream. Through dream, as through art, man can express and realize his secret self: through love, as through art, he can communicate that secret self to others; for art, she believes, is the power to convey love. In "A Still Moment" she brings together the themes of loneliness, love and time, "God's giving Separateness first and then giving Love to follow and heal in its wonder." The tragedy of man is to be separate and lonely, his glory is to be capable of dissolving his loneliness in love.

Legend, a more specific land of mythology, plays a larger part in her later work. In "First Love" and in "A Still Moment" she incorporates legendary figures into the story. "First Love," for instance, is concerned with Joel Mayes, a deaf and dumb boy who is caught up in the romantic and mysterious conspiracy of Aaron Burr. Painfully, through love, the boy achieves self-awareness. The love is, of necessity, unspoken and unacknowledged. His life is touched by the historical past being enacted around him and he achieves self-consciousness, shame, love and adulthood. The unthinking innocence of childhood is lost to him and his life to that point takes on an entirely different meaning. Even the world of nature, to which he was formerly drawn as by a bond of sympathy, now seems completely changed:

> He held the bud, and studied the burned edges of its folds by the pale half-light of the East. The buds came apart in his hand, its layers like small velvet shells, still iridescent, the shrivelled flower inside. He held it tenderly and yet timidly, in a kind of shame, as though all disaster lay pitifully disclosed now to the eyes.

In a way the story re-enacts the Fall of Man, the child moving out of the world of innocence into the world of experience. It is the kind of romantic dynamic associated with Blake who also regarded love as the great regenerative force by virtue of which man could regain a vision of that Eden from which self-conscious knowledge had exiled him. There is a general feeling in Miss Welty's work that man, driven forward by dreams of the future has, with dignity and humor, created a precarious present out of the wilderness and chaos of the past.

Her novel *The Robber Bridegroom* is a direct tribute to the legendary past. Set in Mississippi in 1798 when it was still Spanish, the action is mostly centered on the Old Natchez Trace which ran for two hundred miles through the wilderness between Natchez and Nashville. The story opens in Rodney's Landing—now a ghost town—with a mock-heroic encounter between the two legendary figures, Mike Fink and Jamie Lockhart, and ends in New Orleans with the happy reunion of Jamie Lockhart, the Robber Bridegroom, and Rosamond, his bride. In this brilliant, loving parody of fairy-tale, the legends of the past are recreated with magical simplicity and directness. All the elements of the fairy tale, including its traditional style, are accommodated; the heroes are suitably romantic and heroic; the heroine is virtuous and trusting, with a proper sense of curiosity; the wicked stepmother is, of course, in league with the forces of evil and plotting against the heroine; the father is kind and doting and everyone—at least every one of the virtuous characters—lives happily ever after. Miss Welty's attitude towards her material is detached, even ironic, though she leaves no doubt that it is a parody written without sentimentality but with profound admiration and respect.

In *Delta Wedding,* her second novel, she returns to a study of childhood innocence in contact and often in conflict with the authoritarian world of adult experience. The story is of a nine-year-old girl's visit to the Fairchilds', her introduction to the lives of her cousins and their complex world of aunts and friends. But the novel is much more than the story of a young girl's seven-day stay with relatives, for the journey from Jackson to the Fairchilds' is a journey into the new and frightening world of experience. Delicately, the novel probes expanding possibilities, excitements and responsibilities and with precision of feeling defines the child's vivid responses to the world around her.

Written in a style in which poetry and prose blend, mood and landscape knit in a meaningful whole, so that the reader is able to enter unobstrusively into the private thoughts, discontents and happiness of the characters. The family is dominated by Uncle George and the theme of love is embodied in him. The life of the Fairchilds is ordered, possessive and resentful of outsiders. Uncle George is portrayed as a man of selfless courage and "wild detachment," who is guided not by the social patterns of behavior which the others expect and understand but by some older tradition of personal integrity. The family possessively makes demands on him and cannot forgive him because he "loved the *world. . . .* Not them in particular"; and indeed one of the main themes of the novel is the struggle of his wife to accept the disinterested quality of her husband's love which she felt by rights ought to belong to her alone.

Miss Welty continually stresses the universality of this love which belongs to no one but is available to everyone. Ellen— mother, wife and sister—who is the novel's central character comes to recognize, accept and value the quality of George's love and to see that whatever life and fate handed out to him ("Ready for anything all the time") he would always meet it with that same disinterested passion. The social life at "Shellmound" follows an accepted, almost ritualistic pattern, social relationships are clearly defined; Dabney is marrying "beneath" her in marrying Troy, an overseer, as indeed Uncle George has already shocked the family by marrying Robbie, who worked in the local store.

Uncle George defines to a large extent Miss Welty's conception of the world of love, although as a character he is always in the end remote, mysterious and even mythological. Nevertheless, the central impulse in *Delta Wedding* does not seem strong enough to hold a novel together. The reader is aware of the danger that the novel might fall into sections and episodes which are not strongly interdependent.

Perhaps it was to avoid this tendency that Miss Welty wrote her next book, *The Golden Apples,* in sections rather than in the form of a traditional novel. Undoubtedly the seven separate stories create a unity of a sort, linked as they are by their locale, a small town, Morgana, and by the reappearance of many of the same characters throughout. The stories vary in tone from the broad comedy of "Shower of Gold" to the desperate melancholy of "The Whole World Knows." "Shower of Gold" tells of the disappearance and reappearance of Snowdie MacLain's husband. Like so many of her stories, this one is characterized by a strong feeling for the casual—the mark of the consummate craftsman. The more extraordinary the event, the more the style tends toward the throw-away. The opening of "Shower of Gold" is a fine example:

> That was Miss Snowdie MacLain.
> She comes after her butter, won't let me run over with it from just across the road. Her husband walked out of the house one day and left his hat on the banks of the Big Black River.—That could have started something, too.
>
> We might have had a little run on doing that in Morgana, if it had been so willed. What King did, the copy-cats always might do. Well, King MacLain left a new straw hat on the banks of the Big Black and there are people that consider he headed West.

Her use of the garrulous narrator not only enables her to exploit her uncanny gift for reproducing the authentic accents of colloquial speech but provides her with another source of interest in the character of the narrator as well as another perspective.

In "June Recital," the most complex of these stories, she uses two quite different narrators to define two quite separate attitudes toward the same incident. The young boy, Loch, and his older sister, Cassie, are both spectators of the sinister happening in the deserted house next door. Loch sees a sailor making love to a girl in an upstairs room and an old woman scattering paper around the living room downstairs who then sits down to play the piano. Loch in his innocence accepts these events with wonder but without serious questioning; Cassie, a little more experienced than her brother, questions these events and tries to make sense of them, but her mind is on the hayride for which she is making herself ready. Thus three lives and three points of view are brought together, each working at a different level of consciousness, but each in its separate way affected by the others. One is without experience or anticipation, one with a little experience is filling her life with the excitement of anticipation, the third, old, deranged and embittered, has had her ambitions and expectations cruelly frustrated. Yet the story as a whole affirms the mystery and wonder of life rather than its disappointments.

Similarly, in "The Whole World Knows," which tells the story of Randall MacLain's desertion by Jinny Love and his affair with Maideen Sumrall, the tone is pervasively melancholic, but it is life itself that is affirmed—in spite of the treachery of time and transience. Indeed, the town of Morgana suggests the claustrophobic, painful and distracting landscape in which all of us, in a sense, came to terms with the adult world for the first time. It is a different place for each character as they emerge from their private worlds to face the larger world outside. It is essentially a secure landscape, still to some extent dominated by parents.

What the characters in *The Golden Apples* all learn is that to live in harmony demands a strenuous act of creation; it entails reshaping one's inner world to meet the needs of others. In fact, *The Golden Apples* maps that whole area of consciousness that we vaguely call "growing up." It is in many ways Miss Welty's most complex and satisfying achievement, for she seems to be drawing on all her considerable resources, both technical and thematic, and bringing them together to make a statement about life that is rich and profound in all its fabulous, banal, comic, tragic and human variety.

Morgana becomes finally as complete a map of Eudora Welty's imaginative world as she has given us. The act of creative imagination is seen now to be the act of life itself. The effort of living is an act of imagination, and like the regeneration of the Ancient Mariner (which has often been interpreted as a poem about the workings of the creative imagination) must begin with an act of love.

Allen Tate once observed that "the typical Southern conversation is not going anywhere, it is not about anything. It is about the people who are talking—conversation is only an expression of manners, the purpose of which is to make everybody happy." Miss Welty's hugely comic book, *The Ponder Heart,* is clearly written in this tradition. Breathlessly, Edna Earle describes the life of her Uncle Daniel—a life devoted to making everybody happy. Uncle Daniel is the richest man in the small town of Clay although money means nothing to him, for the world in which he lives is the golden world of the heart where wealth is counted in love, generosity, kindness and happiness. As Edna says, "If he ever did a thing to be sorry for, it's more than he ever intended." Uncle Daniel lives in the world he has created for himself, a beautiful, absurd world of love. According to his niece, his great weaknesses are that he loves people and loves giving things away:

> Things I could think of without being asked that he's given away would be—a string of hams, a fine suit of clothes, a white-face heifer calf, two trips to Memphis, a pair of fantail pigeons, fine Shetland pony (loves children), brooder and incubator, good nanny goat, bad billy, cypress cistern, field of white Dutch clover, two iron wheels and some laying pullets (they were together), cow pasture during drought (he has everlasting springs), innumerable fresh eggs, a pick-up truck —even his own cemetery lot, but they wouldn't accept it . . .

Uncle Daniel's generosity is indiscriminate—the incubator he gave to the postman, not that he "ever got a *letter* in his life." Even the Beulah Hotel that Edna Earle owns was given to her by Uncle Daniel. For the most part the town regards him as simple-minded—his father considered him positively unbalanced and had him put in an asylum—though because some of the magic of his life has rubbed off on them, they also regard him with admiration. Edna Earle is mainly concerned with her uncle's relationship with Bonnie Dee Peacock, her death and Uncle Daniel's trial for her murder. Uncle Daniel found Bonnie Dee working in a ten-cent store and persuaded her to agree to a marriage trial. The marriage trial went on for five years and six months before "Bonnie

Dee, if you please, decided No." When Bonnie Dee leaves him she is persuaded to return by an advertisement placed by Edna in the Memphis *Commercial Appeal*. The advertisement, in the form of a poem entitled "Come Back to Clay," was successful. The first thing she does when she comes back is to force Uncle Daniel to leave. Uncle Daniel moves into the Beulah Hotel but is happy, for, as he explains, "Oh, my bride has come back to me. Pretty as a picture, and I'm happy beyond compare." While to everybody else Bonnie Dee is an empty-headed, stupid, young girl, she remains beautiful in Uncle Daniel's eyes.

Bonnie Dee is incapable of love, though Uncle Daniel has more than enough for two, and, when she is finally bribed to accept him back in the house, he finds her crying with fright at the thunderstorm outside. In order to distract her, Uncle Daniel begins to tickle her and she dies—laughing. At the trial, Uncle Daniel's world of love is exposed to the hard light of logic and reason by Mr. Gladney, the prosecuting lawyer, but it is Uncle Daniel's world that prevails and the world of Mr. Gladney that crumbles away into senseless greed. Uncle Daniel is impregnable and incorruptible for, as Edna Earle explains, "he's been brought up in a world of love." *The Ponder Heart* is a glorious comic invention, a masterpiece of contrived lunacy that affirms love as the source of human activity and Uncle Daniel a fabulous representative of human virtue.

In her latest collection of stories, *The Bride of the Innisfallen,* Miss Welty has broadened the scope, as well as enriched the texture of her writing still further. Her eye and her ear are as sharp as ever, but her compassion leads her to a more subdued consideration of personal suffering. Her work takes on a sculptured, timeless solidity. At the same time, her thematic material becomes denser and more complex, and an increased artistic assurance enables her to treat her narrative more obliquely than in her previous work. She no longer draws her material exclusively from the South and she explores new areas of experience with more somber restraint and from a viewpoint withdrawn from the center of the stories' interest. Taken as a whole the stories are an exciting departure. They are experiments in a kind of impressionistic writing that depends hardly at all on traditional narrative techniques but relies largely on *montage,* an approach to writing that has its parallel in the cinema of the *Nouvelle Vague.* Three of the stories in the volume—"No Place for You, My Love," "The Bride of the Innisfallen," and "Going to Naples"—are concerned with journeys and with strangers briefly and loosely thrown together because of their common destination. The climax of each story is arrived at obliquely as imperceptibly the consciousness of each character leaves its impression on his fellow travelers.

For example, "No Place for You, My Love" is deliberately vague on the conventional level of plot and characterization. A man and a woman, not themselves southerners, meet accidentally in a New Orleans restaurant and take a car ride over the Mississippi toward the South. They drive compulsively onwards through the intense and merciless heat into a country which becomes more unreal the further they travel. They are exposed finally to a wasteland of light without shadows and without purpose—except that they follow the road, until the road just ends. The journey has many of the features of a bad dream as the couple unknown to each other move deeper and deeper into a country which is also unknown. There is little conversation between them and everything that happens appears, as in a nightmare, to be both significant and inconsequential. At the nadir of their journey, which is also the turning point, they dance together in a strange bar. They dance formally, "like professional, Spanish dancers wearing masks," and the dance establishes the relationship between them. This relationship, tenuous, formal, with a quiet undertow of passion, haunts them on their return journey back to normality. It is as if they had visited the underworld together so that when they step back into their old lives and the familiar world, this ghostly relationship "cried like a human, and dropped back."

The story is completely unified at a symbolic, impressionist level and the mood is sustained with great subtlety. Although at the end of the story we know little more about the characters than we did at the beginning, there is a sense also in which we know all there is to know about them. The story is a complete and satisfying "objective correlative" for a certain kind of shock experienced by those with courage enough to face life unprotected by the buffers of habit or custom. Similarly, "The Burning" is a pitiless exposure of a deranged world set at the time of the Civil War when Sherman was marching and burning his way through the South. The tone of these stories is meditative and compassionate and depicts a strange modern Odyssey into disturbing areas of human consciousness.

Each of Miss Welty's works seems to present her with a different challenge and in each she has extended herself in a new direction. For her, writing is a means of exploration and in the stories of *The Bride of the Innisfallen* she reaches deep into a new and darker side of experience.

Miss Welty has stated her belief that:

> . . . each novel written stands as something of a feat. For what has been done? First ask, what was the heart's desire? Not the creating of an illusion, but the restoring of one; something brought off. We are not children once we have pasts; and now as we come looking in fiction with more longing than in any experience save love, but to which love adds, looking for reflections and visions of all life we know compounded through art, performance itself is what we ask for. We ask only that it be magic. Good fiction grants this boon, bad denies it. And performance is what the novelists would like to give . . . a fresh performance; not to show off skill, which would be . . . a thing to be despised, but, out of respect, love, and fearlessness for all that may be tried, to command the best skill.

Between *A Curtain of Green* and *The Bride of the Innisfallen* Miss Welty has developed a vision of life that is matched by her consummate skill. Writing with love, she restores our illusions about the world of love. Her fiction is exuberant with life, rich in comedy, pathos and color, quick with movement and firmly disciplined. Each of her stories creates its own level of reality and succeeds in the business of fiction which is to make reality real. Replete with sensuous and meaningful detail, the meaning itself is often suspended in that private world somewhere between dreaming and waking. Indeed, it is the particular, personal moment that her imagination seizes with concrete and urgent immediacy.

Her writing as a whole is characterized by an elegant and correct compassion that interpenetrates life's disordered vitality in such a way that, in her own words, "life on earth is intensified in its personal meaning and so restored to human terms." Her art shapes the experience, lending it style and direction; life informs her art at every turn, giving it variety and intensity. The most immediate and most lasting impression created by reading her work is an admiration for the sheer abundance of human life. Her achievement has won her comparison with the best writers of the century and the prospect of her future work assures readers of fresh and exciting excellence.

NOVELISTS OF DISJUNCTION

JACK KEROUAC

Unlike most American writers who attain celebrity early, Jack Kerouac published his first novel, *The Town and the City* in 1950 to a quiet critical and public reception. However, his second novel, *On the Road,* which was written in 1951, but not published until 1956, was the sensation of the season. Everyone seemed to have a reaction; even reviews of the book, such as Gilbert Millstein's in *The New York Times* ("Its publication is a historic occasion") were discussed. Since then, the enthusiasms and condemnations have diminished to mere approval or apathy, as Kerouac's novels, poems, numerous magazine articles and his recordings have issued forth. Kerouac was born of French-Canadian extraction in 1922 in Lowell, Massachusetts, where he attended grammar and high schools. After two years at Columbia College, he joined the Merchant Marine and then intermittently devoted himself to the life of the "beat," auto-borne wanderer often described in his books. He is strikingly handsome and, like his movie counterpart, Marlon Brando, has contributed to the cool, or hip, manner. He has been married and divorced twice.

JAMES JONES

James Jones was born in Robinson, Illinois, in 1921. Shortly after his graduation from high school he joined the Regular Army and was shipped to Hawaii, where he was serving at the time of the Japanese attack on Pearl Harbor. A month later, he was in Guadalcanal, saw combat and was wounded. After the Army, Jones lived principally in Illinois and wrote *From Here to Eternity,* the long and realistic novel about professional soldiers' lives, which was considered by some critics as possibly a work of genius. Seven years later, his second novel *Some Came Running* was almost universally treated as an overlong and tedious disappointment. With *The Thin Red Line,* another war novel, Jones's reputation has revived. In recent years Jones has spent much time in Paris.

JAMES JONES AND JACK KEROUAC:

NOVELISTS OF DISJUNCTION

by David L. Stevenson

James Jones and Jack Kerouac are two of the most difficult figures in contemporary American letters to discuss critically, because each one, in his own fashion, is at least as much a highly publicized phenomenon of our postwar years, wearing the guise of a novelist, as he is the genuine thing in itself. Jones, with the publication of his first novel, *From Here to Eternity* (1951), a factual recording of violence and sadism in the Army, and Kerouac with the publication of his second novel, *On the Road* (1957), a celebration of the self-nominated "beat" generation and some of its cult leaders, gained an immediate notoriety. They became identified in the press and in the popular mind less as writers of novels than as spokesmen for eccentric rebellion against the prevailing tone and mood of the fifties: Jones, with his preoccupation with raw sex and four-letter words, as representative of an anti-romantic, tough attitude; Kerouac, asserting a childlike and overly innocent view into the nature of things by intuitive "Zen" flashes of illumination, scornful of traditional thought and traditional dress, as spokesman for an unkempt, hobo romanticism.

To be sure, Jones's *From Here to Eternity* and Kerouac's *On the Road* (though not always their later works) were taken as sufficiently significant fiction to be given full-dress reviews, often with praise, in authoritative magazines and journals. Charles Rolo, for example, writing in *Atlantic Monthly* for March 1951, credited Jones's first novel with "tremendous vitality and driving power and graphic authenticity"; and David Dempsey, in *The New York Times Book Review* for September 8, 1957, found in Kerouac's *On the Road* "a descriptive excitement unmatched since the days of Thomas Wolfe." But it was largely as socio-literary exhibit, and not as mere novelist, that Jones was made the subject of a photographic essay in *Life* (February 11, 1957), and that Kerouac was discussed, along with Allen Ginsberg, Gregory Corso, William S. Burroughs and others, in the collected essays in Thomas Parkinson's *A Case Book on the Beats* (1961). Stephen Spender's *Encounter* published articles on Kerouac and the Beatniks in three successive issues, in the summer of 1959, the final one written by Kerouac himself. Again, however, it was not so much as writer but as high priest of a sect that Kerouac was considered important.

Now that the decade of their first flourishing as notorious figures in the public domain is over, however, it is time to consider seriously the achievement of Jones and Kerouac as novelists of the mid-century. And one's immediate impression on rereading their past work, and on reading their most recent fiction, Jones's *The Thin Red Line* (1962) and Kerouac's *Big Sur* (1962), is that neither man seems to be truly a "writer," a literary person, in any normal use of the term. Their fiction has an oddly opaque quality which comes both from its lack of formal structure as well as from a special kind of non-literary prose in which it is written. At the same time one is aware that in Jones's first novel and at times in his most recent one, and in at least two of Kerouac's novels, *On the Road* and *The Dharma Bums,* there is some elusive element, some tantalizing quality that is not easy to deny. One has the sense that both writers have at least partially succeeded in creating significant fiction in these works despite a nagging primitivism and naïveté in their sheer use of language. In these novels, there is a common ground, difficult to define, where reader and writer seem to be communing together over matters of mutual importance.

We can come at this common ground, I think, by noting many of the sharp and evident contrasts between the fiction of Jones and Kerouac on the one hand, and that of the major young American novelists who are their contemporaries, on the other. It is immediately apparent that Jones, with an ear almost wholly deaf not only to normal syntax but to all the enriching nuances and subtleties of the language, and Kerouac with a puerile fancy for what he calls "spontaneous" prose, seem to be in their use of language mere blunderers into the sophisticated literary scene of the contemporary novel. If one holds up for comparison the careful artistry of Eudora Welty or of Mary McCarthy, of Saul Bellow or of William Styron, one sees that in Jones's prose there is a syntactical crudity so often nearly impenetrable that a reader may find himself lost to the novel and questioning the writer's actual degree of literacy. In Kerouac we are faced with a homemade variety of English in which the tangle of images and ideas which other writers sort out and work through is caught of Kerouac, and set down on the page untouched, at the level of pure tangle. The intensity of a reader's resistance to this kind of thing in Kerouac may lack the sharp peaks to be found in his response to Jones. But if one's resistance follows a more or less straight line in reading Kerouac, it is only because the interrelationship of thought and image in his great splotches of "spontaneous" prose remains steadily, not sporadically, inchoate.

In gross technique, both Jones and Kerouac do write the standard American novel of their contemporaries, the novel of detail, the "realistic" novel which has its mode of being in its mimicry of everyday conversation and in its accumulation of hundreds of references to the appearance of everyday things. But despite the comforting familiarity of their use of

realistic detail, the substance of their fiction, and their special
way of looking at this substance, puts them as far outside the
main stream of the major American fiction of their day as do
their private versions of English. This main stream has been
written with the ideals, traditions, value-myths of our time,
though its most representative writers have most often challenged or denied their validity. But Jones's Private Robert E.
Lee Prewitt and his Sergeant Milton Anthony Warden of
From Here to Eternity, or Jack Kerouac's Sal Paradise and
his Dean Moriarty of *On the Road,* have sensibilities, states
of being, in orbit outside the universe of order and value held
in common by most of their articulate contemporaries. As
created characters, they demonstrate the possibility of actual
disjunction between a particular self and society. And if Jones
and Kerouac have genuine validity as novelists, it is because
their way of looking, their "interpretation" of existence in
their fiction, has an importance which generally overrides the
natural ineptness and the self-imposed difficulties of their
separate prose styles.

If one allows for obvious differences in trends and group-
ings in the American novels written in the past decade, and
for radical differences of mind and perception on the part of
individual writers (as between Saul Bellow, Truman Capote
and John Updike, for example), Jones's and Kerouac's contemporaries have produced a body of fiction almost wholly
Erasmian. That is to say, they have been critical of the value
systems within which they have functioned and within which
they were born. The religious, economic, political, moral systems which have accumulated upon us have been our way of
inventing an American civilization, our way of giving coherence and order to our world. And the values and frames
of this invented world which we inhabit, along with the institutions and rites and ceremonies by which we celebrate
them, are so strong that our major writers at mid-century
have either wanted to fight them or to deny them, but not to
escape them. They have felt their separate identities and been

able to breathe within the system only by accepting as obvious adversary that which also sustains them.

Salinger's Holden Caulfield or his Seymour Glass, Saul Bellow's Augie March or his Henderson, Styron's Peyton Loftis or his Cass Kinsolving, Ralph Ellison's Invisible Man, Herbert Gold's Burr Fuller, Eudora Welty's King MacLain, Capote's Miss Holiday Golightly, John Updike's Rabbit Angstrom, even Nabokov's Lolita, although they all exist in an uneasy relationship to the value contrivances, the mythic codes of behavior which they have inherited, nevertheless exist and have their meaning comically, tragically, anxiously within their boundaries. The codes may not seem wholly viable to them. Ellison's central character, as a Negro, has his problems in trying to prosper within the practices and celebrations of American equality and the American pursuit of happiness. Salinger's Holden Caulfield is lost somewhere among the discrepancies luxuriating between the actual reality and the actual make-believe in the values which are the meaning of American life. Styron's Peyton Loftis exists, in part, to deny her mother's common, garden-variety Protestantism, a combination of moral uplift and formalized magic. But it is with the fighting or the denying of existing traditions and myths (or as in Nabokov's *Lolita,* Mary McCarthy's *A Charmed Life,* Eudora Welty's *The Golden Apples,* the expert teasing of them) that our post-World War II fiction has mainly been preoccupied.

Jones and Kerouac are paired and alike in that they write outside this Erasmian quarrel with the values inherent in traditional culture; and, in their very separate ways, they view the world in a fashion quite eccentric to this quarrel. Jones depicts the disjunctive relationship which his central characters have with a traditional, half-mythic America by creating and eulogizing a whole subculture in black-and-white opposition to the accepted one: in *From Here to Eternity,* the subculture of the barracks, bars, and brothels of Regular Army life; in *Some Came Running,* the subculture of the edge-of-town sleazy bar and café. Kerouac depicts the disjunction as one between the reality of the "beats," the hobo Dharma bums, and the unreality of some other kind of American world as, perhaps, imagined in the pages of the Luce publications.

What we cannot deny in Jones and Kerouac, our common ground, is that we sense a genuine validity in their way of looking. We recognize (if perhaps only below the threshold of an everyday acceptance of our social order) that Kerouac's noisy exuberance in the cause of individuals who steal cars, ride the freights, copulate indiscriminately, is a demonstration of the need of a certain kind of person to survive *sui generis,* uniquely, outside the decorums of society. His fiction, along with that of Jones, is a raucous reminder that we have reached a period in our civilization where many of the eager and thoughtful, and not necessarily neurotic, members of the postwar generation find it increasingly difficult to surrender their whole lives to old values and traditional patterns of action. They find it almost, but not quite, meaningless to compete for grades in college, to assume the ideas, attitudes, stances of a profession, to marry and to breed in a suburbia of a thousand gadgets, to drown forever in the rites of neighborhood religion, business golf, weekend cocktail parties, upper-middle-class romantic adultery.

The general reader, no doubt, would find it impossible to survive at all, as the characters of Jones and Kerouac do happily, in the role of willful person who wants no part of conventional America. But our interest in Jones and Kerouac, what we cannot deny them in their novels, is that they tempt us to be aware of the intensity of our generation's and our own personal unease with the kind of world we do inhabit.

II

Jones's way of looking, his portrait of disjunction between society and the self, emerges least scathed by his prose, I think, in his first novel, *From Here to Eternity*. It is true that the central characters in his first two gigantic novels are all sturdy inhabitants of a subculture in our twentieth century, and outsiders to the proprieties of language and behavior of suburbia. The half-literate Regular Army men in his first novel, as well as the inhabitants of the beer joints of Parkman, Illinois, of his second, enjoy existence largely by gambling, drinking and casual sexual encounters with their own kind. But it is only in *From Here to Eternity* that we feel the author's power to stir our awareness of the slim margin of conviction that holds us to a more decorous life. Perhaps the first of his novels, based as he tells us upon real events and a real barracks, represents some combination of Jones's imagination and memory that could function well within the self-imposed limits of a small barracks world. At any rate, there is a genuine vitality in *From Here to Eternity* that is missing from the gross, spread-eagled substance of *Some Came Running,* from the fastidious smallness of Jones's novelette, *The Pistol,* and from the unrelieved, emotional bludgeoning of his most recent work, *The Thin Red Line.*

From Here to Eternity is a long novel (860 pages) unorganized by any central plot, and broken rather arbitrarily into five books, as if to bring coherence to it from the outside. It is essentially the evocation in vulgate prose of the atmosphere of Regular Army life in Hawaii as it existed just before World War II. There are two central characters, the hero, Prewitt, a "goddam hardhead," through whose perceptions we understand much of the action, and Warden, his sergeant, a driving perfectionist who has the respect from his company which it will never give its commissioned officers. The theme of the novel, if it has a small one, is Prewitt's pride in himself as an outsider, and his courageous refusal to be broken to the Army proprieties as demanded by his company commander, Captain "Dynamite" Holmes, regimental boxing coach. Warden, as the lover of Captain Holmes's wife, Karen, because he too is from the ranks and an outsider, is, like Prewitt, obviously a better "man" than his superior officer.

From Here to Eternity is peopled with dozens of minor

characters: the prostitutes of Mrs. Kipfer's New Congress Hotel; Bloom, a boxer for Holmes, affiliated neither with the "ins" nor the "outs," who in despair blows his head off; Angelo Maggio, discharged from the stockade as insane; Berry, beaten to death by a guard with a grub hoe. But Jones's first novel is in no way an important series of character studies. Neither Prewitt nor Warden, let alone the swarming minor figures, is created interestingly in depth. We hear their voices, but we never really know the undersurface of their minds. And the two women who are involved with Prewitt and Warden, Alma Schmidt from Mrs. Kipfer's brothel and Karen Holmes, have no inner lives at all. They have the fictive intensity of sketches from a comic strip. The added fact that the whole novel is written in a prose so lacking in verbal grace or skill as to force a reader to hold on to himself, and the book, as he turns the pages, may well make one wonder at the feeling that one is also in communion with Jones over matters of genuine importance.

But *From Here to Eternity* does actually achieve a strange authenticity. Riley Hughes, reviewing it adversely in *Catholic World* for June 1951, noted that wherever the scene, "we are present at a moral jungle." He described the whole novel as "the humorless polemic of a mind embittered. The result is not art or even reportage; it is an inhuman cry, anarchic and paranoiac." But it is this inhuman cry that is caught up and somehow actually achieved in the long range of the novel. Its Prewitt and its Warden, drifting in a bleak barracks world almost empty of weather, time or idea, give us at last an understanding, not of themselves, but of the dimensions of their world.

It is not the officers' world of Captain Holmes, jockeying for promotion, nor that of his wife with her well-kept house, her legal husband, her legitimate child, her vain wish to charm her lover Warden into becoming a part of it. It is rather a separate, cut-off world of aimless conversation, of the endless sounds of men's voices, talking to each other in the monotonous and casually pornographic language of the

Army. Jones has captured a Neanderthal culture for us in all its richness, in which romantic love is, after all, only sex with Alma Schmidt, the prostitute, because she too thrives in the outskirts of the accepted system. And the basic excitement of *From Here to Eternity* for the general reader lies in the fact that neither Prewitt nor Warden nor Alma Schmidt ever emerges for long from the social and moral purlieus in which each has his being. They act as provocative comment on our own more seemly culture because they are outsiders by choice: they like it that way.

Jones's second novel, *Some Came Running* (1957), is a curiously maddening attempt to recapture as an element in small-town America the same subculture found in the Schofield Barracks of his first one. And it is an even more obvious celebration of the disjunction between individuals and the social order than that found in *From Here to Eternity*. But Jones's second novel remains inert, a huge sprawl of words (1266 pages of them) which wholly lack the central, smoldering core of atmosphere of the first novel. *Some Came Running* gives us in intolerable detail an almost endless series of dreary episodes in the lives of a handful of people living in the small, midwestern town of Parkman, in southern Illinois, between the end of the Second World War and the Korean War. And where *From Here to Eternity* truly caught the essence of a way of life, *Some Came Running* captures only the reader's rage that Jones would attempt to impose as significant art, and as a way of looking at existence, the routine drinking bouts and banal fornications of the outsiders of his Parkman.

There are again two central male characters in *Some Came Running*, Dave Hirsh, who has once written fiction in imitation of Saroyan, and Frank Hirsh, his older brother, a frayed remnant from a Sinclair Lewis novel, an arrogant small-town go-getter. The narrative concern of the book has to do with Dave Hirsh's attempts to write a new novel under the guidance of two Parkman intellectuals, Gwen French and her father, and at the same time to irritate his brother's pride in belonging. The chief episodes by which Dave's disjunction are revealed to us are those demonstrating his awkward and unsuccessful attempts to seduce Gwen French, and his slovenly and triumphant sexual life with the factory girls of Parkman, carried on under the guidance of a local gambler and local philosopher, 'Bama (for Alabama) Dillert.

Some Came Running fails absolutely, I think, on two counts. In the first place, its characters and events lack the sufficient meaning of successful fiction. It insists that we take as important revelation pages of pitilessly dull comment on love, on writing, on religion, as expounded by Parkman's intellectuals, Gwen French and her father. The novel asks us to hold on in admiration while all the inhabitants of the local beer and whiskey joints have their say on the art of love. It asks us to listen, sometimes for twenty pages at a stretch, to the repulsive 'Bama Dillert, eminently successful at poker, constant finger-stirrer of the whiskey in his glass, utterly fascinating to all the factory girls, give long disquisitions on how to drive a car (e.g. "Well, yore main problem in road-drivin is passing") or, more painfully, on the meaning of life (e.g. "The truth is, most Southerners love niggers a lot more than any white people in the North do").

In the second place, *Some Came Running* fails because of its insistently clumsy syntax, gauche to such a degree that a reader catches himself rewriting as he tunnels through the prose (e.g. "The last rise which when you topped it out onto the flat, suddenly there it [the town] was miles away yet . . ." Or "He never should have come back, not after the way hed [sic] left, he felt bad, a deep depression"). The remorselessly flat, commonplace prose of *From Here to Eternity* was in a vulgate English reasonably appropriate to the scenes described. It actually helped create a world. Jones's prose, grown completely tedious in *Some Came Running,* accumulates for its 1266 pages to no similar purpose. It may be close to a factual recording of the ways in which the interpretations of life are phrased at a crossroads bar. But in submitting oneself to such a recording, it is as if one had been tied down in the booth next to Dave, 'Bama Dillert, and one of the female horrors from the local brassière factory. What they have to say to one another achieves the remorseless intensity of nightmare.

James Jones's *The Pistol* (1958), his third and very short novel (158 pages), is a carefully organized and detailed account of the state of mind of Private Richard Mast immediately following the bombing of Pearl Harbor. He is psychically cut off from his fellows and from any sense of a coherent social order by his terror of "a Jap major bearing down on him with a drawn sword to split him in half." The action of the novel is a string of episodes in which Mast demonstrates his animal cunning in retaining possession of a .45 automatic which is his symbol of survival. A reader is conscious of a new neatness of structure in *The Pistol,* and of heroic efforts to clean up the style. But there is still heavy going in the prose. One accepts the young man's obsession with the pistol as valid, but from the outside. His complete alienation from society and his dry, parching fear remain unknowable. His thoughts spill out in such lines as these:

> a sad, bitter melancholy crept over Mast. . . . a feeling that even the longest life was short and the end of it was death and extinction and then rotting away, and that about all a man could expect . . . was frustration, and bitterness and phoniness in everybody, and hatred.

As in *Some Came Running,* the words pile up. The current of communication runs dimly through them.

Jones's fourth novel *The Thin Red Line* (1962), another long book (about 500 pages), is again concerned with World War II. It is a chronological account of the role played by C-for-Charlie company in helping to drive back the Japanese on Guadalcanal in the late fall of 1942. It is like *From Here to Eternity* in that it is essentially a novel of atmosphere, a rendition of the moment-to-moment "feel" of battle, where the stench and the dripping intestines of human bodies broken open by enemy fire are described in accurate and relentless detail. Fewer characters emerge out of the welter of events in *The Thin Red Line* than in Jones's previous works. And, indeed, he often treats the conglomerate C-for-Charlie company as if it were a single individual.

Jones does not advance the syntactical clarity or grace of his prose in *The Thin Red Line* much beyond that achieved in *The Pistol,* and the novel's authentic observations often seem about to be drowned in a sea of words. Moreover, Jones uses the English four-letter cognate of the Latin *pugno* so frequently in the first few pages of the novel that it inadvertently takes on the air of a euphemism. But Jones once more, despite his insensitivity to the sound and flow of language, somehow manages to create in all its terrifying immediacy the timeless, meaningless world of C-for-Charlie company as it fights for its collective life on Guadalcanal. It is an immediacy which is wholly cut off, for those caught up in it, from even the memory of other possibilities. Jones's characters are totally involved in the impersonal sensuality of the pain and the mutilation of war where existence is viewed as a grotesque dance of death, taking place in a senseless universe.

III

Kerouac's first novel, *The Town and the City* (1951), explores with a young writer's compassion and insight first the bewilderment and then the despair of a Massachusetts mill-town family, the Martins, who have been cut loose from their secure, small-town environment by the failure of the family business. The novel moves to a somber focus with the death of the father in a Brooklyn flat. Peter Martin, the son whose experiences are the central ones of the novel, can find no substitute for his first and lost security. In the last pages of the book we view Peter "on a highway one rainy night" hitchhiking, "on the road again, traveling the continent westward." *The Town and the City* is a formally organized work, a completed section of time in the lives of members of one family, and is written in conventional prose. One might call it an unintentional prelude to Kerouac's subsequent disjunction fiction, all of it concerned with other Peter Martins on the road.

Kerouac's second, and most widely read "beat" novel, *On the Road,* is a radical departure from his first both in language and in way of looking. The language is the trial run, and least extravagant example of his "spontaneous" prose. It is simply the unimpeded flow of observation in which sentence structure, image, and idea drift together, released from established rhetorical patterns of English (e.g. "the evening star must be drooping and shedding her sparkler dims on the prairie, which is just before the coming of complete night that blesses the earth, darkens all rivers, cups the peaks and folds the final shore in, and nobody, nobody knows what's going to happen to anybody besides the forlorn rags of growing old. . . .").

Kerouac's way of looking in *On the Road,* and in his subsequent novels, is to present his characters as absolutely cut off from all the normal pursuits of those affiliated with the social order. Where Jones's Prewitt or Dave Hirsh takes pleasure in holding the crude values of his own subculture against those of organized, competitive, traditional society, Kerouac's Dean Moriarty in *On the Road* (or his Japhy Ryder in *The Dharma Bums,* or his Mardou Fox in *The Subterraneans*) is unaware that traditional society is in existence. Dean Moriarty, the young "jailkid" of *On the Road,* is wholly emancipated from normalcy. His speech itself is a delirium of words (e.g. "Man, wow, there's so many things to do, so many things to write"); his sexuality is irrepressible ("to him sex was the one and only holy and important thing in life"); his stealing food, cigarettes, gasoline, women, cars is no private challenge to conformity but simply "a wild yea-saying overburst of American joy."

The substance of Kerouac's "beat" fiction is actually rather hard to describe because it consists of events which occur more or less at random and which have no retained meaning to the characters who are involved in them. A précis of *On the Road* suggests this odd formlessness, I think. The novel consists of five labeled parts. Part One relates in more or less sequential order the chance happenings on a trip made by Sal Paradise (born Peter Martin) from Paterson, New Jersey, to California, and back, from July to October 1947. One is given in some detail descriptions of the people with whom Paradise hitched rides, wild parties and wild conversations with Dean Moriarty during a stopover in Denver, and again during a stopover in San Francisco, a transient love affair with a Mexican girl Paradise picks up in a bus going to Los Angeles, then his trip back to New York. Part Two gives us a second trip, beginning at Christmas 1948, to San Francisco and back, via New Orleans, in which Paradise is accompanied by Moriarty, and in which both have random conversations about ah life, etc., and random sexual adventures. Part Three consists of similar events with much the same cast, on a third trip, in the spring of 1949, from New York to San Francisco and back. Parts Four and Five give the sexual and philosophical discoveries of still another trip by Sal Paradise to Denver, then with Moriarty to Mexico, and finally back once more to New York.

Disjunction for the characters in *On the Road* goes beyond their mere isolation from the traditional values of our society. Indeed, we view the separate episodes in their lives (as the created, narrative "I" of Kerouac's novel views them) as disjunctive in time itself, existing not as parts of a continuum, but in cut-off fragments of time. The lives of Kerouac's characters are presented as a series of happenings, but ones self-isolated, not explored as if they were interrelated in cause and effect sequences. The events in which Sal Paradise, Dean Moriarty, and the endless Marylous, Camilles, Terrys, Galateas are involved are mutually exclusive and have no communicable fictive significance to the reader beyond their mere occurrence. We know far too much about James Jones's Prewitt, perhaps. We know nothing cumulative or coherent about Sal Paradise or Dean Moriarty at all.

In a sense, in accounting for *On the Road* one has accounted for all of Kerouac's "beat" fiction, because its view of events and people as intermixed in sequential episodes having no fictional importance beyond their having happened establishes the pattern for all his later writing. *The Dharma Bums* (1958), for example, opens with Sal Paradise, now called Ray Smith, hopping a freight in Los Angeles for San Francisco. And the substance of the novel is again a series of disconnected episodes involving the created "I" with his own thoughts, with women, with a Zen Buddhist philosopher, Japhy Ryder, in San Francisco, in Berkeley, in the California Sierras, in retreat in North Carolina, in retreat as a firewatcher on a lookout station in Washington. *The Subterraneans* (1958), shorter and more concentrated in time, is a single sexual episode, played out in San Francisco, between Ray Smith, now Leo Percepied, and Mardou Fox, a Negress. It is told through a haze of language more amorphous than that of *On the Road* or of *The Dharma Bums,* which gives this fourth novel an inframundane quality. Here the real world of the cafés, apartments, hills of San Francisco is looked up at as if seen from under the sea. *Big Sur* (1962) opens with Leo Percepied, now Jack Duluoz, fourteen years after the events of *On the Road,* having meetings in San Francisco with Dean Moriarty, now called Cody, private communings with nature in a cabin south of Carmel, and then wild parties with his San Francisco friends in this same cabin. The novel, recorded in Kerouac's curious version of the language, is a disjunctive medley: scenes of eating and drinking and love-making; Duluoz's thoughts about "life," his subcutaneous reactions to the surf of the Pacific and to the sun, and to the drenching fogs blowing through the coastal redwoods.

Kerouac has published seven more "works" in addition to this "beat" group of novels. Three of them seem to be meant as fiction: *Dr. Sax* (1959), disconnected memories of childhood nightmare written in Kerouac's most "spontaneous" prose, including intentionally incoherent fragments of thought and made-up words; *Maggie Cassidy* (1959), a novel concerned with a high school romance, written more nearly in the style of *The Town and the City; Tristessa* (1960), like *The Subterraneans* a single episode in time, here impressions, as related by the narrative "I" of all of Kerouac's fiction, of a Mexican prostitute and dope addict. *Mexico City Blues* (1959) is a collection of 242 "prose poems," sounds, words, phrases strung together around names (Charlie Parker, Allen Ginsberg, William Carlos Williams, et al.) and around concepts (the void, nothingness, sex, death). *Visions of Cody* (1960) purports to be the reproduction of taped recordings, in selected excerpts, in Kerouac's words from "a 600-page character study of the hero of *On the Road,* 'Dean Moriarty,' whose name is now 'Cody Pomeray.'" *Lonesome Traveler* (1960) is a collection of eight sketches of actual and named places as seen by Jack Kerouac, visitor, some of them, curiously, published in *Holiday* magazine. *Book of Dreams* (1961) is best described by Kerouac himself: "a collection of my dreams that I scribbled after I woke up from my sleep— They were all written spontaneously, nonstop. . . ."

Out of all this material, I would single out only *On the Road* and *The Dharma Bums* as reasonably successful fictional studies in disjunction. They represent Kerouac's view of things with the greatest freshness and vivacity, in spite of passages of intolerable innocence where every hobo becomes a cute little Dharma bum, in spite of the unmotivated sentimentality with which Dean Moriarty and Japhy Ryder are presented. These novels are made interesting to us, I think, because Kerouac's sense of his characters' being cut off, disaffiliated, is clearer here, more available to us as part of the malaise of our times than in his other works. As he moves away from the communicable excitement of these first two "beat" novels into *The Subterraneans,* and then into the flood of his later work, one is aware of a falling off of imaginative drive, an accumulation of new episodes of disjunction to no new purpose. He seems to be consciously moving, in his fiction and his poetry, in the direction of greater and greater incoherence. In his *Visions of Cody,* for example, his "spontaneous" prose becomes violated prose (e.g. "Cody stands in the doorway of the poolhall waiting. . . . and he does not know, does not know, cannot know, even I don't really know, and that thing 12, 13 feet over his head, that spot haunted red wall, what it is that makes the approaching night so exciting, so shivering, so all-fired what-where, so deep."). If one steps out of the lurch and stagger of this rhetoric for a moment, one sometimes has the notion that Kerouac is all set to unravel the verbal coherence of the Western world.

IV

One returns, finally, to weigh the common ground we share with Jones and Kerouac, and that which we share in the fiction of their contemporaries. The serious American novel of the present day, characteristically, has involved itself with states of awareness, with kinds of knowing, on the part of characters flourishing, or trying to, within the confines of the social and moral habits and patterns of our society. Its characters and events have acted as neutral territory where reader and writer could communicate, could exchange and intensify a mutual understanding of the somber and deeply powerful crosscurrents of feeling and idea in which the Augie Marches, the Holden Caulfields, the Sam and Eleanor Slovodas (Mailer's "The Man Who Studied Yoga"), the Rabbit Angstroms have been caught.

But both James Jones and Jack Kerouac have chosen to write outside the interests of this kind of novel. And in so doing, they have exempted their work from any piercing awareness of the nature of "being" within our culture at midcentury. In Jones, such characters as Prewitt and Dave Hirsh are sensitive to immediate personal troubles that need solving. But the troubles are not part of an intramural quarrel with the values and the frames of our society; they are merely the fortuitous happenings within a subculture (or in *The Thin Red Line*, happenings in an abattoir). In Kerouac, the atmosphere of disaffiliation is even heavier, more pervasive. Sal Paradise and Dean Moriarty are truly excommunicants from society. Each day, each new acquaintance exists for them in itself, for itself. They are incapable of an accumulation of thoughts and feelings about themselves, or about others. They live in a world without intellectual or moral dimensions where they sense only the separate moments of their lives. They remain essentially unknowable to themselves and to us.

We associate with the major fiction of Jones's and Kerouac's contemporaries a deep consciousness of what it is like to be alive in our society. For a Salinger, for a Styron, existence, on the negative side, is explored as a transient experience haunted by the anxiety of chance or willed termination at any moment. On the positive side, it is viewed as subject to some human choice, but by a choice which takes its thin edge of excitement and pleasure because of the chanciness of all things. Or, to turn to the elder statesmen, there is a sense of "being" in Hemingway or in Faulkner sufficiently strong to make their characters available to us, at times, even below the level of the articulate myths of our civilization in which their lives have meaning. We *become* the wild, beating mind of Frederic Henry as he turns from the dead Catherine Barkley, in *A Farewell to Arms;* we *become* the wild, beating mind of Joe Christmas as he submits to emasculation and death, in *Light in August.*

Perhaps one can say that Jones and Kerouac are literary figures whose perceptions of the role of the excommunicant from our social order, partially maimed by the qualities of their prose, have been sufficiently powerful to excite flutters of interest. They have been able to please by teasing our private fantasies of disaffiliation. There is also an appealing boldness, a highly romantic but specious honesty, in the disjunctive actions of the characters invented by Jones and Kerouac who prefer the crude delights of a subculture or who choose eager, aimless flight, on the road. But in Jones and in Kerouac we are denied all the turbulent awareness of the real nature of existence found in the best postwar fiction. Their present limitation as writers is that they have not yet been able to produce novels in which the created characters are actually conscious of the basic roots of their own being.

GENERATIONS OF THE FIFTIES

BERNARD MALAMUD

Although Bernard Malamud selects his characters chiefly from a
single hyphenated racial group—the Jewish-American—he makes
no ostentatious display of his own Jewish-American background
nor offers any specific clues to the sources of his inspiration. Born
in Brooklyn, in 1914, he claims a normal American childhood.
Though his mother died when he was very young, his home life
was kept happy by the presence of a devoted, hard-working father.
While attending Erasmus High School, Malamud developed a talent
for writing and published his first stories in the school magazine.
In 1936 he graduated from City College and obtained his Master's
degree from Columbia in 1942. In the meantime, while working
for the government, he started writing for the Washington *Post*
and, soon after, his stories began to appear in *Harper's Bazaar,
Partisan Review, Commentary* and *The New Yorker.* Before publication of his first novel, *The Natural,* in 1952, he began teaching
at Oregon State College, where he subsequently became assistant
professor of English. A *Partisan Review* Fellowship and Rocke-
feller grant enabled him to spend a year in Rome with his wife
and two children, and while there he wrote *The Magic Barrel,* a
collection of short stories which won him the National Book
Award in 1959. He is presently teaching at Bennington and has
just completed a collection of stories, *Idiots First.*

HERBERT GOLD

One of the editors of this book recalls sitting with a small group at Columbia College fifteen years ago—a group devoted to talking about Great Books—and hearing the teacher mention how remarkable it was that Columbia had never turned out a writer. By writer he meant a creative literary artist of renown. In the class at the time was Herbert Gold; and studying at the college, or having studied there recently, were John Hollander, Louis Simpson, Jack Kerouac, John Clellan Holmes and Allen Ginsberg, to mention only some of the poets and novelists Columbia turned out around the immediate postwar years. Whether the teacher is reassured by the accomplishments of these students the editor does not know; but Herbert Gold arrived on the literary scene soon afterwards with the publication of his first novel, *Birth of a Hero,* and has maintained a prominent position ever since. Gold was born in Cleveland in 1924 and attended public schools there before coming to Columbia. He has taught at Cornell, Iowa State, Brandeis, Wayne and Western Reserve. As much as any writer of his generation Gold has assumed the duties of the man of letters—as the role is played in contemporary America. Besides teaching, he lectures, reviews and comments on the public occurrence and private experience with wit and insight. He has allowed contemporary life to rub against him and has used the resultant sparks for their power to ignite and illuminate. Gold has been married once, is divorced, has two children and lives at present in San Francisco.

JOHN UPDIKE

John Updike was born in 1932, raised in Shillington, Pennsylvania, where he attended public schools, and was graduated from Harvard *summa cum laude.* After college he studied for a year at the Ruskin School of Fine Arts in Oxford. Then, from 1955 to 1957, he worked on the staff of *The New Yorker.* The generous and wisely indulgent exposure which *The New Yorker* gave Updike's early fiction should silence, but hasn't, the critics of that magazine who seem to be able to find in it only *"New Yorker"* stories. In fact, it may have been because of this close identification with *The New Yorker* that his first novel, *The Poorhouse Fair,* and his second, *Rabbit, Run,* did not stir up the immediate critical excitement which they deserved and which they might otherwise have had. Even when Updike became a writer to talk about, and talk about at length, a strange kind of dynamic synecdoche limited much of the comment. The focus tended to be on the talent rather than on the books—on the thing contained rather than on the container. Also, one met the uneasy implication that somehow Updike had bitten off less than he could chew—a false notion, since everyman's household, the scene of *Rabbit, Run,* may well be the true battlefield of the contemporary American epic. With the publication of *The Centaur,* however, attention is turning from Updike's manifest abilities to the work itself, where, of course, the attention belongs. Updike now lives in Ipswich, Massachusetts, with his wife and children. "I lead," he says, "a quite life."

GENERATIONS OF THE FIFTIES:

MALAMUD, GOLD, AND UPDIKE

by Granville Hicks

The rate of literary development is erratic, whereas the pace of social change is consistently fast. The three writers I am considering—Bernard Malamud, Herbert Gold and John Updike—are all writers of the fifties, and yet they belong to three distinct generations. Malamud, born in 1914, felt the full effect of the Depression, and one sees its influence in almost everything he has written. Gold, ten years younger, was aware of the Depression, but he came to maturity in the war, and his attitudes have largely been shaped by postwar prosperity and postwar anxiety. Updike, born in 1932, is completely a postwar product. That their first stories appeared at approximately the same time is an accident.

As writers, they have certain things in common. For one thing, they all belong to urban rather than to small-town or rural America: Malamud to Brooklyn, Gold to Cleveland and Detroit, Updike to eastern Pennsylvania. For another, they all write admirable short stories as well as novels. They are all skilled technicians, but they are all more than that. None has demonstrated his full powers, though Malamud, as one would expect in view of the differences in age, has probably come closer than the others.

To understand Malamud, one must read closely his short stories, which began appearing in magazines in the late forties, although it was 1958 before a collection, *The Magic Barrel,* was published. Most of them portray poverty-stricken people living in New York or Brooklyn, and Malamud writes of misery with calm poignancy. Here, for instance, is the Job-like first paragraph of "Angel Levine":

> Manischevitz, a tailor, in his fifty-first year suffered many reverses and indignities. Previously a man of comfortable means, he overnight lost all he had, when his establishment caught fire and, after a metal container of cleaning fluid exploded, burned to the ground. Although Manischevitz was insured against fire, damage suits by two customers who had been hurt in the flames deprived him of every penny he had collected. At almost the same time, his son, of much promise, was killed in the war, and his daughter, without so much as a word of warning, married a lout and disappeared with him as off the face of the earth. Thereafter Manischevitz was victimized by excruciating backaches and found himself unable to work even as a presser—the only kind of work available to him—for more than an hour or two, because beyond that the pain from standing became maddening. His Fanny, a good wife and mother, who had taken in washing and sewing, began before his eyes to waste away. Suffering shortness of breath, she at last became seriously ill and took to her bed. The doctor, a former customer of Manischevitz, who out of pity treated them, at first had difficulty diagnosing her ailment but later put it down as hardening of the arteries at an advanced stage. He took Manischevitz aside, prescribed complete rest for her, and in whispers gave him to know there was little hope.

"Angel Levine" turns out to be a fantasy and a surprisingly successful one, but there is nothing fanciful about Manischevitz's sufferings or about the sufferings of other characters in other stories. What Malamud is always asking himself is how people live with great misery. Some of his people are crushed by it, but most survive, through hope or pride or sheer fortitude. The best, moreover, learn to be compassionate, and compassion is, for Malamud, the first of the virtues.

In view of what his stories show about his deep preoccupations, Malamud chose an astonishing theme for his first novel, *The Natural*, published in 1952. Turning away from the slums, turning away from suffering Jews, he wrote about a boy from the West and his adventures in baseball.

I had read *The Natural* twice, with some enjoyment and some bewilderment, before I was told that it parallels the legend of Sir Perceval. This explains some episodes—for instance the hero's relations with the manager of the Knights, Pop Fisher, the legendary Fisher King—and I realize that I should have seen the parallel myself. But many passages continue to puzzle me, and I am not sure what to make of the book as a whole.

It begins in the manner of a fairy story. Roy Hobbs, an awkward, innocent country boy, starts out to conquer the world, armed with a miraculous weapon, a magic bat called Wonderboy. He triumphs over the first giant he encounters, but he is seduced and symbolically slain by a witch. For a dozen or so years, which are passed over by the novel, he is in a state of evil enchantment.

So far all seems clear, but the bulk of the book is concerned with what happens to Roy after he emerges from the spell in which he has been held, and this part of the story is not so easy to follow. Again Roy conquers a giant, and again he is tempted by a witch, but now he is functioning as a hero should, and, with the aid of Wonderboy, he goes from success to success. Then suddenly he falls into an unaccountable slump, from which he emerges only when he meets a good woman. However, the witch continues to attract him, and at last, after a series of catastrophes, he yields to temptation and agrees to throw a game. At the last moment, because he learns that the good woman is pregnant by him, he tries to redeem himself, but Wonderboy is destroyed in a scene of mock Wagnerian grandeur.

As almost always with a novel based on a myth or a legend, the reader is distracted by the effort he has to make to follow the author's intentions, but if the book is not completely successful, there is much to be said for it.

There is no difficulty in evaluating Malamud's second novel, *The Assistant* (1957); it is one of the strongest and finest novels of recent years. The method is not at all that of *The Natural;* Malamud relies wholly on a solid, highly selective realism. In his first chapter he makes us see Morris Bober, a poor Jewish grocer, sixty years of age, who watches his business dwindle to the vanishing point. Yet he is not crushed by his sufferings, and he is capable of compassion towards those poorer than himself. He is, we see, a good man, but an unlucky one, and at the end of the chapter disaster strikes again when two young thugs rob him of what little money he has and one of them beats him.

It is on one of these bandits that the novel is centered. Frank Alpine has been a drifter, but he is a man who dreams of a better life, and he has a conscience. His conscience impels him to try to make restitution to Morris, not only by secretly returning his share of the stolen money but also by working in the store. He has not altogether changed, for, as business improves, he steals from the till, but he can still tell himself that Morris is better off than he was before. He is interested in Morris not only as his victim but also as a man who suffers.

Frank is also increasingly attracted to Morris's daughter, Helen, who has given up her dream of an education in order to help her struggling family. She is an independent young woman, refusing to make the kind of comfortable marriage her mother wants for her. It is through compromises, she believes, that most people ruin their lives, and she is determined to marry only a man she loves and respects. At first Frank seems to her obviously unsuitable, but gradually, to her mother's horror, she responds to his attentions. And then his rash violence drives her away from him.

Although he has been spurned by Helen, and has been driven from the store by her father, who has discovered his peculation, Frank continues to feel his responsibility to the Bober family, and he is on hand in succeeding emergencies. He has identified himself with Morris and assumed his burdens, and he suffers as Morris suffered. In the end we see him as we saw Morris at the beginning, worrying about the decline of business. In the end, too, he becomes a Jew.

Frank, an Italian, is not anti-Semitic, as is his companion in the holdup, but he has known little about Jews, and it is as a Jew that Morris at first fascinates him. "That's what they live for," he thinks early in the story, "to suffer." Near the end, at Morris's funeral: "Suffering, he thought, is like a piece of goods. I bet the Jews could make a suit of clothes out of it." Then he significantly adds: "The other funny thing is that there are more of them around than anybody knows about."

Morris is not orthodox. When Frank questions him about this, he says, "This is not important to me if I taste pig or if I don't. . . . Nobody will tell me that I am not Jewish because I put in my mouth once in a while, when my tongue is dry, a piece of ham. But they will tell me, and I will believe them, if I forget the Law. This means to do what is right, to be honest, to be good. This means to other people. Our life is hard enough. Why should we hurt somebody else? For everybody should be the best, not only for you or me. We ain't animals. This is why we need the Law. This is what a Jew believes." And the rabbi says at the funeral: "Morris Bober was to me a true Jew because he lived in the Jewish experience, which he remembered, and with the Jewish heart. Maybe not to our formal tradition—for this I don't excuse him—but he was true to the spirit of our life—to want for others that which he wants also for himself. . . . He suffered, he endured, but with hope."

Helen passes a sterner judgment on her father: "He made himself a victim. He could, with a little more courage, have been more than he was." There is truth in this, a truth that Malamud, with all his compassion for Morris, will not overlook. But the great truth is spoken by the rabbi: "He suffered, he endured, but with hope."

Frank Alpine, when he becomes a Jew, is not only accepting suffering but also finding hope. Suffering, Malamud is saying, is the human lot, but we need not surrender to despair. To escape suffering is impossible; to live a good life in spite of it is not. Frank, whose hopes hitherto have been vague daydreams, has found a new way to live. As he knows very well, he has become a changed man, whether others know it or not. "If she [Helen] ever looked at him again she would see the same guy on the outside. He could see out but nobody could see in." Helen does believe at one point that he has changed, and she may believe it again. Whether she does or not, the reader, who can look into Frank's heart, has no doubt.

Malamud handles the tools of his craft with the greatest skill, selecting his details with rigorous economy, making every scene count heavily. He lets us into the mind of each of his characters, yet tells us only what we need to know. His dialogue has both verisimilitude and flavor, and his narrative is lean and supple. The novel makes an unforgettable impact.

Malamud's most recent novel, *A New Life* (1961) is in a sense a further development of the theme of *The Assistant*. Its hero, thirty years of age, "formerly a drunkard," as Malamud tells us in the first line, arrives at Cascadia College in the Far West to become an instructor of English. Out of New York City for the first time, about to teach in a college for the first time, he is beginning a new life. What his old life has been we are not immediately told, but readers of *The Magic Barrel* and *The Assistant* know a good deal about it.

Whatever else he is, Levin is a man who has come to believe in the life of the mind, and it soon becomes apparent that the intellect does not flourish at Cascadia. "We don't pretend," his immediate superior tells him, "we're anything more than a typical American state college. . . . There are no geniuses around here to make you uncomfortable. . . . What we don't want around are troublemakers." Adept with gadgets, good at sports, Levin's colleagues care little for books. At first the countryside charms him—and Malamud describes it affectionately—but even that pleasure fades with the coming of the rains. Meanwhile he has been unhappily involved with two or three women.

When Levin's past is revealed to us, it turns out to have been even grimmer than we had supposed. Not only did he grow up in poverty; his father was a criminal and his mother committed suicide. In sodden despair he took to drink, living, as he says, in self-hatred. "I drank, I stank. I was filthy, skin on bone." But then there was a moment of revelation: "I came to believe what I had hoped to, that life is holy. I then became a man of principle."

To be a man of principle, however, is not easy. Levin has an affair with Pauline Gilley, wife of his superior, and this for a time is a great romantic passion. He decides to become a man of action, a reformer, and he takes part in departmental politics, playing the game as ruthlessly as his colleagues. But the romance falls apart, and scandal destroys his academic hopes. In the end he is left without a job and with a woman he no longer loves. The husband Pauline is leaving tells Levin what he can expect, and his gloomy predictions are no doubt accurate. "Why take that load on yourself?" he asks. And Levin answers, "Because I can, you son of a bitch."

The Assistant ends with Frank's conversion, but it is with Levin's conversion that, properly speaking, *A New Life* begins. The pursuit of goodness, Malamud is showing us, is endlessly difficult, for the past can never be decisively outdistanced. Indeed, all reason seems to say that a new life is impossible, and yet the Levins of this world go on trying.

Levin is a clown, a blunderer—as Stanley Edgar Hyman says, a *schlemihl*. Uncouth in appearance, inept with women, ridiculous in the classroom, he is to outward appearances a joke. Like Frank Alpine, he is not even consistently honest.

And yet, ridiculous as he is, he is a hero of our times. That the reader feels this to the bottom of his being is the measure of Malamud's achievement.

A New Life is more flexible in style than *The Assistant,* and there is greater variety of tone and incident. Malamud lets himself range from lyric descriptions of the landscape to quietly savage accounts of the Cascadia faculty. There is comedy, too, and even farce. It is also true that here Malamud deals more fully and more warmly with love than he has before. On the other hand, he does not drive so intensely to the point as in *The Assistant,* and the impact of the book is less dramatic.

Perhaps it is worth noting that the hero of each of Malamud's three novels is an orphan. They have been thrust alone into a world they could not conceive of making. Roy in *The Natural* has extravagant ambitions, and goes down to defeat. Frank in *The Assistant* expects nothing, but he does learn to come to terms with suffering. Levin seeks virtue, and though he finds the way rocky, he persists.

Writing of the three novels, Hyman has said in the *New Leader:* "In a sense, Malamud has moved from the story of Samson, punished for the misuse of his powers, to Job, suffering because chosen to suffer, to Jesus, suffering voluntarily to redeem." This is flying a little high, but the comment nevertheless suggests the seriousness of Malamud's themes and his steady development as a writer.

Herbert Gold was twenty-seven when "The Heart of the Artichoke" was published in the *Hudson Review,* and he already had a contract for his first novel. The earliest of his stories he has chosen to preserve, it appears in *Fifteen by Three,* which contains work by R. V. Cassill and James B. Hall as well as by Gold, and it is the leading story in *Love and Like,* the collections of stories he published in 1960. In both volumes he has interesting comments to make on the story and its origins. In *Fifteen by Three* he writes: " 'The Heart of the Artichoke' is my most personally crucial story because, by writing it, I learned to be a writer. I had a sense of mastering my experience. Not just examining, not just using, but *riding* my world, with full use of my faculties in the open air. . . . After writing a heavily influenced, heavily constructed first novel—to prove I could learn from others—I was ready to throw a rock at the Henry James hive, a rock even at the great juicy Dostoyevsky swarm, and secrete my own gathered sweets into my own homemade jug."

In *Love and Like* Gold also speaks of his feeling on completing the story that he was his own man, and goes on to talk of his state of mind: "Partly I was nourished by a happy time in my life. I was finished with school, having fun on the G. I. Bill and a Fulbright, author of a book which had just been accepted by a publisher; I was about to become a father; I was rediscovering the American language by learning French and rediscovering the city of Cleveland by riding a bicycle in Paris."

In essentials the story is frankly autobiographical. The hero, Daniel Berman, is twelve. His father runs a store in Cleveland, and both he and Daniel's mother are hard workers. They expect Dan to work, too, but he wants to play as the other boys of the neighborhood in which he lives are able to do, and he is interested in girls. The conflict between the generations is portrayed with warmth and humor, and the climax is beautifully organized.

But I am interested in the story just now because of what it tells us about Gold's background. There he was, in 1936, the son of an immigrant grocer. And here he is, fifteen years later, living in Paris with a wife and a child-to-be. In the meantime he has served in Army Military Intelligence, has taken his A.B. and A.M. at Columbia, has had a Fulbright Fellowship, and has written a novel. It is no wonder that he has so often spoken of the sense of possibility.

He had a sense of possibility in literary matters, too. He had written a novel in one style, and now he was writing a story in quite a different style. The novel, which we shall be looking at in a moment, is about a middle-aged man, and cannot possibly be autobiographical; the story makes frank use of personal experience. There were, Gold may well have felt, no limits to what he could do.

He has done a great deal in the years since he wrote "The Heart of the Artichoke," and I propose to scrutinize his achievement, but first let us look at him at this moment, which he has himself defined as crucial. In the work of many of Gold's contemporaries the world is closing in on the characters. In Gold's novels the world is open. Of course it closes in some times on some characters, but to the last gasp possibility remains.

Birth of a Hero (1951), as I have said, is a novel about a middle-aged man, Reuben Flair, who is living a thoroughly respectable, thoroughly empty life. Then at forty-five he falls in love—for the first time, although he has a wife and children. A woman named Lydia Fortiner discerns in him possibilities—heroic possibilities, she says—that no one else has seen, and, lo and behold, they flourish. It is an extraordinary theme for a man in his middle twenties to choose.

The style of *Birth of a Hero* is disciplined and mature but conventional, and Gold has written no more in this vein. On the other hand, it would be wrong to dismiss the novel as a false start, for it announces themes with which Gold has been persistently concerned. Reuben Flair has never come to terms with himself, and he has never had a fruitful relationship with another person. Lydia Fortiner helps him to discover himself and at the same time frees him to fall in love with her. He becomes a different man and in the end a better husband and father.

Something must also be said about Larry Fortiner, whom Reuben at first believes to be Lydia's brother, though he is in fact her husband. Larry is a ne'er-do-well, irresponsible, antisocial, but he has in him—and always has had—the spark of life. He has failed his wife, and ultimately he destroys himself, but he plays an essential part in the development of Reuben's heroic possibilities.

The Prospect Before Us (1954) seems at first glance to

have been written by a different author. This is the way it begins: "The prospect before us might be Prospect Avenue in Cleveland, where Harry Bowers, that extra-nice fellow, he finally made his fortune. He had the best building, the nicest parcel, the loveliest property you could want there among the fried eggeries, the beer-and-tar strollers, the spitting hopers, and, on a midsummer's morning, the hot grasshopper kids playing in garbage-can fires at the curbs of Prospect." And here is a further word about the hero: "Everyone loved Harry Bowers, not for his snappy Palm Beach and his way with cash, but simply because he was a nice guy to see on Prospect, always good for a big hello and an admirer of fresh pizza and egg rolls to take out."

Gold's use of the vernacular immerses the reader in the garish world of Harry Bowers. Bowers, an immigrant who has prospered just within the boundaries of respectability, is the proprietor of a small hotel. On the surface he is not a prepossessing character: middle-aged and fat, with a kind of professional cheeriness and a stock of corny jokes, with a quick eye for a fast buck and the showy manners of a good spender. But, like Larry Fortiner, he has an inextinguishable vitality, and, like Reuben Flair, he develops a capacity for heroism. Gold has referred to him as "an old country individualist who got in terrible trouble because he insisted on following his stubborn personal morality in business in America."

What happens is that an organization interested in the rights of Negroes decides to make a test in Harry's hotel, and sends a young woman to take a room there. Harry knows what is going on, and he knows the tricks by which hotel proprietors deal with such awkward situations, but he decides to play the game straight. This is partly a matter of pride. He is king on Prospect Avenue, and he believes he can beat the pressures that he knows will be exerted on him. In any case he cannot give in without losing his self-respect. Of course he is defeated. Customers leave, business associates threaten and try violence, the bank bears down. In the end his kingdom is destroyed and he with it.

Although it touches on the evils of segregation, *The Prospect Before Us* is not a novel about the race problem. Its theme is the success-in-failure of Harry Bowers, and it is because he has achieved new stature as a human being that his death has elements of tragedy. However it begins, his gesture of defiance develops into a full-fledged expression of integrity. In the same way his affair with the girl he has befriended becomes a deep and significant relationship. Once more we have witnessed the birth of a hero.

In *The Man Who Was Not With It* (1956) Gold continued his experiment with the vernacular, and here his effect was heightened by his use of the special jargon cultivated by those who work in carnivals. This is his description of Grack, one of the book's leading characters: "He brought his hand with the horny nail of his index finger in a wide circle, swinging an invisible lasso, lopping their belly-eyed gaze and taking it at his eye. They were caught first at the spongy wart on his nose and then in his eyes, working it for themselves now like the flies caught wriggling in sticky-paper. That wart made a stiff flop when he tossed his head in beckon and hitch toward the pungent foot-darkened sawdust at the door of Grack's Zoo, a gobble of cajolery up from his throat and the swollen Adam's apple." As with the description of Harry Bowers, the style becomes part of the characterization. And Grack at the beginning is rather like Bowers—and to a degree like Larry Fortiner—in his vitality.

The central figure in *The Man Who Was Not With It* is a young fellow named Bud, who works for the carnival in various capacities. He has run away from a home that is unsatisfactory to him, but he is not quite at ease in the carnival, and he has found his real refuge in drugs. Grack, who has become a substitute father to him, makes an heroic effort to help him to break the habit. The effort succeeds, and Bud returns to his true father and to the girl he once thought he loved, but, like many another, he discovers that he can't go home again.

However, Bud has begun to change, and, though he returns to the carnival, it is in a different spirit. Proof of the change is found in the fact that he is now capable of falling fully in love, and his relationship with Joy pushes him along the road to maturity. But Grack, in the meantime, has deteriorated; feeling himself betrayed by Bud, he has taken to drugs. Moved by gratitude, affection and a sense of guilt, Bud accepts responsibility for Grack, but at the same time he is aware that his love for Joy also entails responsibilities. His ability to deal with this conflict of loyalties demonstrates that he has achieved manhood.

The Man Who Was Not With It is, in my view, the most impressive of Gold's novels. Like its predecessors, it deals with the twin problems of self-discovery and the capacity for love, and here, it seems to me, Gold has fully succeeded in saying what he wants to say. Bud, as we first see him, is completely alienated; he is not even at home in the make-believe world of the carnival. But when he learns to accept himself, he also learns to accept others. He can become a good husband, a good friend, even a good son.

In *The Optimist* (1959) Gold attempted a study of a man who fails at exactly the point at which Reuben Flair, Harry Bowers and Bud succeed, a man who fails to come to terms with himself and fails to establish a healthy relationship with others. In its range it is his most ambitious novel. We see Burr Fuller first as a college student, and we meet his classmates and the two girls in whom he is interested. Then we see him as a soldier in World War II—and this section contains the best chapters in the book. Finally we see him ten years after the war, a young lawyer with political aspirations and a marriage that is falling apart.

Burr is perhaps a typical young man of his times, intelligent but essentially superficial, always asserting the self and never really understanding it, not irresponsible in any gross way and yet incapable of recognizing his true responsibilities. He not only lacks strong political principles; he is not even truly serious about a political career as a career. The collapse of his marriage and the frustration of his ambitions do not change him. He is still convinced that life will be good to him, still greedy for more and more and more.

If the novel does not quite do what Gold wants it to, there seems to be two explanations. In the first place, the character of Burr is not sharply enough defined; Gold does not put his finger on what are supposed to be Burr's fatal flaws. More important, the political theme is outweighed by the domestic theme. Burr's campaign against his bird-brained opponent never seems completely real, whereas his unhappy relations with Laura are revealed with depressing thoroughness. Moreover, Laura is so wretchedly neurotic that Burr inevitably has the reader's sympathy. He may be acting badly, one feels, but who in his circumstances wouldn't? Since Gold, at the time he was writing the novel, was concerned with domestic problems of his own—about which he wrote an article in the *Atlantic Monthly*—one may reasonably surmise that his troubles crept into the book and for a while dominated it.

Just as Gold has always had, Burr has a sense of possibility. Even at the end, after he has been driven to the thought of suicide, he reaches out with passionate longing and undiminished hope. To some extent the novel may be regarded as a warning against the sense of possibility, not because hopefulness is bad in itself but because it can become bad unless it leads to a disciplined consideration of means. That is the difference, as I see it, between Gold and the character he has created: at the outset and all through the war episodes they are a good deal alike, but Gold has worked hard to make himself a writer whereas Burr expects to have political success and everything else he wants bestowed on him from heaven.

Therefore Be Bold (1960) is a story of youth. The central character, Danny Berman, appeared as early as 1951 in "The Heart of the Artichoke," and we learn from a note that the novel was begun in 1950. Gold has written of the desire to "find the truth by finding the meaning of childhood," and in this novel, which he worked on intermittently over a period of ten years, we have his major effort to record that meaning.

Not surprisingly, he is impressed, as he looks back on his adolescence, by the sense of possibility. Of course he is aware of the frustrations and defeats of youth, but they are less important than the discoveries, the openings up. He is also concerned with the beginnings of the struggle to define the self and bring it into a sound relationship with others.

In order to celebrate the strength of youthful feelings, Gold has chosen a high-pitched style, which has received some criticism. There are points at which objection seems legitimate, but it is the intensity of the style that gives the book its power.

Salt, Gold's latest novel, is a more ambitious book than *Therefore Be Bold* and a more difficult one to evaluate. It is a story of two men in their early thirties, one a bachelor, the other recently divorced. Like its predecessors, it is concerned with love, but it is also in part a satire on modern, prosperous, sex-hungry Manhattan. One of the young men shrinks from any true involvement, whereas the other wants love but, after a disastrous marriage, is afraid of it. The question one has to ask is whether the two men are sharply enough differentiated to make Gold's point. Gold knows his way around New York, and the novel is smartly up-to-date, but in the end it is less satisfying than *The Man Who Was Not With It.*

In addition to his novels. Gold has written many short stories, which have appeared in all sorts of magazines, from gaudy slicks such as *Playboy* to sober quarterlies such as *Hudson Review.* Fifteen of the stories are included in *Love and Like* (1960). Gold makes a sharp distinction between the aims of the novel and the aims of the short story. "What the novelist seems to be doing at his philosophical best," he has written, "is to explore possibility. He cuts loose from the expected and sees another possibility for an entire life. The great novelists, building new worlds, are also great moralists by implication—committed, before all else, to the intense valuation of human experience." The short story, he goes on, makes fewer demands on the reader, offers less of a challenge, but has its own value. "A good story can send out a reassuring flash of feeling to those others out there. We take a peek together, you and I, at the moving image of desire— this is literature. It helps to make sure of life for a time."

The best of his stories are lyric expressions of this kind. I have already spoken of "The Heart of the Artichoke," and I admire equally a companion story, "Aristotle and the Hired Thugs." Among other first-rate stories are "The Burglars and the Boy," "Susanna at the Beach," and "Ti-Moune." The ambitious title story, which throws some light on *The Optimist*, is the story he chose to include in *Fiction of the Fifties*, an anthology he edited in 1960.

Gold has been prolific, and there are times when I wish he would be more self-critical, but much of his work is of high quality. In his contribution to *The Living Novel* (1957) he said: "The novelist must reach for the grownup, risking, athletic personality, surely must in some way be this person, in order to find a hero who gives the sense of men at their best on earth; and catch him finally where his great gifts do not suffice: this is tragedy." He dares to look for heroes, and he finds them in unlikely places. Like Malamud, he dares to believe that men can be better than they are.

After being graduated from Harvard in 1954 and spending a year at the Ruskin School of Drawing and Fine Art in Oxford, John Updike went to work on *The New Yorker*—one of the countless bright young college graduates who have been employed by that magazine. He was soon contributing short stories, poems and parodies. His first book, *The Carpentered Hen*, was a collection of verse. It was followed by a novel, *The Poorhouse Fair*, and by a volume of short stories, *The Same Door*, both in 1959. In 1960 he published a second novel, *Rabbit, Run*. Although he is no longer on the staff of *The New Yorker*, his work, in many genres, frequently appears in that magazine.

The stories in *The Same Door* are nicely done in a manner that is quite suitable to *The New Yorker*. Each has its reward-

ing moment of insight, but none is so compelling as the best
stories of either Malamud or Gold. The most impressive, it
seems to me, are "A Gift from the City," which has depth,
and "The Happiest I've Been," which is warm and tender,
somewhat in the Salinger fashion.

Updike's early short stories made it clear that he was gifted,
but it was with his two novels, and particularly, I feel, the
second, that he made his bid for recognition as a serious
writer.

The Poorhouse Fair is like Gold's first novel, *Birth of a
Hero,* and Malamud's, *The Natural,* in that it does not seem
characteristic of its author. It is a tour de force—a young man
writing about old people—and perhaps this challenge was one
of the attractions the subject had for Updike. Why else it appealed to him I cannot easily imagine.

At bottom the story is simple enough. We have the old people in the poorhouse, a few of them clearly individualized,
and we have the manager of the establishment, the prefect as
he is called, a man named Conner. Conner is truly devoted to
the welfare of the men and women in his charge, but his conception of the good life is narrowly materialistic. The annual
fair is the one great break in the monotony of poorhouse existence, and the old people react to it in their various ways.
Then an unprecedented incident takes place: several of the
old men throw stones at Conner. The wisest old man offers
Conner a sufficient explanation: "Boredom is a terrible force."
But the prefect has been badly shaken.

Updike embroiders his story in various ways: there are
some handsome if not always quite relevant descriptions;
much is made of little happenings such as the escape of a
parakeet; there are some amusing fragments of conversations
that go on among the visitors to the fair. The principal complication, however, is a projection of the story into the indefinite future. We are given few details, but we gather that
there is universal peace, that America is a welfare state, that
prosperity and boredom reign.

Something could surely be done with this, but Updike hasn't

tried hard enough. A poorhouse—the very word has vanished from the vocabulary of social workers—is not a particularly apt symbol for the modern welfare state, and Conner is a feeble embodiment of the bureaucratic spirit. I have an impression that what Updike was trying to say was important to him, but he was unwilling to look squarely at the problem he raised. As a result, the problem seems a distraction, and the book is little more than a promising literary exercise.

Rabbit, Run, on the other hand, is strongly felt. Certain short stories and some passages in *The Poorhouse Fair* have suggested that Updike is concerned with what can be called the religious view of life, though it is by no means sure that he has committed himself to any body of dogma. As epigraph for *Rabbit, Run* he has chosen a passage from Pascal: "The motions of Grace, the hardness of the heart; external circumstances." These elements make up the life of Rabbit Angstrom.

In high school Rabbit was an excellent and locally famous basketball player. Now, at twenty-six, he has a dull job and a wife who has lost all charm for him. These circumstances are more than he can bear, and, hardening his heart, he runs away. He returns, but he runs again and again before the story ends.

The genesis of the novel can be found in an early story called "Ace in the Hole," but there Updike showed us only a young man who has unhappily outlived his days of athletic glory. *Rabbit, Run* goes deeper than that. His prowess on the basketball court has given Rabbit an ideal of excellence. "I *was* great," he tells a girl. "It's the fact. I mean, I'm not good for anything now but I really was good at that." To another character he says: "I once played a game real well. I really did. And after you're first-rate at something, no matter what, it kind of takes the kick out of being second-rate."

Rabbit has an inner life of considerable intensity. After his fashion he is religious; a friendly clergyman, perhaps not wholly reliable, calls him a mystic. At any rate he has a feeling for what he believes to be "rightness" in a situation, and he is convinced that his impulses are somehow inspired. "He is a good man," the clergyman says, and it is true that he aspires to goodness. He responds, however erratically and uncertainly, to "the motions of Grace."

Rabbit is not converted, as are certain of Malamud's heroes; such grace as he has is in him from the beginning, and the novel is concerned with its fitful operation. He is not redeemed; in fact, at the end he is running once more. But, after all that has happened, he has not surrendered to despair. I think Updike is saying that, in a world so empty and aimless as Rabbit's, even this modicum of grace is better than nothing, but he may be saying that it is not enough. However this may be, we are made to feel the reality of Rabbit's ordeal. He inflicts plenty of suffering on others, but he also suffers himself, and his hope, such as it is, is hard won.

Like Gold, Updike committed himself early to the literary life, and he has been even more precociously successful. At first it was not certain that he sought a deeper involvement than would suit the pages of *The New Yorker*, but with *Rabbit, Run* he showed his seriousness, and in some of the recent stories in *The New Yorker* itself he has pushed very far indeed beyond any easy formula. These stories, as collected in *Pigeon Feathers* (1962), give me great hope for his future.

Take, for instance, the title story, which is a poignant and wholly convincing description of a boy's religious experience. Or take "Lifeguard," really one long, beautifully sustained metaphor, concerned on several levels with great problems of human destiny. Most impressive of all are the two long stories at the end, one in three parts, the other in four. In each of these stories apparently unrelated experiences are juxtaposed, and the unity derives from the author's vision of life, whose virtue it is that it can embrace just such complexity. Of the brilliance of Updike's writing there has never been any question, but now we find him setting himself more and more difficult tasks and looking more and more deeply into the minds and hearts of men.

When *The Centaur* appeared (1963), there was again

much admiration expressed for the writing, which is indeed superb. The first chapter, in which the central character is alternately a harried schoolteacher and a centaur, is a magnificent tour de force, and, in quite a different vein, the description of the Pennsylvania countryside after a snowstorm is a rich achievement. What many critics had doubts about was the use of mythology, not so much the reliance on the central Chiron-Prometheus myth as the sometimes mechanical identification of every single character in the novel with a god or hero. But in any case the story of the boy and his father is clear and touching. Updike has said that he thought of the book as a companion piece to *Rabbit, Run,* the point being, I suppose, that Peter is saved by his father's sacrifice from Rabbit's fate. Even if the novel was not the major work Updike's admirers have been hoping for, it was a brilliant performance.

As I suggested at the beginning, the grouping of these three writers is pretty arbitrary, but it has by now become clear that they have more in common than was at first apparent. In particular, all are preoccupied with the theme of redemption. Updike began by simply pointing out the need for redemption, but of late he has undertaken bolder explorations. Gold has shown redemption as achieved through the inseparable processes of discovery of self and love of others. Malamud has left the mechanism of redemption a mystery, but he has shown us the reality of redemption in the most unlikely circumstances.

Redemption, of course, is also the theme of other contemporary novelists. There is nothing surprising about this. The ebbing of the sea of faith left mankind with the problem of salvation on earth. Many thinkers in the past two centuries have argued that the way to save the individual was to save society. Few great writers, however, have believed this, and today, for obvious reasons, most of us are skeptics. We do not believe that society will be saved, and we doubt that the salvation of society would achieve the redemption of the individual. If the individual is to be redeemed, he must find the path. Malamud, Gold and Updike are all looking for paths, and Malamud and Gold, at least, convince us, by the power of their imaginations, that paths can be found.

THE NOVELS OF MARY MCCARTHY

Mary McCarthy's reputation in American letters rests as securely on her non-fiction—her literary and social criticism, impressions of travel abroad and autobiographical writing—as on her novels and short stories. But it was with her fiction that she first attracted wide notice: her first book, *The Company She Keeps,* published in 1942, marked her at once as a social satirist with Stendhalian psychological insights. Born in Seattle, Washington, in 1912, of an Irish father and part-Jewish mother, Miss McCarthy was orphaned at six and educated at Forest Ridge Convent in Seattle and Annie Wright Seminary in Tacoma. Her earliest recollections center around the austere Victorian household of her father's aunt and uncle in Minneapolis where she and her three brothers lived for five years. *Memories of a Catholic Girlhood* is partly a record of those bleak years. At Vassar, from which she was graduated with highest honors in 1933, she pursued her early interest in the classics and in the French psychological novelists. In New York, she straightway established herself as a book and drama critic for the *Nation* and the *New Republic,* and in 1937 became an editor of *Partisan Review.* Married first to actor-playwright, Harold Johnrod (whom she divorced in 1936) and later to the critic, Edmund Wilson, she moved in left-wing intellectual circles but never fully committed herself to Stalinist dogma. "My Confession," a magazine article published in 1953, is her candid account of the largely fortuitous nature of her political "conversions" from her earliest radical days to her present-day liberal position. After 1942 she abandoned regular reviewing and took up teaching, first at Bard College, then at Sarah Lawrence. In the 1950s, besides a novel, an autobiography and a book of critical pieces, she published two unique works of travel and art criticism, *Venice Observed* and *Stones of Florence*. Since her divorce from Edmund Wilson in 1938, she has married twice. Presently, as Mrs. James West, she is living in Paris where she completed her new novel, *The Group*.

THE NOVELS OF

MARY MCCARTHY

by *John Chamberlain*

Satire, so one tends to assume, is what results when a person
with a sure hold on his values decides to mock a world which
outrages those values at every important turn. A conscious
perspective is supposedly all-important: the satirist, by implication, must have his clear view of utopia, a private vision of
perfection guaranteed to impart gusto and savagery to the assault on the knaveries of the comic villain or the shortcomings
of the bumbler who is a veritable caricature of all bumblers.

Such assumptions and definitions are all very well, but
what is one to do when they fail to net the fish? The case
of Mary McCarthy, for example, offers a piquant commentary
on the conventional thinking about satire. For here we have
a young woman (one will always think of her as young as
long as she retains her engaging insouciance and her killer instinct) who has written five satirical novels and a collection of
shorter fictional essays in controlled malice without any conscious recognition of the disparity between her professed beliefs and the actual touchstones that give point to her ironies.
Three of the novels—*The Company She Keeps, The Oasis,
The Groves of Academe*—are first-rate in their candid and

witty exposure of types of fashionable radicals; and the shorter fictions (see the purely fictional first half of *Cast a Cold Eye*) have the merit of sustained mood pieces carried out with a cauterizing detachment. A new novel, *The Group,* which is Mary McCarthy's most ambitious work, sometimes deserts satire for a straight realism that is infused with a surprisingly poignant tenderness, but insofar as it is a satirical story of what it was like to come of age in the New Deal decade it makes an implicit case for an older America that is not sustained when Miss McCarthy speaks in what she calls her "own voice." Another novel, *A Charmed Life,* which preceded *The Group* in point of writing, is full of incidental good things, but it must rank as an ambitious failure for the simple reason that the heroine (if that is the word for Martha Sinnott) never quite comes into focus. Yet even in *A Charmed Life* Miss McCarthy's fiction is living proof that one can be good, and sometimes very good, without quite being conscious of one's actual frame of moral reference. One can build better than one knows.

To make the point plain, one has only to compare the fiction of Mary McCarthy with that of her English opposite number, Evelyn Waugh. The Englishman's satirical themes are, of course, much broader than Miss McCarthy's, his chosen enemies much more powerful. Nevertheless the two writers are alike when it comes to mocking the more orthodox Leftists and their allies among the crypto-Stalinists (or crypto-Khrushchevists) of the so-called Liberal Establishment. With Waugh, the mockery demonstrably proceeds from a sure belief in a utopian alternative to the present. A Roman Catholic in religion, an Old School Empire man in external politics, a supporter of know-your-place-and-métier in matters of internal social organization, Waugh has fashioned his private utopia by imagining a marriage of Hilaire Belloc's image of a merry and quite religiously orthodox pre-Tudor England to the nineteenth-century Empire of Rudyard Kipling. The assumption that the Plantagenet kings might have shouldered the White Man's Burden may seem fantastic after three centuries and more of Tudors, Stuarts and Hanoverians, to say nothing of Labour Party and welfare state, but it enables Mr. Waugh to bring certainty of aim to his Crouchback trilogy. To Guy Crouchback, good English Catholic, World War II was justified when the rats (the Nazis, the Communists) were all aboard the same ship by virtue of the Nazi-Soviet Pact. But when a no longer gallant England refused to fight a war within a war once the Soviets had been compelled by events to switch sides, Crouchback (as Waugh's alter ego) lost interest in the struggle. The enemy suddenly appeared on the home front in the local Liberal Establishment supporters of the likes of Tito. And Churchill, who had once spoken of Stalin as a "monster," was unaccountably one of the "liberals" who was willing to sup with the devil to gain a shortsighted end.

Like Evelyn Waugh, Mary McCarthy would apply the "rat" appellation to both Nazis and Stalinists; one can imagine her writing a Crouchback trilogy with much the same political emphasis in identifying the villains. But her private utopia, unlike Waugh's, is, to quote from her own statement to Elisabeth Niebuhr in the Winter-Spring 1962 issue of the *Paris Review,* "a kind of libertarian socialism, a decentralized socialism." Her politics is "dissident," and, like the American tourist in her short story, "The Cicerone," she would oppose the Italian Communist Togliatti "from the *left.*" The italics are Mary McCarthy's, a fierce emphasis on her own idea of radical purity.

Logically considered, Mary McCarthy's dream of a decentralized socialism must rank as a fantasy, for if the world were to be organized as a collection of autonomous Brook Farms or Fourieristic "phalanxes," the problem of handling the relationships, productive and otherwise, between the utopian communities would soon engage the "centralist" energies of people who insist on such things as order, the standard of living or merely the seizure of power. But this is not the place to argue with Miss McCarthy's views on political economy. For purposes of fictional satire it is certainly just as valid to expose Stalinism and "liberal" conniving with Stalinists from the "libertarian socialist" left as it is to attack them from the right. The good satirist doesn't argue; he shows—and if his animating dream is hardly a realistic possibility it may still serve as a useful literary springboard.

But if the realism of Miss McCarthy's political economy is not at issue here, its actual aesthetic relevance to her stories must be questioned. The point is that Mary McCarthy's fiction never achieves its force or meaning from her professed political orientation. Her utopia is never really brought to bear on her subject matter. And her conclusions follow, not from her romantic identification with Trotskyism (in an earlier phase) or with "libertarian socialism" (in a later), but from an unconscious application of far less revolutionary common sense. She achieves Waugh-like effects because, actually, she respects a rather traditional sense of personal morality. And it may be significant that she had a Catholic upbringing (see her extraordinarily interesting and revealing autobiography of her young years, *Memories of a Catholic Girlhood* [1957], which is in many ways her best book).

Here some synopses and individual specifications are in order. Miss McCarthy's first fiction, *The Company She Keeps* (1942), is a linked cycle of short stories, called a novel by courtesy, about a young woman of Manhattan named Margaret Sargent. A creature of the nineteen-thirties, Miss Sargent is a romantic adherent of the Trotsky movement. She will defend Trotsky (or the Spanish anarchists, or anyone else who is "dissident" Left) against the callously bureaucratic Stalinists at the drop of a handkerchief. But Miss McCarthy crosses up her values by causing Meg Sargent to say, in a moment of canny self-revelation, that she is "not even political." It is just that she has a temperamental need to identify herself with lost causes, with outcasts. In nineteenth-century Ireland she would have been a Fenian; in Civil War Atlanta she would have sung sad songs about the Confederate soldier's pin-up, Lorena. The reason for Meg Sargent's espousal of a chronic underdoggery, as is suggested in the final episode

in *The Company She Keeps,* is Freudian in nature. Meg
Sargent's Catholic mother died young, her father (a Protestant and a puritan) turned the girl over to an unsympathetic
Catholic aunt for a convent-dominated upbringing out of a
misplaced sense of loyalty to the presumed wishes of the
mother. Thus the father image has been defiled for the
daughter, who quickly loses her faith in both Church and
family. So, though Miss McCarthy still exalts her "libertarian
socialist" utopia as the value-giving "alternative" to her satires
on the present, it is not really socialist politics or socialist
ethics that gives meaning to *The Company She Keeps.*
What galvanizes everything is Miss Sargent's troubled and
defective childhood—which, incidentally, seems lifted with
only slight distortions from Mary McCarthy's own autobiography.

Meg Sargent is in search of an identity, of wholeness—and
this very human predicament is hardly a subject for satire.
But the other characters in the book, the "company she
keeps," can still be satirized. True enough, Mr. Sheer, the
shady dealer in *objets d'art* who employed Meg Sargent for
a time, gets favorable treatment, but this is because he too is
a certifiable underdog. The satirist's acids really begin to work
on the "Man in the Brooks Brothers Shirt," a steel company
executive whose sin is that he is a bourgeois, a Babbitt. Meg
Sargent, in her romantic Trotskyist affiliation, would like to
send this Brooks Brothers fellow from an adulterous Pullman
compartment bed to Spain, to lead a Republican cadre against
the fascist Franco. That would be a real redemption; in her
daydreams Meg Sargent imagines the kudos that would come
to her for having made a Byronic convert of a porcine
middle-aged commercial traveler.

Then there is Jim Barnett, the "Intellectual as a Yale Man,"
who in due course gets the works for being in Meg Sargent's
kept company. Jim Barnett lacks the courage to become an
out-and-out Marxist in either theory or action. As Mabel
Dodge Luhan once said of the young socialist, Walter Lipp-
mann, Jim Barnett would never lose an eye in a fight. Another

member of the kept company is Pflaumen, the "genial host," a wealthy eclectic in his appreciation of radical types. Though she is "not even political" when she is honest about herself, Meg Sargent lets politics shape her attitude toward the steel executive and the Yale intellectual and the genial rich man who slums among types on the Left.

The fact that Meg Sargent is an ambivalent young woman does not destroy the validity of *The Company She Keeps* as realism. But Miss McCarthy, Meg's creator, is ambivalent, too—and it is never quite certain which particular split in the heroine's personality is supposed to be the dominating factor in the book's ironic design. Indeed, Mary McCarthy has herself confessed (in the *Paris Review* interview) to having been swept into the Trotskyite movement "by accident." At a party she had told James Farrell, author of *Studs Lonigan,* that she thought Trotsky was entitled to a hearing and to the right of asylum. This was in the mid-thirties, at the time of the furore over the Moscow trials. The next thing she knew she was on a letterhead of something calling itself the American Committee for the Defense of Leon Trotsky. Although Farrell's presumption made her furious for a moment, she decided to stay on the letterhead when a number of pusillanimous people began to withdraw because of Stalinist pressure. She has remained a member of the anti-Stalinist Left ever since.

Consciously, then, Mary McCarthy would have liked to pack the Brooks Brothers Shirt capitalist off to Spain to side, not with the Stalinists, but with the anarcho-syndicalists. She would have liked to steal Jim Barnett, the Yale "intellectual," from Henry Luce in order to add him to the staff of the *Partisan Review* or to Dwight Macdonald's libertarian-left *Politics,* a short-lived magazine which took fiendish pleasure in burlesquing the mental fog that resulted when the warm winds of liberal doctrine came into contact with the Soviet glacier. But Mary McCarthy's conscious preferences in utopianism are not what make Meg Sargent's friends satirizable. What renders the Brooks Brothers Shirt character a fit candidate for ironical treatment is his flibberty-jibberty approach to all matters of the intellect. He doesn't know what he thinks or why he thinks it. This intellectual flabbiness has nothing to do with the steel business as a capitalist manifestation. As for Jim Barnett, the Yale man, it is his lack of fundamental seriousness that is his basic fault. This, as Mary McCarthy shows, is a matter for truly valid satirical exposure. But it has nothing whatsoever to do with the viability of any radical utopia.

What makes Jim Barnett an object for pity is his self-delusion, which is evident to Miss McCarthy's unconscious common sense. No doubt this should gall me personally, for Miss McCarthy has said (again in that *Paris Review* interview) that she used "John Chamberlain's boyish looks and a few of the features of his career" as a take-off for her story of a "broad Yale type." But since my own indentification with the Left in those days was purely out of a depression-induced pessimism (as I wrote in the last chapter of *Farewell to Reform,* I didn't think the capitalists were up to making their own preferable economic system work), I have never been able to see myself in Jim Barnett's shoes. I thought socialism was a stomach appeal, and said so. Where Jim Barnett "sold out," I merely recovered my optimism—or maybe it was my nerve. For that matter, Miss McCarthy is probably wrong in thinking that Yale produces any specific type of intellectual. Thomas Beer, Sinclair Lewis, Waldo Frank, George Soule, Selden Rodman, Archibald MacLeish, Dean Acheson, Max Lerner, John Hersey and Dwight Macdonald are all identifiable as Yale "intellectuals"—but just what common denominator makes them a "broad type"?

To continue with synopses and specifications, Miss McCarthy's second novel, *The Oasis* (1949), is the product of a period (the post-World War II years before the Soviets had purloined the secrets of "the bomb") when the author still had hopes that it might be possible to "change the world on a small scale." But her profession of a belief in the possibility of making oases of "libertarian socialism" is not what gives meaning to the satire in *The Oasis*. Miss McCarthy packs her Leftist intellectuals off to their colony with a sardonic certainty that every last one of them will end up constituting a quarreling minority of one. They can argue, but they cannot co-operate. It is a foregone conclusion that in the end the colony will go to pieces because of the property sense. Some intruders try to steal the colonists' strawberries, and the group —which would probably have subscribed orally to Proudhon's maxim, "Property is theft"—is not up to socialist sharing of the free boons of nature. This is what provokes the crisis atmosphere in the last pages of the fable. The satire of *The Oasis* is delicious, but it takes its force from Miss McCarthy's disenchanted common sense about intellectuals she has known, not from her professed belief in the momentary possibility of saving the world through a socialist variety of decentralization.

Mary McCarthy's third novel, *The Groves of Academe* (1952), is structurally her best. But, again, its satirical points make no visible connection with the author's professions about teaching and the proper stance for a good radical. Miss McCarthy's fictional "progressive" college, situated in the Mennonite country of Pennsylvania, is supposed to be "quite a bit like Bard." And in the *Paris Review* interview Mary McCarthy quite approves of Bard, where she taught courses in the novel in 1945 and 1946. Unlike Sarah Lawrence, where she taught in 1948, Bard was "very exciting." "The students were fun. The bright ones were bright. . . . I liked teaching because I loved this business of studying. I found it quite impossible to give a course unless I'd read the material the night before."

The "very exciting" aspects of Bard, however, do not bulk very large when Mary McCarthy is through transferring them to the fictional Jocelyn College in the Mennonite country. True, the rather impromptu courses are good for the Jocelyn teachers, who have to get up some new subject material every year or so in order to cater to the random choices of the students. But Jocelyn, as an institution, is a paradise for

fools of a most shallow type. The plot of the book is dominated by the comic villainies of a professor who, rightly,
should be unemployable in any institution of learning on
quite evident grounds of incompetence. But Henry Mulcahy,
to save himself from being dropped by President Maynard
Hoar at the end of the year (there is no matter of tenure involved), manages to spread the word abroad that he had
been, at one time, a member of the Party. The unappetizing
Hen Mulcahy knows that, in the America of a supposed
"conformist" Reign of Terror, it is actually safer in college
circles to have been a Communist than not to have been one.
For the ex-Communist becomes an automatic knee-jerk beneficiary of the code of "academic freedom"; no self-respecting
college president would dare fire even the most incompetent
"ex" for fear of losing caste as a liberal. On the American
campus, so Miss McCarthy is telling us, the liberal creed has
become the entrenched orthodoxy of the age.

Since the faculty members are mostly taken in by Mulcahy,
it is certain that Mary McCarthy regards them as a most
gullible lot. There is Domna Rejnev, for example, a Russian
girl of twenty-three whose classic beauty has the quality "not
of radiance or softness but of incorruptibility." Domna, who
teaches Russian and French literature (she is a Radcliffe
B.A.), is a "smoldering anachronism, a throwback to one of
those ardent young women of the Sixties, Turgenev's hero-
ines . . . who dreamed resolutely of 'a new day' for peasants,
workers and technicians." Mulcahy, in fastening upon Domna
to handle his problems for him vis-à-vis President Maynard
Hoar, correctly estimates that this is a girl "who could very
easily throw herself away." In short, Domna is admirable in
every respect save one: she has no talent for judging character. Manipulated by the comic villain Mulcahy, Domna
wrongs the very decent President Hoar. Other members of
the faculty who take up for Mulcahy for one reason or another (his "sins of omission" are mere "technicalities," it
would be a "vindication for the critics . . . of the rights of
the dissident to teach" if he were to be fired) are just as

remiss in their judgment of personalities. Yet these are the people into whose cares the young of the land are being entrusted.

An artist with the rapier, Miss McCarthy is never clumsy with her thrusts. But no professional enemy of the egghead could be more severe on a group of double domes than is Mary McCarthy in her collective portrait of the Jocelyn faculty. These "brains" blow up trivia to monumental proportions, they vote for continuing the traditional "progressive" college February field period for the students merely to save their own precious midwinter vacations. And when it comes to faculty manipulation of the curriculum on "behalf of the student Jocelyn's disorganized ways," it is not done with improved "individual instruction" in mind. What the teachers want is to be allowed the "pure nightly joy" of pursuing "the world's history down its recondite byways" under the "cover of duty." As Mary McCarthy sums up the "progressive" college, it is "the faculty, paradoxically" that profits from "untrammelled and individualistic arrangements, the students being on the whole too disorderly or lazy or ill-trained to carry anything very far without the spur of discipline."

So Mary McCarthy, the radical, satirizes the radical educational creed of the Deweyite generation. Though her onslaught may be unfair to the nubbin of truth in Deweyism, no "reactionary" could have criticized with more telling impact. Politically, the cream of the jest is that Mulcahy had never been considered by the Communists to be sufficiently reliable material for party recruitment. He has saved himself at Jocelyn by turning Senator McCarthy's technique of exaggerated accusation inside out, telling a lie about himself to make it seem that he is now a fit candidate for assuming self-righteous shelter behind the Fifth Amendment. Bewildered by the martyrdom that Mulcahy has untruthfully manufactured to suit his political needs, the Jocelyn prexy decides that he himself had better resign. The whole fracas has been too much for President Maynard Hoar's uncomplicated sense of rectitude. Miss McCarthy has made it clear that "intellect," as represented by the Jocelyn faculty, is no synonym for intelligence. Evelyn Waugh, from his position on the Right, could hardly have had greater sport with the whole tissue of "liberal" academic attitudes and beliefs.

Miss McCarthy's next novel, *A Charmed Life* (1955), is, in its more delightful aspect, a spoof on the bohemian community, where the one sure way of getting suicidally involved in a fatal head-on automobile collision is to drive quite legally on the right hand side of the road. The description of bohemian types, both of the summer colony variety and of those who elect to make a Cape Cod village their permanent all-year-round residence, is enormously entertaining. But the main satirical thrust of this particular Mary McCarthy book is elusive.

Though Miss McCarthy has herself praised the education she got at Vassar, *A Charmed Life* seems to mock women's Ivy League sophistication as represented by Martha Sinnott. This young woman has returned to the colony of New Leeds with a new husband. The odd thing about the choice of residence is that New Leeds has unhappy memories for Martha, for it was there that her first marriage came to grief. Nor can John Sinnott, the second husband, feel easy about the return, for Miles Murphy, the man from whom Martha had fled in the night, is a neighbor. Martha and Miles are bound to meet again.

The motivation behind the return is perverse, to say the least. And it is with more perversity that Martha, on a night when John Sinnott is absent in Boston, lets Miles go to bed with her on the engagingly mathematical theory that sleeping with an ex-husband can only add the merest mite to a long string of integers in an extremely familiar equation. In her complaisance Martha Sinnott is rather like one of those Dreiserian women, the Carrie Meebers and the Jennie Gerhardts who give in to men just to be pleasing. But there is a significant difference: in her complaisance Martha Sinnott is dry of heart.

Mary McCarthy deals with Martha Sinnott at arms length.

The woman has never been loyal: when she was engaged to a boy in her college years she had sleazy extracurricular affairs, and the pattern has always continued. Doubt has never bothered Martha Sinnott in a relativistic universe. Why, then, should she have been so concerned about the paternity of her as yet unborn child after her interlude with Miles Murphy? No doubt there are good reasons (a child ought to know its own father), but Miss McCarthy does not make the reasons fit the case of Martha Sinnott, who remains a rather repellent enigma.

Martha Sinnott is not a comic villainess; she is just an ugly character with a fair façade. And unlike the Margaret Sargent of *The Company She Keeps,* she offers no Freudian justification for her misadventures—and her termagant quarrels—with men. Since she remains unexplained, the satire—if any—does not come clear.

Yet it is clear that the intention is satiric. As in all of her fiction, Mary McCarthy is casting a cold eye on Bohemia itself. She, the girl who sought refuge below Manhattan's Fourteenth Street from the life of the bourgeois after her graduation from Vassar, sees clear through the Greenwich Village country of her adoption. Her works constitute a sort of ferocious history of the bohemian movement in America between the time of its decline from the high days of Max Eastman, John Reed and Edna St. Vincent Millay to the coming of the beatniks, when marijuana replaced Marx. To anyone who has known the company Mary McCarthy has kept, the "broad types" of her novels have tantalizingly individual idiosyncrasies. The disputatious habits of Dwight Macdonald appear in more than one of the novels. Martha Sinnott's ex-husband, Miles Murphy, is, like Ernest Hemingway, an amateur pugilist. But he is represented as being good with "the history of ideas" and at "amassing information," which suggests Edmund Wilson, to whom Mary McCarthy was herself once married. And, like a flash, Miles Murphy is represented as envying in Martha Sinnott two qualities that are certainly Mary McCarthy's own—"a sharp ear and a lively natural style." These are not *romans à clef*. But they make use of contemporary history, which is another way of saying that they seek to be authentic.

The most recent Mary McCarthy novel, *The Group,* is an extended contemporary history that could be taken as a satire on a Vassar education if it were not for the fact that the whole modern movement of ideas is the real villain of the piece. The eight Vassar girls whose paths continue to cross after graduation into the Rooseveltian world of 1933 are a mixed lot—and they provoke Mary McCarthy to some interesting implicit judgments that are revealed in subtle alterations in tone. There is a strong, steady note of pity when the author is dealing with Kay Strong, who can't admit to having made a bad marriage; there is tenderness in the portrait of Polly Andrews, an adorable and loyal woman whose values force a curiously respectful shift in the normally disrespectful McCarthy style; there is contempt in the bits about Libby MacAusland, who becomes a literary agent; there is good-natured dismissal of "Pokey" Prothero, a rather brainless daughter of a rich family that looks to its butler for guidance; there is fascinated horror in the revelation of the elegant "Lakey" Eastlake's Lesbianism; there is cool affection in the characterizations of Dottie Renfrew and Helena Davison and Priss Hartshorn Crockett, who might have lived very happily in the world of their mothers. Once again, the disparity between the touchstone of Mary McCarthy's innate common sense and her professed "libertarian socialism" is clearly on display.

Since all of Mary McCarthy's novels are the products of a keen, if somewhat unanchored, intelligence, it is hardly to be wondered at that Mary McCarthy is her own best critic on occasion. The feminine novel, which is long on bric-a-brac, is not for Miss McCarthy; she insists on structure and idea. Her defense of Jane Austen cuts through the nonsense of those Janeites who think of Miss Austen as the progenitor of the Anglican tea-time manner in describing things of purely feminine interest. As Mary McCarthy insists, Jane Austen is always possessed of an idea: *Sense and Sensibility* is a defense of the intelligence against the vapors of the romantic movement; *Pride and Prejudice* is a disarmingly playful sermon directed against both pride and prejudice; *Emma* is a warning against playing God; *Mansfield Park* shows that bread cast upon the waters will be returned some day; *Northanger Abbey* is directed against the habit of letting one's imagination run riot; *Persuasion* underscores the folly of not making decisions on one's own. In assessing Jane Austen for what she was at a time when the novel was young, Mary McCarthy points the way to a comparably valid assessment of her own work now that the novel is older. *The Company She Keeps* is a judgment on the playgirl as romantic revolutionary; *The Oasis* is a preachment on the futility of political escape; *The Groves of Academe* insists that teaching should not be left to those who think that the discipline of "keeping school" is an outmoded Victorian prejudice; *A Charmed Life,* though its heroine is unmotivated, has something to say about the folly of rearing a marriage on doubt; *The Group* says that it is better for a woman to be a woman, but having a good man might help. Austenish novels, all of them, even though the bite and savor of Mary McCarthy is a far cry from Miss Austen's far gentler irony.

The animating force of Mary McCarthy's "lively natural style" (her own phrase) derives from an intransigent will to candor. She will have no idols beyond the idol of the writer as dedicated non-careerist and non-politician when it comes to practicing his vocation. The defect of this insistence on purity is that it becomes self-conscious to the point of destroying compassion for compromising mortals. And so it is, in Mary McCarthy's words about herself, that "something happens in my writing—I don't mean it to—a sort of distortion, a sort of writing on the bias, seeing things with a sort of swerve and swoop . . . the description takes on a sort of extravagance—I don't know exactly how it happens. I know I don't mean it to happen." The "swerve and swoop," however, take off from accurate inventories of both the inte-

rior and exterior worlds—and there is always the deepening
effect of the good classical education that, in the past two
generations, has seemingly been limited to Catholic schools.
The McCarthy style, which draws on resources of both observation and memory, manages to incorporate acute and
extended analysis without any slackening in narrative pace.
Selectivity combined with good syntax means that Miss
McCarthy's style has all the traditional virtues. It is conservative in the best sense. As for the ideas animating Miss
McCarthy's novels, they too are fundamentally conservative
ideas. Still enacting the role of the revolutionary playgirl for
that *Paris Review* interviewer, however, Miss McCarthy has
—for reasons that have to do with intellectual fashion?—
seen fit to deny her fundamental conservatism. She doesn't
see herself as clearly as she sees Jane Austen.

This curious blindness does not matter much, for when
Mary McCarthy deals with a specific problem in her fiction
her impish and inimitable common sense always triumphs.
The only problem raised by Miss McCarthy's continuing
loyalty toward her friends of the "libertarian socialist" and
"dissident" Left is the inhibiting effect it has on her choice
of subject. If she moved in wider circles, she would have
more important things to write about. As Emerson remarked
of Thoreau, "Pounding beans is all very well to the end of
pounding empires, but what if, at the end, it is only pounding beans?" Evelyn Waugh has pounded both beans and
empires—but Mary McCarthy had yet to take on an adversary
that is worthy of her scorn.

BIBLIOGRAPHIES

JAMES BALDWIN

Go Tell It on the Mountain   *New York: Knopf, 1953.*
Giovanni's Room   *New York: Dial, 1956.*
Another Country   *New York: Dial, 1962.*
Going to Meet the Man   *Dial, 1965.*
Tell Me How Long the Train's Been Gone   *Dial, 1968.*
No Name in the Street   *Dial, 1972.*

Non-Fiction
Notes of a Native Son   *Boston: Beacon, 1955.*
Nobody Knows My Name   *New York: Dial, 1961.*
The Fire Next Time   *New York: Dial, 1963.*
Blues for Mister Charlie   *Dial, 1964.*
Amen Corner   *Dial, 1968.*

RALPH ELLISON

Invisible Man   *New York: Random House, 1952.*

Non-Fiction
Shadow and Act   *Random, 1964.*

WILLARD MOTLEY

Knock on Any Door   *New York: Appleton, 1947.*
We Fished All Night   *New York: Appleton, 1951.*
Let No Man Write My Epitaph   *New York: Random House, 1958.*

J. D. SALINGER

THE CATCHER IN THE RYE   *Boston: Little, Brown, 1951.*
NINE STORIES   *Boston: Little, Brown, 1953*
FRANNY AND ZOOEY   *Boston: Little, Brown, 1961.*
RAISE HIGH THE ROOFBEAM, CARPENTERS, and SEYMOUR, AN
INTRODUCTION   *Boston: Little, Brown, 1963.*

VLADIMIR NABOKOV

LAUGHTER IN THE DARK   *Indianapolis: Bobbs-Merrill, 1938.*
THE REAL LIFE OF SEBASTIAN KNIGHT   *New York: New Directions, 1941.*
BEND SINISTER   *New York: Holt, 1947.*
NINE STORIES   *New York: New Directions, 1947.*
PNIN   *New York: Doubleday, 1957.*
NABOKOV'S DOZEN   *New York: Doubleday, 1958.*
LOLITA   *New York: Putnam, 1958.*
INVITATION TO A BEHEADING   *New York: Putnam, 1959.*
PALE FIRE   *New York: Putnam, 1962.*
THE GIFT   *New York: Putnam, 1963.*
ADA   *McGraw-Hill, 1969.*
KING, QUEEN, KNAVE   *McGraw-Hill, 1969.*
MARY   *McGraw-Hill, 1970.*
GLORY   *McGraw-Hill, 1972.*
TRANSPARENT THINGS   *McGraw-Hill, 1972.*

Non-Fiction
NIKOLAI GOGOL   *New York: New Directions, 1944.*
CONCLUSIVE EVIDENCE   *New York: Harper, 1951.*
POEMS   *New York: Doubleday, 1959.*
POEMS AND PROBLEMS   *McGraw-Hill, 1972.*

CARSON MCCULLERS

THE HEART IS A LONELY HUNTER   *Boston: Houghton, Mifflin, 1940.*

REFLECTIONS IN A GOLDEN EYE *Boston: Houghton, Mifflin, 1941.*
THE MEMBER OF THE WEDDING *Boston: Houghton, Mifflin, 1946.*
THE BALLAD OF THE SAD CAFE *Boston: Houghton, Mifflin, 1951.*
CLOCK WITHOUT HANDS *Boston: Houghton, Mifflin, 1961.*
THE MORTGAGED HEART *Houghton, Mifflin, 1971.*

Non-Fiction
THE SQUARE ROOT OF WONDERFUL *Boston: Houghton, Mifflin, 1958.*
SWEET AS A PICKLE AND CLEAN AS A PIG *Houghton, Mifflin, 1964.*

TRUMAN CAPOTE

OTHER VOICES, OTHER ROOMS *New York: Random House, 1948.*
A TREE OF NIGHT *New York: Random House, 1949.*
THE GRASS HARP *New York: Random House, 1951.*
BREAKFAST AT TIFFANY'S *New York: Random House, 1958.*
IN COLD BLOOD *Random, 1967.*

Non-Fiction
LOCAL COLOR *New York: Random House, 1950.*
THE GRASS HARP [a play] *New York: Random House, 1952.*
THE MUSES ARE HEARD *New York: Random House, 1956.*
THANKSGIVING VISITOR *Random, 1968.*

SAUL BELLOW

DANGLING MAN *New York: Vanguard, 1944.*
THE VICTIM *New York: Vanguard, 1947.*
THE ADVENTURES OF AUGIE MARCH *New York: Viking, 1953.*
SEIZE THE DAY *New York: Viking, 1956.*
HENDERSON THE RAIN KING *New York: Viking, 1959.*

HERZOG   *Viking, 1964.*
MOSBY'S MEMOIRS AND OTHER STORIES   *Viking, 1968.*
MR. SAMMLER'S PLANET   *Viking, 1970.*

Non-Fiction
LAST ANALYSIS   *Viking, 1965.*

WILLIAM STYRON

LIE DOWN IN DARKNESS   *Indianapolis: Bobbs-Merrill, 1951.*
THE LONG MARCH   *New York: Random House, 1952,*
SET THIS HOUSE ON FIRE   *New York: Random House, 1960.*
CONFESSIONS OF NAT TURNER   *Random, 1967.*

NORMAN MAILER

THE NAKED AND THE DEAD   *New York: Rinehart, 1948.*
BARBARY SHORE   *New York: Rinehart, 1951.*
THE DEER PARK   *New York: Putnam, 1955.*
AN AMERICAN DREAM   *Dial, 1964.*
WHY ARE WE IN VIETNAM?   *Putnam, 1967.*

Non-Fiction
ADVERTISEMENTS FOR MYSELF   *New York: Putnam, 1959.*
DEATHS FOR THE LADIES (AND OTHER DISASTERS)   *New York: Putnam, 1962.*
CANNIBALS AND CHRISTIANS   *Dial, 1966.*
ARMIES OF THE NIGHT   *World, 1968.*
MIAMI AND THE SIEGE OF CHICAGO   *World, 1968.*
OF A FIRE ON THE MOON   *Little, Brown & Co., 1970.*
THE PRISONER OF SEX   *Little, Brown & Co., 1971.*
EXISTENTIAL ERRANDS   *Little, Brown & Co., 1972.*
ST. GEORGE AND THE GODFATHER   *New American Library, 1972.*

EUDORA WELTY

A CURTAIN OF GREEN   *New York: Doubleday, 1941.*

THE ROBBER BRIDEGROOM   *New York: Doubleday, 1942.*
THE WIDE NET AND OTHER STORIES   *New York: Harcourt, Brace. 1943.*
DELTA WEDDING   *New York: Harcourt, Brace, 1946.*
THE GOLDEN APPLES   *New York: Harcourt, Brace, 1949.*
THE PONDER HEART   *New York: Harcourt, Brace, 1954.*
THE BRIDE OF THE INNISFALLEN   *New York: Harcourt, Brace, 1955.*
LOSING BATTLES   *Random, 1970.*
THE OPTIMIST'S DAUGHTER   *Random, 1972.*

Non-Fiction
SHORT STORIES   *New York: Harcourt, Brace, 1950.*
PLACE IN FICTION   *New York: House of Books, 1957* (limited edition).
ONE TIME, ONE PLACE: MISSISSIPPI IN THE DEPRESSION   *A Snapshot Album. Random, 1971.*

JAMES JONES

FROM HERE TO ETERNITY   *New York: Scribner, 1951.*
SOME CAME RUNNING   *New York: Scribner, 1958.*
THE PISTOL   *New York: Scribner, 1959.*
THE THIN RED LINE   *New York: Scribner, 1962.*
GO TO THE WINDOW-MAKER   *Scribner, 1967.*
ICE-CREAM HEADACHE AND OTHER STORIES   *Delacorte, 1968.*

JACK KEROUAC

THE TOWN AND THE CITY   *New York: Harcourt, Brace, 1950.*
ON THE ROAD   *New York: Viking, 1957.*
THE DHARMA BUMS   *New York: Viking, 1958.*
THE SUBTERRANEANS   *New York: Grove, 1958.*
DOCTOR SAX   *New York: Grove, 1959.*
MAGGIE CASSIDY   *New York: Avon, 1960.*
BIG SUR   *New York: Farrar, Straus, 1962.*
DESOLATION ANGELS   *Coward-McCann, 1965.*
VANITY OF DULUOZ   *Coward-McCann, 1968.*

Non-Fiction

MEXICO CITY BLUES   *New York: Grove, 1959.*
EXCERPTS FROM VISIONS OF CODY   *New York: New Directions, 1960.*
LONESOME TRAVELER   *New York: McGraw-Hill, 1960.*
BOOK OF DREAMS   *San Francisco: City Lights, 1961.*
PULL MY DAISY   *New York: Grove, 1961.*
VISIONS OF GERARD   *Farrar, Straus &Giroux, 1963.*

BERNARD MALAMUD

THE NATURAL   *New York: Harcourt, Brace, 1952.*
THE ASSISTANT   *New York: Farrar, Straus, 1957.*
THE MAGIC BARREL   *New York: Farrar, Straus, 1958.*
A NEW LIFE   *New York: Farrar, Straus, 1962.*
IDIOTS FIRST   *Farrar, Straus & Giroux, 1963.*
THE FIXER   *Farrar, Straus & Giroux, 1968.*
PICTURES OF FIDELMAN   *Farrar, Straus & Giroux, 1969.*
THE TENANT   *Farrar, Straus & Giroux, 1971.*

HERBERT GOLD

BIRTH OF A HERO   *New York: Viking, 1951.*
THE PROSPECT BEFORE US   *Cleveland: World, 1954.*
THE MAN WHO WAS NOT WITH IT   *Boston: Little, Brown, 1956.*
THE OPTIMIST   *New York: Dial, 1959.*
LOVE AND LIKE   *New York: Dial, 1960.*
THEREFORE BE BOLD   *New York: Dial, 1960.*
SALT   *New York: Dial, 1963.*
THE FATHERS   *Random, 1967.*
THE GREAT AMERICAN JACKPOT   *Random, 1970.*
THE MAGIC WILL   *Random, 1971.*

Non-Fiction

THE AGE OF HAPPY PROBLEMS   *New York: Dial, 1962.*
FIRST PERSON SINGULAR   *New York: Dial, 1963.*
MY LAST TWO THOUSAND YEARS   *Random, 1972.*

JOHN UPDIKE

THE POORHOUSE FAIR   *New York: Knopf, 1959.*
RABBIT, RUN   *New York: Knopf, 1960.*
PIGEON FEATHERS   *New York: Knopf, 1962.*
THE CENTAUR   *New York: Knopf, 1963.*
OF THE FARM   *Knopf, 1965.*
A CHILD'S CALENDAR   *Knopf, 1965.*
THE MUSIC SCHOOL   *Knopf, 1965.*
ASSORTED PROSE   *Knopf, 1965.*
COUPLES   *Knopf, 1969.*
BECK   *Knopf, 1970.*
RABBIT REDUX   *Knopf, 1971.*
MUSEUMS AND WOMEN   *Knopf, 1972.*

Non-Fiction
THE CARPENTERED HEN   *New York: Harper, 1958.*
THE MAGIC FLUTE   *Knopf, 1962.*
TELEPHONE POLES AND OTHER POEMS   *Knopf, 1963.*
THE RING   *Knopf, 1964.*
BOTTOM'S DREAM   *Knopf, 1969.*
MIDPOINT AND OTHER POEMS   *Knopf, 1969.*

MARY McCARTHY

THE COMPANY SHE KEEPS   *New York: Harcourt, Brace, 1942.*
THE OASIS   *New York: Random House, 1949.*
CAST A COLD EYE   *New York: Harcourt, Brace, 1950.*
THE GROVES OF ACADEME   *New York: Harcourt, Brace, 1952.*
A CHARMED LIFE   *New York: Harcourt, Brace, 1955.*
THE GROUP   *New York: Harcourt, Brace, 1963.*
BIRDS OF AMERICA   *Harcourt, Brace Jovanovich, 1970.*

Non-Fiction

SIGHTS AND SPECTACLES   *New York: Farrar, Straus, 1956.*

VENICE OBSERVED   *New York: Reynal, 1956.*

MEMORIES OF A CATHOLIC GIRLHOOD   *New York: Harcourt, Brace, 1957.*

THE STONES OF FLORENCE   *New York: Harcourt, Brace, 1959.*

ON THE CONTRARY   *New York: Farrar, Straus, 1961.*

VIETNAM   *Harcourt, Brace & World, 1967.*

HANOI   *Harcourt, Brace & World, 1968.*

MEDINA   *Harcourt, Brace Jovanovich, 1972.*

SOME USEFUL BOOKS PUBLISHED WITHIN THE LAST 10 YEARS ON THE WRITERS IN THIS VOLUME

(not including individual studies):

Aldridge, John W.   *The Devil in the Fire.* Harper's Magazine Press, 1972.

Baumbach, Jonathan.   *The Landscape of Nightmare: Studies in the Contemporary American Novel.* New York University Press. 1965.

Eisinger, Chester E.   *Fiction of the Forties.* University of Chicago Press. 1963.

Galloway, David.   *The Absurd Hero in American Fiction.* University of Texas Press. 1966.

Harper, Howard M. Jr.   *Desperate Faith: A Study of Bellow, Salinger, Mailer, Baldwin & Updike.* University of North Carolina Press. 1967.

Klein, Marcus.   After Alienation: *American Novels in Mid-Century.* 1964.

Moore, Harry T., editor, *Contemporary American Novelists*. Southern Illinois University Press. 1967.

Rupp, Richard H. *Celebration in Postwar American Fiction, 1945-1967*. University of Miami Press. 1970.

Tanner, Tony. *City of Words: American Fiction, 1950-1970*. Harper and Row. 1971.

Weinberg, Helen. *The New Novel in America: The Kafkan Mode in Contemporary Fiction*. Cornell University Press. 1970.

BOOKS ON THE THEORY AND PRACTICE OF THE MOST RECENT FICTION:

Friedman, Bruce Jay, editor. *Black Humor*. Bantam Books. 1963.

Harris, Charles B. *Contemporary American Novelists of the Absurd*. College and University Press, 1971.

Nin, Anais. *The Novel of the Future*. MacMillan. 1969.

Scholes, Robert. *The Fabulators*. Oxford University Press. 1967.

Spencer, Sharon. *Space, Time and Structure in the Modern Novel*. New York University Press. 1971.

CONTRIBUTORS

DONALD BARR taught in the English department at Columbia University, then became assistant dean of Engineering and Applied Science. He is currently on leave from Columbia to serve as associate program director of the National Science Foundation. He has written extensively on contemporary fiction and current educational problems.

HARVEY BREIT was for many years assistant editor of *The New York Times Book Review* and is the author of a book of poems, *There Falls Tom Fool* and a collection of talks with authors, *The Writer Observed.* He collaborated with Budd Schulberg on the play, *The Disenchanted.*

JOHN CHAMBERLAIN has been a book critic for dailies, weeklies and monthlies (with sometimes a foray in a quarterly). He has also written on economics and politics for *Fortune, Life* and *The Wall Street Journal* and is currently a columnist for the King Features Syndicate. He is the author of *Farewell to Reform* and *The Enterprising Americans.*

ROBERT GORHAM DAVIS' reviews of American and British fiction appear frequently in *The New York Times Book Review* and other literary magazines. He is professor of English at Columbia University and the author of a study of John Dos Passos.

GRANVILLE HICKS, who has been contributing editor of *The Saturday Review* since 1958, is the author of many books, among them *The Great Tradition—an Interpretation of American Literature Since the Civil War,* a novel *There Was a Man in Our Town,* and two autobiographical works *Small Town* and *Where We Came Out.* He is also the editor of *The Living Novel.*

ALUN R. JONES, lecturer at Hull University, England, is currently visiting professor at the University of Rochester. He is the author of *The Life and Opinions of T. E. Hulme* and co-editor of *Lyrical Ballads 1798–1805.*

ALAN PRYCE-JONES was for twelve years editor of *The (London) Times Literary Supplement.* From 1961–63 he served as program associate in the Humanities and Arts Program of the Ford Foundation. At present he is drama critic of *Theatre Arts* magazine. He is the author of books of poetry, criticism, biography, travel, and fiction.

MARK SCHORER is chairman of the English department at the University of California, Berkeley. He is the author of a number of books, among them a novel, *Wars of Love,* and a biography of Sinclair Lewis.

DAVID L. STEVENSON is professor of English at Hunter College. He is the author of *The Love-Game Comedy* and coeditor with Herbert Gold of *Stories of Modern America.*

DIANA TRILLING'S articles on literary, political, and sociological subjects have appeared in *The Nation* (of which she was fiction critic from 1941–49), *Partisan Review, Commentary, Encounter, Harper's, The New York Times* and other publications here and abroad. She is the editor of *The Viking Portable D. H. Lawrence* and *The Selected Letters of D. H. Lawrence.*